1990 *Wilton* Yearbook of Cake Decorating

Creative Director . . . . . . Richard Tracy
Copy Director . . . . Marie DeBenedictis
Copywriter . . . . .Linda Skender
Production Coordinator .Mary Stahulak
Senior Cake Decorators . . . . Amy Rohr
                              Susan Matusiak
Cake Decorators . . . . . . Mary Gavenda
                              Corky Kagay
                              Sandra O'Toole
Photographer . . . . . . .Thomas Zamiar
Photography Assistant . . . . Dan Bakke
Photo Stylist. . . . . .Pat Burke
Design/Production . . . RNB Graphics
Color Separations . . . . . NCL Graphics
Printing . . . . Moebius Printing

Copyright ©1989 Wilton Enterprises, Inc. All rights reserved. No part of this publication may be reproduced or transmitted in any form, or by any means, electronic or mechanical, including photocopy, recording or any information storage and retrieval system, without the written permission of Wilton Enterprises, Inc., 2240 W. 75th Street, Woodridge, IL 60517
For photography purposes, many cakes in this book were decorated with royal icing.

Toddler Treats

JACK-IN-THE-BOX

- **10 in. Square Pans,** p. 169
- **Happy Clown Pan,** p. 178
- **Tips 3, 16, 21,** p. 132-133
- **Christmas Red, Royal Blue, Kelly Green Icing Colors,** p. 131
- **'90 Pattern Book (Collar & Back Brace Patterns),** p. 121
- **7 in. Square Separator Plate,** p. 166
- **Dowel Rods,** p. 159
- **Heart Cookie Cutter Set,** p. 119
- **Cake Boards, Fanci-Foil Wrap,** p. 139
- **Birthday Candles,** p. 145
- **Gingerbread Recipe,** p. 108
- **Gumdrop, candy-coated chocolates**
- **Buttercream, Royal Icings**

- **To Make Clown:** Spray inside of clown pan with vegetable oil. Roll out gingerbread dough on lightly floured surface to ⅜ in. thickness. Transfer dough to inside of pan; press into indentations. Smooth edges, (dough should not be up the sides); pierce with a fork. Bake 17 to 20 minutes or until edges begin to pull away from sides. Turn out onto a rack to cool.

- Out of dough, also cut 2 back braces and four 4¼ in. hearts. Bake and cool.

- Use royal icing to decorate gingerbread. **For clown plaque:** With a pin, scratch Collar Pattern guidelines. Outline hat, face and collar with tip 3 strings. Pipe in eyes, face and tongue (smooth with finger dipped in cornstarch). Cover hat, face and collar with tip 16 stars. Add tip 3 outline lashes. Add candy trims. Let dry. Generously ice straight sides of back braces and push onto back of clown. Ice hearts smooth and let dry.

- **For box:** Cut a 10 in. square from cake board and cover with Fanci-Foil Wrap for lid. Ice 4-layer square cake smooth. Push in dowel rods. Put separator plate on top. On cake sides: Push heart cookies into icing. Print tip 3 message on front heart. Pipe tip 16 pairs of scrolls above hearts. Trim corners with tip 16 C-shells. Add tip 16 rosettes and stars. Edge hearts with tip 16 C-shells.

- On cake top (around plate, too) and sides, pipe tip 16 shells. Edge base with tip 21 shell border. Push lollipop sticks into the back edge of cake top so box lid will rest on them. Position box lid. Place Clown on plate. Pipe tip 21 spiral "candleholder" and push in candle. *Serves 56.*

ROCK-A-BYE

- **Rocking Horse Pan,** p. 181
- **Tips 3, 4, 17, 21,** p. 132-133
- **Christmas Red, Brown, Lemon Yellow, Royal Blue, Kelly Green Icing Colors,** p. 131
- **'90 Pattern Book (Folk Hearts Pattern),** p. 121

- **Buttercream Icing**
- Ice sides and background areas on cake top blue. With toothpick, mark Folk Hearts around saddle and heart on rocker (for easier marking, lightly ice areas).
- Outline horse, bridle, saddle and rocker with tip 4 strings. Pipe tip 3 bead heart flowers with tip 3 outline stems and leaves. Outline folk hearts with tip 3 strings. Add tip 3 bead eye. Print tip 3 message.
- Fill in hooves with tip 3 zigzags. Cover horse, bridle, saddle and rockers with tip 17 stars.
- Pipe tip 3 elongated bead leaves on rocker. Cover mane with tip 21 reverse shells. Pipe tip 21 elongated swirled scrolls on tail (overpipe for dimension). Edge base with tip 21 star border. *Serves 12.*

PAMPERED PANDA

- **Double Tier Round Pan,** p. 175
- **Aluminum Panda Mold,** p. 116
- **Tips 3, 4, 14, 16,** p. 132-133
- **Christmas Red, Kelly Green, Royal Blue, Lemon Yellow (add small amounts for pastel shades),** p. 131
- **Alphabet Cookie Cutters,** p. 119
- **Roll-Out Cookie Dough Recipe,** p. 109
- **Buttercream, Royal Icings**
- Cut letters out of cookie dough. Bake and cool. Using royal icing, outline letters with tip 4 and fill in with tip 14 stars.

- **For panda cake:** With tip 3 outline face, body and paws; pipe dot eyes; add bead heart nose. Pipe in ears and feet (smooth with finger dipped in cornstarch). Cover with tip 14 stars.
- Ice "tier" cake smooth. With tip 16, edge bases with shells, tops with stars. Pipe tip 3 bead hearts randomly on tops and sides. Position panda; add cookies and push in candle. *Serves 12.*

HONEY BUNNY

- **Cottontail Bunny Pan,** p. 188
- **Tips 4, 6, 16, 86 or 87, 225, 349,** p. 132-136
- **Christmas Red, Brown, Kelly Green Icing Colors,** p. 131
- **Buttercream Icing**
- Make 6 tip 225 drop flowers with tip 4 dot centers.
- Ice sides, background areas and eye smooth with pink icing. Outline bunny and bow with tip 4 strings. Pipe tip 4 dot eye and tip 6 nose (flatten with finger dipped in cornstarch).
- Cover inside of ear and bow with tip 16 stars.
- Inside of outlines, with tip 6, pipe two rows of mocha icing. With spatula, fill in the rest of bunny with beige icing. Pull end of tip through icing to blend shades together and give a fur-like effect.
- Edge base with tip 86 or 87 zigzag border. Add flowers. Pipe tip 4 outline stems and tip 349 leaves. Print tip 4 message. *Serves 12.*

BLAST FROM THE PAST

- 11 x 15 in. Sheet Pan, p. 169
- Tips 2, 3, 6, 14, 17, p. 132-133
- Sky Blue, Teal, Orange, Lemon Yellow, Brown Icing Colors, p. 131
- Dinosaur Cookie Cutters, p. 119
- Message Pattern Press Set, p. 140
- Birthday Candles, p. 145
- Buttercream Icing

- Ice cake smooth; sky area and sides blue; ledge and ground brown (pat and swirl in yellow icing to create a rugged texture).
- Imprint dinosaurs with cookie cutters and message with pattern press. Outline letters and write name with tip 3.

- Outline dinosaurs with tip 2. Pipe in spots on brontosaurus with tip 2 (smooth with finger dipped in cornstarch). Add tip 2 dot eyes. Fill in dinosaurs with tip 14 stars.
- Pipe tip 3 outline "plants." Pipe tip 17 zigzag clouds.
- Edge cake top with tip 6 bead border; base with tip 17 rosette border. Push candles into clouds. *Serves 30.*

STAR SEARCH

- Shooting Star Pan, p. 174
- Tips 3, 19, p. 132-133
- Pink, Lemon Yellow, Royal Blue, Kelly Green Icing Colors, p. 131

- Cake Board, Fanci-Foil Wrap, p. 139
- Buttercream Icing

- Ice sides and star area smooth. Outline star with tip 3. Write tip 3 message.
- Cover rainbow with tip 19 stars. Edge base with tip 19 C-motion border. *Serves 12.*

ON THE RIGHT TRACK

- Long Loaf Pan, p. 172
- Tips 3, 6, 46, 67, p. 132-137
- Kelly Green, Brown Icing Colors, 131
- '90 Pattern Book (Tracks Pattern), p. 121
- Buttercream, Royal Icings
- Graham crackers and crumbs, candy discs

- **To make train:** Use 3 whole crackers. Cut 2 triangle shapes out of a 4th of a cracker for smokestack and cowcatcher. Cut disc candies in halves and quarters. With royal icing, attach candy and decorate train. Outline engine and cars with tip 3. Trim smokestack and window of engine with tip 3 zigzags.
- Ice cake smooth. With toothpick, mark Tracks Pattern on cake top. Outline rails with tip 3 and tracks with tip 46 ribbed stripes.
- Print 46 ribbed stripe name on side. Edge top with tip 6 bead border; base with tip 67 shell-motion border.
- Position train cars (push a 4th section of graham cracker into cake behind each car for support). Sprinkle graham cracker crumbs on cake top. *Serves 18.*

Let the Party Begin!

Circus Clowns

CLOWNING AROUND

- Happy Clown Pan, p. 178
- Tips 4, 12, 16, 124, 233, p. 132-136
- Lemon Yellow, Royal Blue, Orange, Red-Red and Black Icing Colors, p. 131
- Buttercream Icing
- Large red gumball

- Ice cake sides smooth. Outline hat and facial features with tip 4 strings.
- Pipe in tip 12 hat brim, eyes, mouth and tongue (smooth with finger dipped in cornstarch).
- Cover hat and face with with tip 16 stars; add tip 4 dots. Print tip 4 name.
- Pipe tip 124 ruffles. For hair: Fill bag with ½ red and ½ orange icing and cover head with tip 233 pull-out strands. Add gumball nose. *Serves 12.*

CIRCUS CIRCUS

- Two Cake Mix Round Tier Set, p. 167
- Tips 3, 6, 12, 14, 19, 101, p. 132-136
- Lemon Yellow, Wilton Red, Royal Blue Icing Colors, p. 131
- Small Derby Clowns, p. 142
- Zany Zoo Cookie Cutters, p. 118
- Alphabet Cookie Cutters, p. 119
- Decorator's Brush, Cake Dividing Set, p. 140
- 6, 8, 12 in. Cake Circles, Fanci-Foil Wrap, p. 139
- Dowel Rod (for pole), p. 165
- Roll-out Cookie Dough Recipe, p. 109
- Ribbon, gumdrops
- Buttercream, Royal Icings

- With cookie cutters, cut 8 animal shapes and letters for name from cookie dough. Bake and cool. Outline cookies with tip 3 royal icing strings; fill in letters with tip 14 stars.
- Ice cakes smooth (on cake circles and separator plates). Push pillars into tiers. Using Cake Dividing Set, dot mark top tier into 6ths, center tier in 8ths.
- Edge cake tops with tip 6 bead borders; bases with tip 12 bulb borders.
- Brush-stripe icing; and figure pipe tip 19 clowns in desired positions on cakes (see p. 105). Push in Derby Clown heads. Pipe tip 3 dot hands, buttons and shoes. Trim sleeves and legs with tip 101 ruffles.
- Attach cookes to sides with icing. **For pole:** "Glue" ribbon around and streamers to end of dowel rod with royal icing. Attach candy knob with icing. *Serves 24.*

BIRTHDAY
Sesame Street®

PARTY PALS

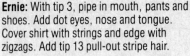

- 10 in. Round Pans, p. 168
- Cookie Sheets, p. 172
- Tips 3, 13, 18, 21, 65, p. 132-134
- Lemon Yellow, Royal Blue, Brown, Kelly Green, Orange, Sky Blue, Wilton Red Icing Colors, p. 131
- Alphabet, Numbers and Sesame Street Cookie Cutters, p. 119
- Birthday Candles, p. 145
- Roll-Out Cookie Dough Recipe, p. 109
- Buttercream, Royal Icings
- Hard candy sticks

- Cut letters, number and characters out of cookie dough. Bake and cool. Decorate cookies with royal icing. Outline details on characters with tip 3.

For Bert: With tip 3, pipe dot eyes, nose, shirt stripes, pants and shoes. Add tip 13 pull-out stripe hair.

Ernie: With tip 3, pipe in mouth, pants and shoes. Add dot eyes, nose and tongue. Cover shirt with strings and edge with zigzags. Add tip 13 pull-out stripe hair.

Big Bird: Pipe tip 3 dot eyes. Fill in beak, hands and feet with tip 3. Cover with tip 65 leaf feathers.

Cookie Monster: With tip 3, pipe in cap, apron, mouth and rolling pin. Add dot eyes. Cover fur with tip 13 stars.

For letters and number: Outline with tip 3 and fill in with tip 13 stars.

- Let icing dry. Attach candy sticks to backs of characters with icing.
- Ice 2-layer cake smooth with buttercream icing. Edge with shell borders–tip 18 at top, tip 21 base. Attach name and number to side with icing. Push characters into cake top. Pipe tip 21 spiral candleholders. Push in candles. *Serves 24.*

MUFFIN MUPPETS

- Jumbo Muffin Pan, p. 173
- Tips 2, 16, p. 133
- Lemon Yellow, Royal Blue, Wilton Red Icing Colors, p. 131
- Big Bird and Cookie Monster Picks, p. 142
- Buttercream Icing

- Ice top of cupcakes smooth. Pipe tip 2 names. Add tip 16 star and shell borders. Position Big Bird and Cookie Monster Picks.

BIG BIRD™ REVS IT!

- Big Bird Pan, p. 183
- Tips 3, 4, 18, 67, p. 132-134
- Lemon Yellow, Brown, Red-Red, Pink, Orange, Sky Blue Icing Colors, p. 131
- Chocolate sandwich cookies, candy disks, jelly beans

- Ice message area and side white, nest area brown. Outline eyes, beak, arm, body and hands with tip 3 strings.
- Pipe in tip 4 hand and beak areas; flatten with finger dipped in cornstarch
- Pipe in tip 4 eyeballs (smooth with finger dipped in cornstarch). Add tip 3 dot pupils; flatten with finger. Outline eyelids and brows with tip 3 strings. Pipe in mouth with tip 3.
- Write tip 3 message. Pipe in dashboard of car with tip 4. Cover car with tip 18 stars. Attach cookie wheels, candy lights and hubcaps with dots of icing.
- Cover Big Bird with tip 67 pull-out leaf feathers. Add tip 18 shell base border around sky area. *Serves 12.*

HAPPY JUGGLER

- Cookie Monster Pan, p. 183
- Tips 4, 12, 17, 233, p. 132-133
- Royal Blue, Brown Icing Colors, p. 131
- Ready-made cookies
- Buttercream Icing

- Ice hat and mouth smooth. Outline hat, eyes and mouth with tip 4 strings.
- Pipe in eyeball with tip 12 (smooth and flatten with finger dipped in cornstarch). Add tip 4 dot pupils.
- Cover Cookie Monster with tip 233 pull-out fur. Position cookies and pipe tip 233 pull-out fur hands. Pipe tip 4 numbers.
- Edge cap with tip 17 shell border. *Serves 12.*

© 1985 Children's Television Workshop. COOKIE MONSTER, BIG BIRD, BERT, ERNIE are trademarks of Muppets, Inc. SESAME STREET and SESAME STREET SIGN are trademarks and service marks of the Children's Television Workshop. All rights reserved.

Happy Birthday Danny

2 3 1

RICH
AMY
MARY
SUE
MARIE
CORKY
DAVE
TERRY
MARY
SANDY

9

Happy
Birthday
Shari

HAPPY
BIRTHDAY
DAVID

Jessica
is
4

Birthday Balloons

HOLD ON TIGHT!

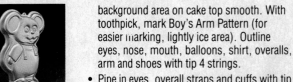

- **Up 'N Away Balloon Pan, p. 174**
- **Tips 2, 4, 8, 21, p. 132-133**
- **Sky Blue, Lemon Yellow Icing Colors, p. 131**
- **'90 Pattern Book (Hand Pattern), p. 121**
- **Buttercream Icing**
- **Marshmallow creme**

- Ice cake smooth. With toothpick, mark Hand Pattern on top and side. Outline hand with tip 4. Pipe in hand with tip 8 (smooth and shape with finger dipped in cornstarch).
- Outline balloon with tip 2 icing. To flow in balloon with melted marshmallow creme, see p. 108. Let set before printing tip 4 dot message. Pipe tip 4 outline balloon string.
- Edge cake top with tip 4 bead border. Pipe tip 21 zigzag puffs on top and at base. *Serves 12.*

DANCING ON AIR

- **8-in Round Pans, p. 168**
- **Tips 3, 16, p. 132-133**
- **Pink, Orange Icing Colors, p. 131**
- **Candy disks**

- Ice 2-layer cake smooth. Print tip 3 message.
- Edge top and base with tip 16 rosettes. Pipe tip 3 scallops around rosettes. Trim rosettes with tip 3 dots.
- Arrange candy balloons on cake top. Add tip 3 balloon strings and small bows. Pipe tip 16 large bow. *Serves 12.*

BEARLOONS, BEARLOONS!

- **Huggable Bear Pan, p. 174**
- **Tips 3, 4, 17, p. 132-133**
- **Lemon Yellow, Orange Icing Colors, p. 131**
- **Circus Balloons, p. 142**

- Ice inside of ears, snout, paws and tummy smooth. Outline ears, face, paws and tummy with tip 4 strings.
- Pipe in eyes and nose with tip 4 (smooth with finger dipped in cornstarch). Print tip 3 message.
- Cover heads, paws and body with tip 17 stars. Push in Circus Balloons. *Serves 12.*

BOY-OH-BOY!

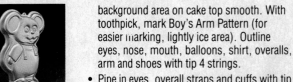

- **Little Mouse Pan, p. 180**
- **Tips 4, 7, 16, p. 132-133**
- **Royal Blue, Orange, Lemon Yellow, Copper, Brown, Pink Icing Colors, p. 131**
- **'90 Pattern Book (Boy Pattern), p. 121**
- **Buttercream Icing**
- **Shoestring licorice**

- Ice sides, balloons (mouse's ears) and background area on cake top smooth. With toothpick, mark Boy's Arm Pattern (for easier marking, lightly ice area). Outline eyes, nose, mouth, balloons, shirt, overalls, arm and shoes with tip 4 strings.
- Pipe in eyes, overall straps and cuffs with tip 4 (flatten with finger dipped in cornstarch).
- Cover face, shirt, overall and shoes with tip 16 stars. Pipe tip 16 pull-out stripe hair.
- Print tip 4 message. Add tip 7 number on balloon. Place licorice balloon strings on cake top. Edge base with tip 16 shell border. *Serves 12.*

HAPPY BIRTHDAY

Tom

12

Cake & Ice Cream

COLOSSAL ICE CREAM SANDWICHES

- 6 in. Square Pans p. 169 or Square MicroBakes™, p. 171
- Tip 3, p. 132
- Birthday Candles, p. 145
- Message Pattern Press, p. 140
- Buttercream Icing
- ½ gallon of ice cream, aluminum foil

- Bake two chocolate cakes or brownies. Torte each in half. Ice the top of each half. Use message press to imprint message on one. Print and write tip 3 messages on each.

- **To mold ice cream square:** Line square pan with foil. Soften ice cream and stir until creamy. Pour 2 pts. of ice cream into each pan and freeze until firm.

- **To serve:** Unmold ice cream onto cake. Remove foil and add sandwich top. Push in candles. *Each serves 6.*

YOU'RE A DOLL

- Shortcakes 'N Treats Pan, p. 173
- Tips 4, 16, 86 p. 132-136
- Lemon Yellow, Pink Icing Colors, p. 131
- Small Doll Picks, p. 145

- Buttercream Icing
- Ice cream scoops, chopped nuts, candy sprinkles
- **On doll picks:** Ice bodices smooth or cover with tip 16 stars. Pat some with chopped nuts or candy. Trim with tip 4 dots, tip 16 stars or tip 86 ruffles.

- Fill shortcakes with ice cream; sprinkle with candy. Add picks.

- Pipe tip 16 star, zigzag, swirled shell and stripe trims; add tip 86 ruffle border around cake bases. *Each serves 1.*

GO BANANAS

- Continental Flan Pan, p. 173
- Tip 2110, p. 133
- Buttercream Icing or Stabilized Whipped Cream
- Bananas, scoops of vanilla, chocolate and strawberry ice cream, maraschino cherries, chopped nuts, chocolate sauce

- Ice top of cake with buttercream icing or stabilized whipped cream. Arrange bananas around cake top.

- Place scoops of ice cream on cake. Pipe tip 2110 rosettes in center of cake; pipe stars between ice cream scoops.

- Arrange cherries on top of rosettes. Sprinkle with chopped nuts. Drizzle with chocolate sauce.

JITTER BUG

- 10 x 15 Jelly Roll Pan, p. 172
- Tip 4, p. 132
- Leaf Green Icing Color, p. 131
- Buttercream Icing
- Birthday Candles, p. 145
- 2 pts. vanilla ice cream, 3 in. round sugar cookie, mini marshmallows, 12 pecans, candy-coated chocolates, tinted coconut flakes

- Prepare Jelly Roll Chocolate Sponge Cake Recipe on the back of the Jelly Roll Pan label. Let cool. To tint coconut, see p. 104

- Soften ice cream, then stir until soft and creamy, but not melted. Unroll cooled cake. Spread ice cream on top (leave ½ in. from edge uncovered). Roll cake and ice outside smooth with chocolate buttercream. Return to freezer until ice cream is frozen.

- To decorate face (buttercream icing can be used, but royal icing would hold up better): Flatten 2 mini marshmallows and attach "eyes" to cookie with icing. Outline eyes and mouth with tip 4. Add tip 4 dot pupils to marshmallow eyes and nose. Pipe tip 4 string lashes. Attach (candy-coated chocolates) cheeks with dots of icing. Edge face with tip 4 outline scallops.

- **To serve:** Print tip 4 name. Push candle antennae into cake. Add candy "spots" and pecan feet. Cover serving base with tinted coconut. Attach cookie face with icing. *Serves 10.*

13

READY-IN-MINUTES TEDDY

- MicroBakes™ Teddy Bear Pan, p. 171
- Brown Icing Color, p. 131
- Birthday Candles, p. 145
- Buttercream Icing
- Candy-coated chocolates, candy discs, shoestring licorice

- Ice face, tummy and paws smooth. Ice remaining cake generously and pat with spatula for a fluffy effect.
- Push candy on ears, face and paws. Add candles. *Serves 8.*

Animal Friends

WHAT'S HOPPENIN'?

- Sunny Bunny Pan, p. 188
- Tips 4, 16, 18, p. 132-133
- Black, Pink, Lemon Yellow Icing Colors, p. 131
- Buttercream Icing

- Ice sides, background areas on top and eyes smooth. With toothpick, mark eyeballs.
- Outline ears, face, tie, paws and body with tip 4 strings. Pipe in eyeballs, nose and tongue with tip 4 (flatten with finger dipped in cornstarch). Add tip 4 dot pupils to eyes. Pipe tip 4 beads and dots on bottom of paws.
- Cover ears, face, tie, body and paws with tip 16 stars. Trim tie with tip 4 dots. Print tip 4 message.
- Edge base with tip 18 "comma-motion" shell border. *Serves 12.*

ALL THE RIGHT MOO'S!

- Cuddles the Cow Pan, p. 180
- Tips 3, 4, 17, 21, p. 132-133
- Brown, Sky Blue, Black Icing Colors, p. 131
- Buttercream Icing
- Party hat

- Ice sides and background areas on top smooth. Outline horns, face and tie with tip 4 strings.
- Pipe in eyes, nostrils and inside of mouth with tip 4 (smooth with finger dipped in cornstarch).
- Fill in tuft of hair with tip 17 stripes. Cover horns, ears, face and tie with tip 17 stars.
- Print tip 3 message. Add tip 3 outline lashes. Edge base with tip 21 shell border. *Serves 12.*

ROARIN' GOOD TIME

- Kitty Cat Pan, p. 179
- Tips 3, 17, 21, p. 132-133
- Brown, Golden Yellow Icing Colors, p. 131
- Buttercream Icing

- Ice side smooth. Outline facial features, paws, body, legs and tail with tip 3 strings.
- Pipe in eyes, nose and mouth with tip 3 (smooth with finger dipped in cornstarch).
- Cover face, paws, body, legs and tail with tip 17 stars. Pipe tip 17 spatula-striped pull-out stripe mane and tail tuft.
- Print tip 3 message. Pipe tip 3 dot and whiskers on face. Edge base with tip 21 shell border. *Serves 12.*

COURTLY CAROUSEL

- 8 & 12 in. Round Pans, p. 167
- Tips 5, 16, 21, p. 132-133
- Golden Yellow, Red-Red Icing Colors, p. 131
- Carousel Separator Set, p. 142
- Variety Lollipops II, Hearts Hard Candy Molds, p. 117
- Birthday Candles, p. 145
- Cake Dividing Set, p. 140
- Dowel Rods, p. 165
- 8 & 14 in. Cake Circles, Tuk 'n Ruffle, Fanci-Foil Wrap, p. 139
- Hard Candy Recipe, p. 111
- Buttercream Icing

- Mold 4 diamond and 4 heart candies (see p. 111).
- Cover 14 in. cake circle with Fanci-Foil Wrap and trim with Tuk 'n' Ruffle. Ice 2-layer cakes smooth and prepare them for pillar construction (see p. 106).
- Using Cake Dividing Set, mark sides of 8 in. round into 8ths. Position candies at marks. Outline with tip 5 strings. Trim diamonds with tip 5 fleur-de-lis. Connect with tip 5 dots.
- Print tip 16 message on side of 12 in. cake. Edge separator plate with tip 21 elongated shells (work from edge of plate towards edge of cake). Pipe tip 21 elongated shell border on 8 in. top (work from outer edge towards center). Trim elongated shells with tip 16 outline. Add tip 16 rosettes to tails of shells.

On 12 in. cake top, pipe another row of tip 16 rosettes. Between shells on 12 in. top, pipe tip 16 stars.
- Edge bases with tip 16 rosettes. With tip 16, outline rosettes and trim centers with stars. Assemble tier on pillars. Push in candles. *Serves 48.*

PRINCE

- 11 x 15 in. Sheet Pan, p. 169
- Tips 2, 4, 14, 19, 104, p. 132-136
- Royal Blue, Golden Yellow, Red-Red, Black Icing Colors, p. 131
- '90 Pattern Book (Horse, Banner & Diamond Patterns), p. 121
- Cake Boards, Fanci-Foil Wrap, p. 139
- Color Flow Mix, p. 131
- Buttercream, Color Flow Icings

- Using color flow icing and tip 2, outline and flow in Horse, Banner and Diamond Patterns (see p. 108). Let dry completely.
- Ice cake smooth. Edge cake top with tip 104 ruffles. Trim with tip 4 beads. Pipe pairs of tip 19 C-motion shells in each corner. Trim centers of shells with tip 19 rosettes (will be covered with color flow "diamonds"). Pipe tip 2 scallops around cake top.
- Edge base with tip 19 shell border. Trim shells with tip 14 zigzags.
- At serving time, place sugar cubes on cake top to support color flow pieces. Position color flow. *Serves 30.*

*Note: Since buttercream icing will break down color flow, either position pieces on cake shortly before serving or place a piece of plastic wrap cut to fit on area first.

BIRTHDAY
Carousel Horses

MANDY

- Precious Pony Pan, p. 181
- Tips 4, 16, 17, 21, p. 132-133
- Golden Yellow, Brown, Wilton Red, Sky Blue, p. 131
- Piping Gel, p. 131
- Buttercream Icing
- Grease-resistant ribbon, pretzel rods
- Attach ribbon to pretzel rods with dots of icing. Let dry.
- Ice sides smooth. With toothpick, mark bridle, saddle and pole (for easier marking, lightly ice areas). Cover marks and outline pony with tip 4 strings.
- Pipe in eye with tip 4 (smooth with finger dipped in cornstarch). Cover ear, face, saddle, body, legs and hooves with tip 17 stars.
- For mane and tail, spatula-stripe white icing with yellow piping gel. Pipe tip 21 elongated shells on mane; curved stripes on tail.
- Edge base with tip 21 shell border. Pipe tip 16 star flowers on bridle and saddle. Dot centers with tip 4. Push in pretzel "poles." *Serves 12.*

MAJOR LEAGUER

- Baseball Glove Pan, p. 184
- Tips 1, 3, 12, p. 132-133
- Wilton Red Icing Color, p. 131
- Candy Melts™ * – White, Light Cocoa (1 bag of each), p. 115
- Candy Color Kit, p. 114
- Buttercream Icing

Fill "ball" with melted white Candy Melts. Let set. Mix remaining melted white candy and 1 bag of Light Cocoa together. Optional: Add orange Candy Color for a more authentic "leather" color. To mold glove out of candy, see p. 111.

- Ice cake smooth. Position candy glove on top. Outline seams and stitches on ball with tip 3 strings. Write tip 3 name.
- Edge base with tip 12 "base" ball border. Trim with tip 1 curved outlines. *Serves 12.*

ROOKIE COOKIES

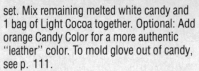

- Sports Cookie Cutter Set, p. 119
- Cookie Sheet, p. 172
- Tips 2, 4, 16, p. 132-133
- Lemon Yellow, Terra Cotta, Sky Blue, Red-Red, Orange Icing Colors, p. 131
- Roll-Out Cookie Dough Recipe, p. 109
- Royal Icing

- Out of cookie dough, cut shapes and bake per recipe directions. Let cool.
- **Bowling:** Outline with tip 4. Pipe in holes with tip 4 (smooth with finger dipped in cornstarch). Cover with tip 16 stars.
- **Football:** Outline with tip 4; fill in with tip 16 stars.
- **Basketball:** Outline with tip 4. Pipe tip 4 latticework net. Cover ball with tip 16 stars.
- **Baseball:** Outline with tip 4. Pipe in ball with tip 4 (smooth with finger). Add tip 2 outline stitches. Fill in with tip 16 stars.
- **Tennis:** Outline with tip 4. Pipe tip 4 latticework strings. Cover handle with tip 16 side-by-side stripes. Fill in ball with tip 16 stars.

— B I R T H D A Y —

Sports

MAKE A RACKET!

- 9 x 13 in. Sheet Pan, p. 169
- Tips 4, 16, p. 132-133
- Sky Blue, Kelly Green, Lemon Yellow, Brown Icing Colors, p. 131
- '90 Pattern Book (Net Pattern), p. 121
- Message Pattern Press Set, p. 140
- Sports Cookie Cutter Set, p. 119
- Buttercream Icing

- Ice cake smooth; sky, blue; grass, green. With toothpick, mark Net Pattern. Using Tennis Racket Cookie Cutter as a pattern press and Happy Birthday Message Press, imprint designs on cake top.
- Outline racket and ball with tip 4 strings. Cover racket handle with tip 16 side-by-side stripes. Fill in ball with tip 16 stars. Outline net and racket strings with tip 4 latticework. Add tip 4 side-by-side strings to top of net.
- Outline message with tip 4 and write name. Pipe tip 16 zigzag clouds. Edge top with tip 4 bead border; base with tip 16 shells. *Serves 20.*

SECOND HOME

- Golf Bag Pan, p. 184
- Tips 4, 233, p. 132,
- Kelly Green, Brown, Royal Blue Icing Colors, p. 131
- Golf Set, p. 144
- Piping Gel, p. 131
- Script Message Pattern Press, p. 140
- Granulated light brown sugar

- Ice top and sides smooth. Imprint message with pattern press. Write message and name with tip 4.
- Outline "sand traps and pond" with tip 4. Pipe in sand traps with tip 4 (smooth with finger dipped in cornstarch). Sprinkle "sand traps" with granulated light brown sugar. With tip 4, pipe in pond with tinted piping gel "water."
- Cover sides and add random clumps of pull-out grass with tip 233. Position golfer and flag on cake top. *Serves 12.*

Comic Characters

RAINBOW DINO

- Partysaurus Pan, p. 180
- Tips 3, 4, 17, p. 132-133
- Lemon Yellow, Kelly Green, Brown Icing Colors, p. 131
- Gumdrops
- Ice sides, scales and background areas on top smooth.

- Outline head, facial features, legs, body and tail with tip 4 strings.
- Pipe in nostril with tip 4 (smooth with finger dipped in cornstarch). Cover with tip 17 stars.
- Flatten about 20 gumdrops with a rolling pin for scales. Slice one gumdrop in half for eye. Position candy on cake top.
- Edge base with tip 17 shell border. Add tip 3 message. *Serves 12.*

HAPPY RETURNS FROM BATMAN*

- Super Heroes Pan, p. 182
- Tips 4, 16, p. 132-133
- Royal Blue, Lemon Yellow, Black Icing Colors, p. 121

- Cake Board, Fanci-Foil Wrap, p. 139
- Buttercream Icing
- Ice area where face mask will go (top and sides) and in between arms with blue icing.
- Outline suit, gloves and belt with tip 4 strings.
- Cover cape, gloves, suit and belt with tip 16 stars. Add tip 16 pull-out stars to gloves.
- Position face mask and emblem. *Serves 12.*

*Trademark licensed by DC Comics, Inc.
© 1978

MICHELANGELO™ IS RARIN' TO CELEBRATE!

- Teenage Mutant Ninja Turtles® Pan, p. 183
- Tips 3, 16, 21, p. 132-133
- Kelly Green, Brown, Orange, Wilton Red, Golden Yellow Icing Colors, p. 131
- Buttercream Icing

- Ice sides and message area smooth. Outline with tip 3 strings. Pipe in eyes and mouth with tip 3 (smooth with finger dipped in cornstarch).
- Cover face, bandanna, body, shell, bandolier, arms and legs with tip 16 stars.
- Print tip 3 initial and message. Edge base with tip 21 shell borders. *Serves 12.*

© 1989 Teenage Mutant Ninja Turtles® is a registered trademark of Mirage Studio, U.S.A. Michelangelo™ is a trademark of Mirage Studio, U.S.A.

COWABUNGA!
IT'S YOUR
BIRTHDAY
DUDE!

PRESENTING
BUGS BUNNY®

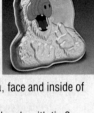

- **Bugs Bunny Pan,**
  p. 182
- **Tips 3, 16, 21,**
  p. 132-133
- **Sky Blue, Pink,**
  Wilton Red, Black Icing Colors, p. 131
- **Buttercream Icing**
- **Gift**
- Outline Bugs and message balloon with tip 3. Pipe in inside of ears, eyes, teeth, tongue and mouth with tip 3 (smooth with finger dipped in cornstarch).
- Cover Bugs and background on top with tip 16 stars; sides with tip 21 stars.
- Add tip 3 outline eyebrows and whiskers. Pipe tip 16 pull-out stripes on head. Position gift (atop a piece of plastic wrap). *Serves 12.*

® Trademark of Warner Bros. Inc.
© 1989

GIVIN' ALF®

- **ALF Pan, p. 183**
- **Tips 3, 16, 21,**
  p. 132-133
- **Brown* , Royal Blue**
  Icing Colors, p. 131
- **Gift**
- Ice sides, message area, face and inside of ear smooth.
- Outline head, body and hands with tip 3 strings. Print tip 3 message.
- Position ALF'S facemaker. With tip 16, cover outside of ear and add two stars inside of ear.
- Cover hands, body and face with tip 16 pull-out star"fur." Add tip 21 pull-out (side-by-side) stripe strands of hair. Pipe tip 21 elongated shell eyebrows.
- Edge base with tip 16 rosettes border. Trim with tip 3 dots. Position gift (atop a piece of plastic wrap) on cake top. *Serves 12.*

*or substitute chocolate icing

ALF is a Registered Trademark of Alien Productions
© 1987 Alien Productions. All Rights Reserved.

MARIO® IS
MAD TO PARTY!

- **Super Mario**
  Bros.® Pan, p. 194
- **Tips 3, 16, 21,**
  p. 132-133
- **Brown, Sky Blue,**
  Golden Yellow, Wilton Red, p. 131
- **Buttercream Icing**
- **Gift**
- Ice sides, background areas and soles of shoes smooth. Outline Mario with tip 3 strings.
- Pipe in eyes, emblem on cap, teeth and tongue with tip 3 (flatten with finger dipped in cornstarch). Add tip 3 dots to eyes (flatten with finger).
- Cover cap, face, hands, shirt, pants and shoes with tip 16 stars. Add tip 3 dot buttons. Print tip 3 message and "M" on cap.
- Pipe tip 16 brown stripes hair and mustache. Add tip 16 shell-motion eyebrows. Edge base with tip 21 shell border. Position gift beside cake. *Serves 12.*

© 1989 Nintendo of America Inc.

BIRTHDAY
Party Superstars

Say It With A Smile

RAISIN' CANE

- Oval Pan Set, p. 171
- Tips 2, 4, p. 132
- Burgundy, Black Icing Colors, p. 131
- '90 Pattern Book (Raisin Pattern), p. 121
- Color Flow Mix, p. 131
- Buttercream, Color Flow Icings

- Using Raisin Patterns and tip 2, make eyes, mouth, hands and tie out of color flow icing (see p. 108). Let dry.
- Generously ice 2-layer cake. Fluff with spatula to create a wrinkled effect.
- Position color flow pieces on cake top. Pipe tip 4 outline brows and mouth creases. *Serves 12.*

Note: Since buttercream icing will break down color flow, either position pieces on cake shortly before serving or place a piece of plastic wrap cut to fit on area first.

TOP BILLING

- 10 in. Square Pans, p. 169
- Tips 4, 10, 16, p. 132-133
- Kelly Green Icing Color, p. 131
- '90 Pattern Book (Money Pattern), p. 121
- Photograph*, green cellophane
*A photocopy of a photograph can be substituted.

- Position two cakes side by side; ice smooth. With a toothpick, mark Money Pattern on cake top.
- Trim photo to fit into the picture"frame" (adjust area to accommodate your photo). Cover photo with cellophane.
- Outline money and photo with tip 4 strings. Cover border, banner and numbers with tip 16 stars. Print tip 4 messages.
- Edge top with tip 4 bead border. Edge base with tip 10 ball border. Add tip 4 dollar signs. *Serves 14.*

BAG LADY

- 10 in. Round Pans, p. 168
- Tips 2, 3, 17, 19, p. 132-133
- Golden Yellow Icing Color, p. 131
- Script Pattern Press Message Set, p. 140
- Candy Melts™*–White (1 bag), p. 115
- Candy Colors Kit, p. 114
- Cake Dividing Set, p. 140
- Buttercream Icing
- Shoestring licorice, tissue paper

- Make shopping bags and charge plates following directions for Candy Cut-Out Method on p. 111. Complete by writing tip 2 messages with melted candy. Bend licorice for handles and attach with dots of candy. Stuff bags with tissue.
- Ice 2-layer cake smooth. Using Cake Dividing Set, mark sides into 8ths. Imprint message with pattern press. Write message and name with tip 3.
- Edge top with a row of tip 17 C-shells and a row of tip 17 shells. At marks, pipe tip 19 fleur-de-lis. Edge base with tip 19 shell border.
- Position bags and charge plates. *Serves 24.*

*brand confectionery coating.

MOUTHING OFF

- Happiness Heart Pan Set, p. 186
- Tips 3, 4, 16, p. 132-133
- Pink, Brown Icing Colors, p. 131
- '90 Pattern Book (Lips Pattern), p. 121
- Buttercream Icing
- Marshmallow creme

- Slice away point on heart. Ice 2-layer cake with brown or chocolate icing. With toothpick, mark Lips Pattern on top.
- With icing, outline lips and teeth using tip 4. Heat marshmallow creme in a double boiler. To flow in teeth and lips with melted marshmallow creme, see p. 108. With tip 3, flow in teeth with marshmallow creme. Tint remaining marshmallow creme pink and flow in lips with tip 3.
- Imprint message with pattern press. Print and write messages with tip 3. Edge base with tip 16 e-motion border. *Serves 12.*

17 THOUSAND DOLLARS 17

HAPPY BIRTHDAY CAROL

Born To Shop

Happy Birthday Linda

CREDIT

CHARGE

Read My Lips, George Happy Birthday

WHAT'S SHAKIN'?

- **Super Heroes Pan™,** p. 182
- **Tips 1, 2, 4, 16, 18,** p. 132-133
- **Copper, Black, Golden Yellow, Teal Icing Colors,** p. 131
- **'90 Pattern Book (Rock Star Pattern),** p. 121
- **Color Flow Mix,** p. 131
- **Buttercream, Color Flow Icings**

- With color flow icing and tip 2, make glasses, scarf, guitar buckle and message balloon with Rock Star Patterns (see p. 108).
- Ice sides and background areas on top smooth. With toothpick, mark neckline of shirt. Outline facial features, shirt, cape, belt and hands with tip 4.
- Cover face, neck, shirt, cape, hands and belt with tip 16 stars. Pipe tip 16 pull-out stripe hair (overpipe for dimension). Pipe tip 1 rope chains. Trim neck and cuffs with tip 2 dots. Pipe tip 4 dot medallion (flatten with finger dipped in cornstarch).
- Edge base with tip 18 shell border. Position

color flow pieces. With color flow icing, print tip 2 message on "balloon." Add tip 2 string fringe to scarf. *Serves 12.*

Note: Since buttercream icing will break down color flow, either postion pieces on cake shortly before serving or place a piece of plastic wrap cut to fit on area first.

*TRADEMARKS LICENSED BY DC COMICS, INC. © 1978

BE THERE OR BE SQUARE

- **11 x 15 in. Sheet Pan,** p. 169
- **7 in. Round Pan,** p. 168
- **Tips 1, 2, 3, 6, 18,** p. 132-133
- **'90 Pattern Book (Drive-In Patterns),** p. 121
- **Orange, Teal, Lemon Yellow, Wilton Red Icing Colors,** p. 131
- **Treats Hard Candy Molds,** p. 117
- **Lollipop Sticks,** p. 114
- **Color Flow Mix,** p. 131
- **Script Message Pattern Press,** p. 140
- **Hard Candy Recipe,** p. 111
- **Buttercream, Color Flow Icings**
- **Mini and large marshmallows, uncooked spaghetti, sugar cubes**

- Mold 3 lollipops out of hard candy.
- To Make Drive-In Patterns out of color flow icing, see p. 108. Use tip 2 to outline and flow in each piece. To make arches (6 are needed), pipe three tip 2 outlines, side-by-side. Let pieces dry.
- **For cars:** Fasten mini marshmallow wheels to large marshmallows with pieces of uncooked spaghetti. Using color flow icing, outline cars with tip 2. Let dry.
- Ice round (on a 6 in. cake circle) and sheet (on a foil-covered cake board) cakes smooth. Cut and position dowel rods in sheet where round will go. Place cakes together.
- With toothpick, mark windows and doors on side of round. Outline with tip 3. Print tip 1 words on doors and windows. Imprint message on sheet with pattern press. Outline with tip 3.
- Edge top and base of "diner" with tip 6 rope border. Pipe tip 18 rope borders at top and base of sheet.
- Position arches around diner. Place sugar cubes or mini marshmallows around top of diner to support color flow roof. Add roof. Push in lollipops. Lean sign against lollipops. Add cars. *Serves 35.*

AHHH, HOW REFRESHING!

- **Bowling Pan Set,** p. 184
- **Tip 4,** p. 132
- **Brown* Icing Color,** p. 131
- **Buttercream Icing**
- **Bendable drinking straws**

- Ice cakes smooth. Add bottle grooves with spatula. Outline labels with tip 4 strings. Write tip 4 "Cola."
- Mound white icing to resemble foam (swirl and pat for a fluffy effect). Cut straws and push into cake. *Both serve 12.*

*Or use chocolate icing.

Note: One "cola" cake is shown, but we suggest you decorate two to serve more.

HOLD THE MAYO

- **Hamburger Pan,** p. 177
- **Tips 3, 16, 124,** p. 132-136
- **Golden Yellow, Kelly Green, Brown, Wilton Red Icing Colors,** p. 131
- **Buttercream Icing**

- Ice bun areas smooth; outline bun, cheese, mustard, tomato and meat with tip 3 strings.
- Pipe in tip 3 cheese, mustard and ketchup areas (smooth with finger dipped in cornstarch).
- Pipe in inside of tomatoes with tip 3 (smooth with finger dipped in cornstarch). Fill in the rest with tip 16 stars.
- Cover meat areas with tip 16 zigzags. Pipe tip 124 ruffle lettuce. Add tip 3 dot message. *Serves 12.*

BIRTHDAY

Fabulous 50's

Milestones

21-CANDLE SALUTE

- **11 x 15 in. Sheet Pan, p. 169**
- **Tips 2, 4, 21, p. 132-133**
- **Orange, Pink, Kelly Green, Lemon Yellow Icing Colors, p. 131**
- **'90 Pattern Book (Color Flow 21/Panels & Geometric Design), p. 121**
- **Color Flow Mix, p. 131**
- **Birthday Candles, p. 145**
- **Color Flow Icing Recipe, p. 108**
- **Buttercream Icing**

- Make 21, triangle and message panels out of color flow with tip 2 (see p. 108). Let dry. Add tip 2 message with stiffened color flow icing.

- Ice cake smooth. With toothpick, mark Geometric Design Patterns on cake top. Outline diamonds and corners with tip 4 strings. Fill in with tip 21 stars.

- Edge green area at top and base with tip 4 bead borders. Position color flow pieces*. Push in candles. *Serves 20-30.*

*Note: Since buttercream icing will break down color flow, either position pieces on cake shortly before serving or place a piece of plastic wrap cut to fit on area first.

FLIRTY THIRTY

- **10 in. Round Pans, p. 168**
- **Tips 2, 4, 16, 19, 66, p. 132-134**
- **Kelly Green, Brown, Violet, Sky Blue,** Orange, Lemon Yellow, Pink Icing Colors, p. 131
- **'90 Pattern Book (Rainbow Pattern), p. 121**
- **Birthday Candles, p. 145**
- **Buttercream Icing**
- **Candy-coated gum**

- Ice 2-layer cake smooth. With toothpick, mark Rainbow Pattern on cake top.

- Outline rainbow with tip 4. Fill in rainbow stripes on top and side with tip 19 stars.

- Pipe tip 16 side-by-side stripe tree trunks and branches on top and sides. Cover tree tops with tip 66 pull-out leaves. Write tip 2 messages.

- Edge base with tip 66 shell-motion border. Add candy-coated gum path on top and side. Push in candles. *Serves 24.*

STILL IN BLOOM
- Horseshoe Pan, p. 174
- Tips 2, 4, 12, 67, 104, 225, 362, p. 132-136
- Flower Nail No. 7, p. 138
- Creamy Peach, Kelly Green, Violet, Lemon Yellow Icing Colors, p. 131
- Birthday Numbers Set, p. 145
- Edible Glitter, p. 130
- Script Message Pattern Press, p. 140
- Buttercream, Royal (for daisies) Icings
- Candles, greenery

- **Make flowers:** 3 tips 12 and 104 roses; 3 tip 104 daisies with tip 4 dot centers (pat centers with edible glitter); 6 tip 225 drop flowers with tip 2 dot centers.
- Ice cake smooth. Imprint message and write tip 2 message and name. Pipe tip 104 half roses and rosebuds. Add tip 4 calyxes,

sepals and stems. Position roses, daisies and drop flowers. Trim with tip 67 leaves.
- With toothpick, mark ½ in. intervals on sides. Connect marks with tip 2 overlapping drop strings. Edge top and base with tip 362 shell borders. Push in numbers; add greenery and candles. *Serves 12.*

R. I. P.
- Long Loaf Pan, p. 172
- Tips 3, 4, 5, 9, 125, p. 132-139
- Brown, Golden Yellow, Kelly Green Icing Colors, p. 131
- '90 Pattern Book (Calla Lily Petals Patterns), p. 121
- Gum Paste Flower Kit, Flower Formers, Gum Paste Accessory Kit, Gum Paste Mix or Glucose & Gum-Tex™, p. 130
- Birthday Numbers Set, p. 145
- Cake Boards, Fanci-Foil Wrap, p. 139
- Gum Paste Recipe, p. 109
- Buttercream & Royal Icings

- Make 3 leaves and 3 calla lilies out of gum paste (see p. 109).
- **For lid:** Cut an 8 x 4 in. rectangle from cake board and cover with white Fanci-Foil.
- **For "coffin:"** Ice cake smooth, half of top white, rest brown. Mound icing on white area. Shape and flatten with finger dipped in cornstarch to form pillow (approximately 3 x 2 in.).
- Print tip 4 message on side. Add tip 5 outline handles. Edge white area with tip 5 bead border. Pipe tip 3 beads on remainder of top and on corners.
- Spatula-stripe stiffened buttercream; edge lid and white area with tip 125 ruffles. Trim ruffles with tip 4 beads.
- Place flowers on cake top and pipe tip 125 ribbon bow. Edge base with tip 9 bead border. Push in Birthday Numbers. Position lid so that it rests on numbers. *Serves 12.*

JUST DUCKY

- **Country Goose Pan,**
  p. 179
- **Tips 4, 6, 67,**
  p. 132-134
- **Teal, Golden Yellow,**
  Brown, Kelly Green
  Icing Colors, p. 131
- **Buttercream Icing**
- Ice sides and background area on cake top smooth. With toothpick, turn goose into

a duck by shortening neck and thickening body slightly.
- Outline duck with tip 4 strings. Pipe in bill and eye with tip 4 (smooth with finger dipped in cornstarch).
- With tip 6, pipe in head and body. For mottled effect on head, pipe a few rows of blue; the rest green. Feather icing by pulling end of tip through the icing.
- Pipe tip 67 pull-out leaves on sides. Edge base with tip 67 shell-motion border. *Serves 12.*

FOXY GUY

- **10 in. Square Pans,**
  p. 169
- **Tips 3, 6, 12, 66,**
  102, 104, 106,
  p. 132-136
- **Ivory, Brown, Teal,**
  Terra Cotta Icing Colors, p. 131
- **'90 Pattern Book (Horn Pattern), p. 121**
- **Script Message Pattern Press, p. 140**
- **Buttercream Icing**
- Make 10 tip 106 drop flowers with tip 3 dot centers.

- Ice 2-layer cake smooth. With toothpick, mark Horn Pattern. With message press, imprint message. Write tip 3 message; print tip 3 dot name.
- Figure pipe horn with tip 12 (see p. 105). Add tip 3 outline stems. Position drop flowers. Trim with tip 66 leaves. Pipe eucalyptus – tip 3 stems; tips 102 and 104 flute leaves. Add tip 104 ribbon bow.
- Pipe tip 6 beads down corners. Edge top with tip 6 reverse bead border. Add tip 3 dots. Edge base with tip 12 beads; trim with tip 104 flutes. *Serves 24.*

Gentlemen's Choice

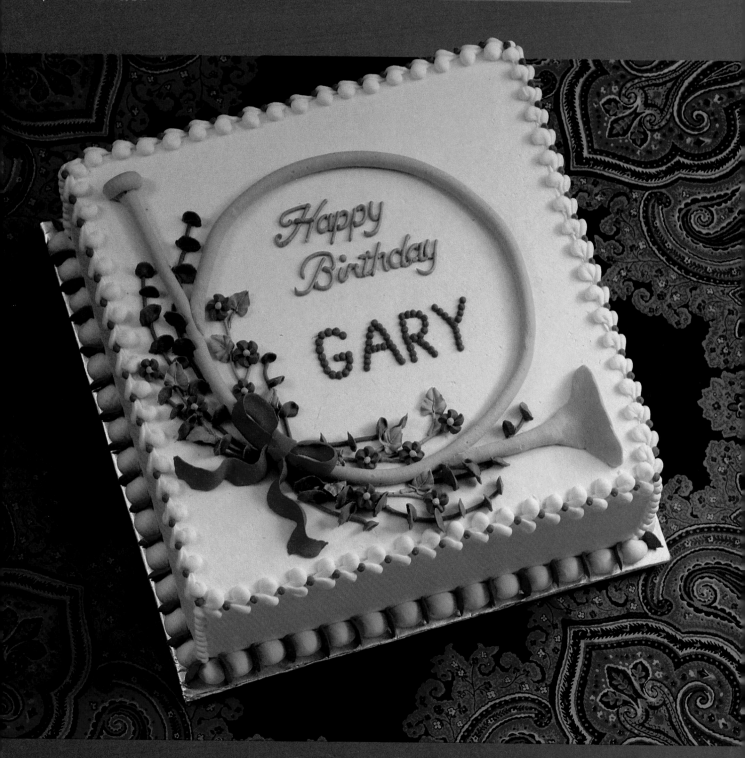

BIRTHDAY

Victorian Romance

MY FAIR LADY

- 8 & 12 in. 3 in. deep Round Pans, p. 170
- Tips 3, 13, 16, 32, 66, 68, 102, 103, 224, p. 132-135
- 1 pc. Lily Nail, p. 138
- Burgundy Icing Color, p. 131
- Pearl White Stamens, p. 130
- 8, 12 in. Cake Circles, p. 139
- Dowel Rods, p. 159
- Birthday Candles, p. 145.
- Buttercream, Royal Icings

- With royal icing, make 6 tip 102 and 8 tip 103 petunias. Add tip 13 star centers. Trim with pearl white stamens. Let dry. Make 20 tip 224 drop flowers with tip 3 dot centers.
- Ice cakes smooth.
- To prepare 3 in. deep cakes for stacked tiered cake assembly, see p. 106.
- Print tip 3 message on top tier. Edge top of 8 in. and sides of 12 in. with tip 32 crown border. Trim with tip 16 stars. Between tiers, pipe tip 32 comma-motion scrolls. Edge base with tip 32 reverse shell border.
- Arrange flowers on tops. Pipe tip 68 leaves on petunias, tip 66 leaves on drop flowers. *Serves 32.*

This cake (in different colors) is shown on the cover celebrating our Yearbook's 20th anniversary.

TIMELESS ELEGANCE

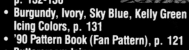

- **18 in. Half Round Pan, p. 170**
- **Tips 2, 3, 4, 6, 21, 103, 125, 224 p. 132-136**
- **Burgundy, Ivory, Sky Blue, Kelly Green Icing Colors, p. 131**
- **'90 Pattern Book (Fan Pattern), p. 121**
- **Buttercream Icing**
- Make 15 tip 224 drop flowers with tip 3 dot centers.
- Ice cake smooth–sides ivory, top, light burgundy. Mark Fan Pattern on cake top.

- Ice small semicircle dark burgundy. Score "crease lines" (use points of scallops as a guide) with a knife or spatula.
- Cover scalloped bands with tip 2 cornelli lace. Edge "bottom" of fan with tip 6 bead border. Pipe tip 103 ruffle in center and tip 125 ruffle around edge. Trim large ruffle with tip 2 zigzags, small ruffle with tip 4 beads.
- Edge cornelli bands with tip 4 beads. Pipe tip 103 ribbon bow.
- Edge base with tip 21 C-motion scrolls. Trim each with tip 103 ruffles. Add flowers. *Serves 50.*

This unforgettable collection was designed by renowned chocolatier, Elaine Gonzalez. Each confection is a reflection of talent and tastefulness.

EXCLAMATION

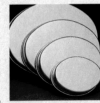

- 8 in. Square Pans, p. 169
- Tips 1, 6, 12, p. 132
- Parchment Triangles, p. 141
- Candy Melts™ * – White, Light Cocoa, (2 bags each), p. 115
- Candy Colors Kit, p. 115
- 11 in. Square Separator Plate, p. 166
- Modeling Candy Recipe (1½ recipes), p. 112
- '90 Pattern Book (Hat Pattern), p. 121
- Buttercream Icing
- Pour melted coating over separator plate, rotate until evenly covered, then pour off excess. Let set.
- Mold party hat out of white melted coating (see p. 113). To pipe streamers on hat, tint ¼ cup of coating green. Use cocoa coating (left over from covering plate) to add message. Use tip 1 or a cut bag to pipe coating (see p. 110).

- For blower, confetti, streamers and fringe on hat, make 1 recipe of modeling candy with white Candy Melts. Reserve ¼ of recipe, then tint ½ recipe red and ¼ yellow. For ribbon, bow and streamers, make ½ recipe of cocoa modeling candy. See p. 112 for creating these unique trims.
- Place 2-layer cake on candy-coated plate and ice smooth. Add modeling candy ribbon on top and sides. Pipe tip 6 rows of beads on corners of sides. Edge top and base with tip 12 bulb borders.
- Add bow, hat, blower, confetti and streamers. *Serves 16.*

INSPIRATION

- Oval Pan Set (13 x 9⅞ & 16 x 12⅜ in. are used), p. 171
- Tip 6, p. 132
- Candy Melts™ – Light Cocoa (4 bags), p. 115

- Decorator's Brush, p. 140
- Modeling Candy Recipe, p. 112
- Ganache Recipe, p. 113
- Candle, lemon leaves
- Out of modeling candy, make 1 large, 4 medium size roses and 8 rosebuds (see p. 112).
- For plate: Pour (approximately 2 bags) melted candy into largest oval pan. Let set and unmold (see p. 111).
- Cut leaves to desired size and paint with melted candy (see p. 112).
- Place oval cake on a wire rack over a drip pan and cover with Ganache Glaze. Whip ganache, and pipe tip 6 bead border at base.
- Arrange flowers and leaves on top and side. *Serves 20.*

FASCINATION

- 9 in. Heart Pan, p. 187
- '90 Pattern Book (Heart, Lacy Collar & Scallop Patterns), p. 121
- Candy Melts™ * – Cocoa (2 bags), p. 115
- Flower Formers, p. 140
- 11 in. Heart Separator Plate, p. 166
- Buttercream Icing
- To pipe Heart, Lacy Collar and 12 Scallops with Candy Melts, see p. 112.
- Pour melted coating over separator plate, rotate until evenly covered, then pour off excess. Let set.
- Ice cake smooth. Carefully position Heart in center, Lacy Collar around edges (cover seams with melted coating) and Scallops at base. *Serves 16.*

DEDICATION

- 9 in. Petal Pan, p. 171
- Parchment Triangles, p. 141
- Candy Melts™ * – Light & Dark Cocoa, White, p. 115
- '90 Pattern Book (Dogwood & Easel Patterns), p. 121
- For easel: Outline Easel Pattern, then flow in with melted coating. Make two. When set, turn over and repeat procedure. Attach halves together with melted coating, stand up immediately and adjust angle of sides.
- For plaque: Pour melted coating into pan. Let set. Unmold. To "engrave" Dogwood Pattern on plaque, see p. 113. Outline pattern and let set. Flow in flowers and leaves, let set. Add dot flower centers and berries. Write name. Edge petal with scrolls.
- When easel and plaque are completely set, position together.

*brand confectionery coating

BIRTHDAY
Candy Artistry

You're Very Special

FRANK'S PLACE

- **Football Hero Pan, p. 184**
- **Tips 2, 4, 16, 18, 21, 233, p. 132-133**
- **Leaf Green, Brown, Orange Icing Colors, p. 131**
- **'90 Pattern Book (Monster Pattern), p. 121**
- **Buttercream Icing**

- Ice sides and background areas on top orange. With toothpick, mark Monster Pattern (for easier marking, lightly ice area white). To square off head, build up area with brown icing. On tombstone, add a small amount of brown to white icing. Blend slightly to give a marble effect.

- Cover marks with tip 4 strings. Pipe in eye and fingernails with tip 4 (smooth with finger dipped in cornstarch). Add tip 16 pull-out stars eyebrow. Print message and dates on tombstone with tip 2.

- Cover face, neck, shirt and hands with tip 16 stars. Outline ear with tip 16. Add tip 16 rosette bolt at neck.

- Pipe tip 233 pull-out hair (overpipe to add dimension). Pipe tip 4 outline scars. Cover jacket with tip 18 pull-out stars (work in rows from bottom to top). Edge base with tip 21 shell borders. *Serves 12.*

POSSESSED ADDRESS

- **Haunted House Kit, p. 185**
- **Cookie Sheets, p. 172**
- **Tips 3, 16, 48, 67, 233, p. 132-137**
- **Violet, Moss Green, Orange and Brown Icing Colors, p. 131**
- **12 in. Cake Circles, Fanci-Foil Wrap, p. 139**
- **Royal Icing**

- Following recipe and instructions included with your Haunted House Kit, prepare gingerbread; cut, bake and assemble house.

- Outline ghosts with tip 3. Flow in bodies with thinned icing. Let set. Add tip 3 dot facial features. On tombstones: Write messages and pipe designs with tip 1.

- On trees: Pipe tip 16 side-by-side tree trunks and branches. Add tip 67 leaves.

- Cover roofs and canopy with rows of tip 48 stripe "shingles." Attach candy and cookies to house and "yard" with dots of icing. Pipe tip 233 spatula-striped, pull-out grass. Add brown sugar mounds and gum path.

FRIGHT FLIGHT

- **9 x 13 in. Sheet Pan, p. 169**
- **Tips 2, 12, 13, 17, 67, p. 132-134**
- **Leaf Green, Brown, Orange, Lemon Yellow Icing Colors, p. 131**
- **Witch Cookie Cutter, p. 118**
- **Buttercream Icing**

- Ice sheet cake smooth. Print tip 3 message. Press Witch Cutter onto cake top to imprint design. Outline with tip 2. Cover face, hands, dress, moon, broom band and hat with tip 13 stars. Cover broom straws with tip 13 side-by-side stripes.

- Figure pipe tip 12 pumpkins. Edge "ground" area on cake top with tip 67 shell-motion border. Pipe tip 17 shell borders around remainder of cake top and base.

- Figure pipe tip 12 ghosts on top and sides. Add tip 3 dot eyes. Pipe tip 3 outline vines on pumpkins. Trim with tip 67 leaves. *Serves 14.*

Happy Spirits

WOODLAND HAUNT

- **7 in. Round Pans, p. 168**
- **Petite Doll Pan, p. 175**
- **Tips 3, 12, p. 133**
- **Brown Icing Color, p. 131**
- **6 in. Cake Circles, p. 139**
- **Decorating Triangle, p. 141**
- **Jack-O-Lantern Picks, p. 143**
- **Buttercream, Chocolate Buttercream Icings**
- **Spice drops**
- **For Tree Stump:** Ice top of 2-layer cake smooth. Use decorating triangle to imprint tree "rings" on top.
- Generously ice sides and "roots" on serving tray (or 14 in. foil-covered cake circle). Use decorating triangle to carve facial features and pull out bark indentations. Add candy eyes.
- **For Ghosts:** Place mini cakes on cake circles cut to fit. Position beside "stump" cake. Ice smooth, pulling icing out at base of cakes. Figure pipe arms with tip 12. Add candy eyes. Pipe tip 3 outline brows, mouth and dot pupils.

- Position beside and atop stump. Push cake picks into ghosts. *Serves 13.*

CANDLELIGHT CREEPIES

- **Ball Pan, p. 184**
- **Tips 2A, 3, 21, p. 132-133**
- **Orange, Lemon Yellow, Brown Icing Colors, p. 131**
- **'90 Pattern Book (Pumpkin Face Pattern), p. 121**
- **12 in. Hexagon Separator Plate, p. 166**
- **3 & 5 in. Grecian Pillars (2 of each size), p. 165**
- **14 in. Cake Circle, Gold Fanci-Foil Wrap, p. 139**
- **1 bag Light Cocoa Candy Melts™*, p. 115**
- **Wacky Witch Cake Top, p. 143**
- **Decorator's Brush, p. 140**
- **Dowel Rod, p. 165**
- **Buttercream Icing**
- **Marshmallow, candles, 2 silk leaves**

- Cut cake circle into 12 in. hexagon (use separator plate as a guide) and cover with gold foil.
- Melt Candy Melts. Dip marshmallow into candy. "Paint" pillars. Let set. Pour candy onto hexagon base plate. Rotate to coat evenly. Tap gently on counter to break air bubbles. Let set.
- Allow ball cake to cool completely. With knife, slice off round part on one half of ball so it sits level on plate (secure to plate with icing). Ice halves together. Attach dipped marshmallow to top with icing.
- Lightly ice an area on side for the face. With toothpick, mark Face Pattern. Outline with tip 3. Pipe in facial features with tip 3 (smooth with finger dipped in cornstarch). Cover with tip 21 stars.
- Position pillars in plate. Figure pipe tip 2A ghosts on pillars (see p. 105). Add tip 3 facial features. Position Wacky Witch. Shave ends of candles to fit into pillars. Push in candles. *Serves 12.*

*brand confectionery coating

HALLOWEEN
Ghost Stories

PLAYFUL POLTERGEIST

- Boo Ghost Pan, p. 185
- Tips 4, 18, p. 132-133
- Orange Icing Color, p. 131
- Buttercream Icing
- Outline facial features, "boo" and hands with tip 4. Pipe in eyes, mouth and tongue with tip 4 (smooth with finger dipped in cornstarch).
- Cover ghost and "boo" with tip 18 stars. *Serves 12.*

HALLOWEEN
Thrillers

ALL SMILES
- Jack-O-Lantern Pan, p. 185
- Oval Pan Set, p. 171
- Tips 2, 6, p. 132
- Orange Icing Color, p. 131
- Candy Melts™*–Light Cocoa, Fall Mix, p. 115
- Pumpkin, Halloween Variety Set Candy Molds, p. 117
- Roll-Out Cookie Dough Recipe, p. 109
- Candy-coated chocolates

- **To Make Box:** Tint dough orange. Roll dough out on a lightly floured surface to ⅜ in. thickness (use pan as a guide to size). Carefully transfer dough to inside of Jack-O-Lantern pan, then press into indentations. Smooth edges with finger (dough should not be up the sides). Puncture dough with a fork. Bake 15-20 minutes or until edges begin to pull away from the pan. Turn out onto a rack to cool. Repeat procedure for bottom of box.

- **For sides:** Cut 1½ in. wide strips. On the outside, grease the sides of an oval pan. Gently press strips around outside. Smooth seams when adding a new strip. Cover strips with foil and bake 10-13 minutes. Slide onto a rack to cool.

- **To assemble box:** Center sides on flat side of cookie bottom. Pour melted candy inside and rotate to coat evenly. Pour out excess.

- Decorate with melted coating. Pipe bead borders on bottom of box, tip 4 at top, tip 8 at base. On lid, outline facial features, stem and grooves with tip 2. Fill with candy and let set. Print message with tip 2. Attach candy-coated chocolates for eyes.

- Mold a variety of colorful Halloween treats (see p. 110). Place inside your pumpkin cookie box. Cover with lid.

SO MANY WAYS TO USE SCARECROW PAN

Putting on quite a show, our Scarecrow (p. 185) knows how to be bewitching or beguiling, too. You're bound to think of other new faces. All designs are decorated with Buttercream icing. Each *serves 12.*

WITCH
- Tips 3, 16, 21, p. 132-133
- Violet, Black, Leaf Green, Orange Icing Colors, p. 131

- With toothpick, mark facial features (for easier marking lightly ice area). Outline witch with tip 3. Pipe in eyes and mouth with tip 3 (smooth with finger dipped in cornstarch). Add tip 3 dot teeth.

- Pipe in collar with tip 21. Cover face and shoes with tip 16 stars, hat and dress with tip 21 stars. Add tip 16 pull-out star hair and hands. Print tip 3 message.

SCARECROW
- Tips 3, 16, 102, p. 132-136
- Leaf Green, Golden Yellow, Violet, Orange, Brown Icing Colors, p. 131

- Ice background areas on top white. Outline scarecrow with tip 3 strings.

- Cover band of hat and pant cuffs with tip 16 zigzags. Cover hat, face, shirt, overalls with tip 16 stars.

- Pipe tip 16 pull-out star straw hair, hands and feet. Trim shirt with tip 102 ruffles. Add tip 16 star eyes and tip 3 dot buttons.

VAMPIRE
- Tips 4, 16, 21, p. 132-133
- Black, Leaf Green, Wilton Red Icing Colors, p. 131
- '90 Pattern Book (Vampire Pattern), p. 121

- Ice background area on cake top white. With toothpick, mark Vampire Pattern and shoes (for easier marking, lightly ice areas). Cover marks with tip 4 strings.

- Pipe in eyes and mouth with tip 4 (smooth with finger dipped in cornstarch). Cover face, shirt, suit and shoes with tip 16 stars.

- Print tip 4 message. Pipe tip 4 dot buttons on shirt. Add tip 4 dot pupils to eyes and pull-out bead fangs. Overpipe eyebrows and nose with tip 4.

- Cover cape with tip 21 elongated zigzags. Pipe tip 21 spatula-striped pull-out star hair.

GOBBLE, GOBBLE

- **9 x 13 in. Sheet Pan, p. 169**
- **Tips 3, 8, 12, 18, 20, 352, p. 132-134**
- **Leaf Green, Brown, Orange, Golden Yellow Icing Colors, p. 131**
- **'90 Pattern Book (Turkey, Pumpkins, Message Patterns), p. 121**
- **Buttercream Icing**

- Ice cake smooth. With toothpick, mark Turkey, Pumpkin and Message Patterns on cake top. Outline letters with tip 3.
- Figure pipe tips 3 and 12 turkey (see p. 105). Edge feathers with tip 3 white zigzags.
- Figure pipe pumpkins with tip 8. Add tip 3 stems.
- Pipe tip 3 outline vines. Trim with tip 352 leaves.
- With tip 21, edge top with reserve shell border; base with shells. *Serves 14.*

HOLLY-DAY MINCEMEAT

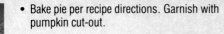

- **Holly Cookie Cutter, p. 118**
- **Favorite mincemeat pie recipe**

- Roll out pie crust to ¼ in. thickness. With holly cutters, cut 3 out of pie crust. Prepare pie per recipe directions.
- Place "holly" on pie and bake, following recipe.

PUMPKIN PRIDE

- **Cookie Sheet, p. 172**
- **Pumpkin Cookie Cutter, p. 118**
- **Pumpkin pie**

- Cut pumpkin out of pie dough. Bake separately on cookie sheet until golden brown.

- Bake pie per recipe directions. Garnish with pumpkin cut-out.

HAVE A TREE-FOR-ALL

- **Mini Christmas Tree Pan, p. 191**
- **Tip 2, p. 132**
- **Crescent Coffee Cake Recipe, p. 109**
- **Confectioner's Glaze**

- Prepare trees, following recipe directions. Omit glaze and substitute chopped cherries for raisins. Bake at 375° for 8 to 10 minutes. Unmold and cool on wire rack.
- To decorate: Use tip 2 and drizzle thinned icing over cakes. *Each serves 1.*

DATE NUT BREAD BOY

- **Gingerbread Boy Pan, p. 191**
- **Tip 21, p. 133**
- **Cream Cheese Icing**
- **2 packages of date nut bread mix, nuts for garnish.**

- Bake bread. Note: Place on serving plate with crown side up (don't level).

- With cream cheese icing and tip 21, pipe star eyes, rosette nose and buttons, outline mouth. Edge base with rosettes. Add nuts.

THANKSGIVING
and
CHRISTMAS

Holiday Time

KALEIDOSCOPE GOODIES

- Cookie Sheets, p. 169
- Star & Round Cookie Cutter Sets, p. 119
- Tip 2, p. 132
- Wilton Red, Kelly Green Icing Colors, p. 131
- '90 Pattern Book (Cookie Patterns), p. 121
- Color Flow Mix or Meringue Powder, p. 131
- Roll-Out Cookie Recipe, p. 109
- Color Flow or Royal Icing
- Straight pin

- Out of cookie dough, cut a variety of round and star shapes. Bake and cool per recipe directions. Outline edge of each cookie with tip 2.
- Use color flow or thin royal to color flow consistency and decorate one cookie at a time. With a cut bag, flow in white icing, then immediately pipe lines or dots with tip 2 tinted icing (not thinned). Pull a straight pin down through lines of design (from center out to edge). The direction will vary with the effect you want to achieve, (see p. 108 for more details).
- Let set 24 hours or until dry to touch.

CHRISTMAS HOUSE

- Cookie Sheets, p. 169
- Gingerbread House Kit, p. 191
- Spritz Cookie Press, p. 118
- Tips 4, 12, 18, p. 132-133
- Wilton Red, Leaf Green Icing Colors, p. 131
- Cake Boards and Fanci-Foil Wrap, p. 139
- Royal Icing (3 recipes needed)
- Grandma's Gingerbread and Spritz Cookie Recipes p. 109
- Spice drops, candy canes, red and green sugar, fruit-flavored sticks, dragees, peppermint sticks

- To pipe "roof shingles" out of spritz cookie dough, use bar cookie disc in cookie press.

Hold straight up and squeeze trigger twice. Make 48 cookie shingles. Sprinkle with red and green sugar before baking. For door and side windows, use same disc but hold press at a 45° angle. Squeeze out three 3 in. bars (make extras, if you want to decorate back wall). For front windows, tint cookie dough with green icing color. Use "cross" disc in cookie press; hold straight to squeeze out square windows. Bake and cool.

- **Gingerbread House:** Make one gingerbread recipe. Cut pieces, following directions in Gingerbread House Kit for the Country Church. Bake and cool. Place pieces on racks in drip pans. Pour thinned royal icing evenly over each piece. Allow to dry thoroughly.
- On foil-covered board, assemble house, following instructions in booklet (excluding steeple). Attach cookie doors and windows with royal icing. Outline windowpanes and scallops around door with tip 4 strings. Add tip 4 bead heart to door. Pipe tip 18 zigzags "shutters." Edge doorway with tip 18 stars. Cut spice drops in half. Press dragees onto the cut side.
- **On Roof:** Attach cookie "shingles" to roof (alternate colors). Edge eaves, roof and corners of walls with tip 18 zigags. Pipe tip 12 snowdrifts, pull tip down to form peaks. Attach candies to roof, eaves and windows with dots of icing (if necessary).
- Generously ice cake board with spatula, fluff icing for snowy effect. Add candy to base as shown. Connect "fence post" candy sticks with tip 4 drop strings (add light corn syrup to icing to prevent breakage).

STAR GAZE

- Cookie Sheets, p. 169
- Christmas Cookie Tree Kit, p.
- Tip 16, p. 133
- Wilton Red Icing Color, p. 131
- Roll-Out Cookie Dough Recipe, p. 109
- Quick Pour & Royal Icings
- Green tinted sugar

- Use the recipes and follow instructions included in your Christmas Cookie Tree Kit for making and baking cookies.
- **To ice:** Place cookie stars on a cake rack over a drip pan. Pour white icing over all but the smallest cookie. Ice smallest cookie red. Start in the center of each and work toward edges with spatula; be sure to cover sides. When almost dry, sprinkle white cookies with tinted sugar. Let dry completely, approximately 1 hour.
- Stack stars (largest to the smallest) securing them together with a little icing. Trim with tip 16 royal icing rosettes. Attach red cookie on top with icing.

WINTER WONDERLAND

- 11 x 15 in. Sheet Pan, p.
- Tips 2, 4, 14, 17, p. 132-133
- Kelly Green, Leaf Green, Wilton Red Icing Colors, p. 131
- Snowman, Cottage Cookie Cutters, p. 119
- Buttercream Icing

- Ice cake smooth—sky area green blue (use Kelly Green), snow-covered ground and sides white.
- With toothpick, mark hills and draw triangle trees in different sizes. Use cookie cutters as pattern presses to imprint guidelines for house and snowman.
- Outline hills, trees with tip 4 garlands, cottage and snowman with tip 4 strings.
- **On cottage:** Pipe in windows, doorstep and snow with tip 4 (use a heavy pressure to build up snow). Outline windowpanes with tip 4. Cover with tip 14 stars.
- **On snowman:** Pipe tip 2 dot facial features and buttons. Add tip 2 outline mouth. Cover with tip 14 stars. Add tip 2 string fringe to scarf and dot berries on hat.
- Pipe tip 14 star snowflakes randomly on sky and snow. Add tip 2 message. Edge top with tip 17 zigzags. Edge base with tip 17 rosette border. Trim with tip 2 strings and dots. *Serves 24.*

ANGELINA

- **Wonder Mold Pan,** p. 175
- **Tips 2, 16, 125,** p. 132-136
- **Freckle-Face Doll Pick, p. 145**
- **Gold Fanci-Foil Wrap, p. 139**
- **Swirls (2 needed), p. 160**
- **Buttercream Icing**
- **Gold doilies, ribbon**

- Cut 9 snowflake medallions out of doilies. Note: Any doily pattern will work. The snowflake design we've used was cut from the centers of large round doilies. Pin one to doll's head. Make necklace out of a small band from doily. Attach with dots of icing. Cut and fold gold Fanci-Foil to make book. Using a Swirl as a guide, cut wings out of foil. Glue together.

- Ice cake smooth. Push doll into cake. Build up waist with icing for a smooth look. Cover bodice and sleeves with tip 16 stars.

- Edge base with 2 rows of tip 125 ruffles. Press snowflake medallions onto skirt, just above ruffles. Pipe tip 2 strings and dots around snowflakes. Randomly pipe tip 2 dot and string snowflake designs on skirt.

- Attach ribbon bow, book and wings with dots of icing. *Serves 12.*

*Fancy That! Our Filigree Curved Triangles (p. 160) were glued together to create the lovely Victorian tree ornaments shown. We fancied them with flowers and ribbons.

Golden Elegance

ALL THAT GLITTERS

- **Holiday Tree Pan Kit,** p. 191
- **Two 10 in. Round Separator Plates,** p. 166
- **Four Dancing Cupid Pillars,** p. 161
- **Poured Fondant, Buttercream Icings**
- **Gold metallic ribbon (approximately 3 yds.), greenery, satin ornaments, three 10 in. gold doilies**

- Tie gold ribbon bow and attach streamers.
- Follow step-by-step baking and assembly instructions included in Holiday Tree Kit. Ice cake with a thin layer of buttercream, then cover with poured fondant per recipe directions. Let set completely.
- Cut three doilies in half and gather around plate. Place cake atop plate. Attach bow and streamers (for curled effect, dot cake at 2 in. intervals, push ribbon into waves and press onto icing.)
- Cover bottom separator plate with doily, greenery and satin balls. Position cake plate on pillars. *Serves 24.*

*So Romantic: Our Satin Bells (p. 158) and Angelinos (p. 161) are lavished with golden accents and lovely lace.

SNOWY BEAR
- Teddy Bear Stand-Up Pan, p. 181
- Tips 4, 17, 18, p. 132-133
- Pink, Teal Icing Color, p. 131
- Cake Board, Fanci-Foil Wrap, p. 139
- Buttercream Icing
- Candy cane

- Ice inside of ears and bottom of paws smooth. Outline ears, facial features, tie and paws with tip 4.
- Pipe in eyes, nose and tongue (flatten with finger dipped in cornstarch). Add tip 4 dot irises and pupils to eyes and pads on bottoms of paws (smooth with finger dipped in cornstarch).
- Cover head, body and front paws with tip 18 stars, bow tie with tip 17 stars.
- Add tip 4 elongated bead eyebrows. Attach candy cane to paw with icing. *Serves 12.*

A REAL SOFTIE
- Jolly Santa Pan, p. 190
- Tips 2, 6, p. 132
- Pink Icing Color, p. 131
- Buttercream Icing
- Mini marshmallows

- Ice cake smooth—sides, beard, eyebrows and "fur" on cap white, cap pink and face light pink.
- Pipe tip 6 dot eyes and mouth, ball nose and cheeks (flatten with finger dipped in cornstarch). Add tip 2 outline eyelashes.
- Edge base with tip 6 bulb border. Cover white areas on cake top and eyebrows with mini marshmallows. *Serves 12.*

JOLLY SNOWBALL
- Merry Snowman Pan, p. 190
- Tip 16, p. 133
- Wilton Red Icing Color, p. 131
- Buttercream Icing
- Shredded coconut, candied cherries, shoestring licorice

- Ice snow areas smooth. Cover with coconut flakes.
- Cover crown of hat with tip 16 stars. Pipe tip 16 zigzag hat brim and scarf. Add tip 16 rosette nose and buttons. Edge base with tip 16 star border.
- Add cherry eyes, licorice mouth and scarf fringe. *Serves 12.*

CHRISTMAS

Winter Whites

FRILLY FIR
- Treeliteful Pan, p. 190
- Tips 6, 86 or 87, 349, p. 132-136
- Christmas Red, Teal Icing Colors, p. 131
- Quick-Pour Fondant and Buttercream (for decorating) Icings
- Cinnamon-flavored candies

- Ice cake with a thin layer of buttercream icing. Pour fondant icing on cake. Edge base with tip 6 bead border.
- Pipe tip 86 ruffle garlands and rows of ruffles (work from bottom row, up) on trunk.
- Attach cinnamon candies with dots of icing. Trim with tip 349 leaves. *Serves 12.*

CHRISTMAS FANCIES
- Mini Bell Pan, p. 176
- Mini Christmas Tree Pan, p. 191
- Tips 14, 16, 349, p. 133-134
- Christmas Red, Teal Icing Colors, p. 131
- Buttercream Icing
- Cinnamon-flavored candy

- **For Bells:** Cover clappers with tip 16 spirals. Pipe tip 16 stars on side and "inside." Add tip 16 rosette posies to tops. Place cinnamon candies in centers. Trim with tip 349 leaves.
- **For Trees:** Cover with tip 16 stars. Add tip 14 zigzag garlands. Trim with cinnamon candies. *Each serves 1.*

CHRISTMAS PARTY

- **10 in. Round Pan, p. 168**
- **Tips 3, 18, 21, 349, 352, p. 132-134**
- **Leaf Green, Wilton Red Icing Colors, p. 131**
- **Decorating Comb, p. 140**
- **Sesame Street Toppers*, p. 143**
- **Christmas Tree Candle**
- **Buttercream Icing**

- Pipe tip 3 hats on Sesame Street characters. Add tip 3 zigzag borders at base of hats. Pipe tip 3 ball at top of hats.
- Pipe tip 349 leaves around sides and top of Big Bird's cake and a wreath on Oscar's garbage can. Add tip 3 berries.
- Ice 2-layer cake smooth. Use Decorating Comb to make ribbed effect on cake sides.
- Edge cake top with tip 18 reverse shells. Trim with tip 3 dots. Edge base with tip 21 e-motion border.
- With tip 352, pipe holly leaves on sides of cake. Add tip 3 dot berries. *Serves 24.*

*1982, 1984 Children's Television Workshop BIG BIRD, COOKIE MONSTER, OSCAR THE GROUCH, BERT AND ERNIE
© 1982, 1984 Muppets, Inc. All rights reserved.

GUIDING LIGHT

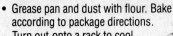

- **Rudy Reindeer Pan, p. 190**
- **Tip 16, p. 133**
- **Chocolate Buttercream Icing**
- **2 small boxes or 1 large brownie mix, candied cherry**

- Grease pan and dust with flour. Bake according to package directions. Turn out onto a rack to cool.

- With tip 16, outline antlers, ear, face and bow. Fill in nose and eye. Cover antlers and bow with stars. Edge with shells. Add cherry to nose.

TWINKLING TEDDY TREE

- **MicroBakes™ Christmas Tree Pan, p. 171**
- **Leaf Green Icing Color, p. 131**
- **Buttercream Icing**
- **Chewy candy bears, shoestring licorice**

- Ice cake. Tie bow out of licorice. Add licorice bands to trunk and garlands to boughs. Trim garlands with candy bears. *Serves 8.*

THE CLAUS CLAN

- **Cookie Sheets, p. 172**
- **Tip 3, p. 132**
- **Wilton Red, Kelly Green Icing Colors, p. 131**
- **Gingerbread Family Cookie Cutter Set, p. 118**
- **Chocolate Cookie Recipe, p. 109**
- **Cookie Icing**

- Roll out dough on lightly floured surface per recipe directions. Bake and cool on racks.
- Decorate cookies with tip 3. Pipe dot eyes, noses, mouths and buttons. With cookie icing, outline outfits, mouths and caps. Fill in hats, collars, belts and bands on clothes. Add e-motion hair.

HO, HO, HO-ABOARD!

- **Choo-Choo Train Pan, p. 178**
- **Tips 17, 21, 352, p. 133-134**
- **Wilton Red, Leaf Green Icing Colors, p. 131**
- **Santa Candle, p. 143**
- **Tree Formers, p. 130**
- **Rectangle Cake Board, Fanci-Foil Wrap, p. 139**
- **Buttercream, Royal (for trees) Icings**
- **Chocolate chips, chocolate sandwich cookies**

- **To make trees:** Wrap waxed paper around tree formers. Secure by tucking paper under base or use tape. Pipe a guideline around base with tip 352. Cover line with a row of tip 352 leaves, turning former counterclockwise as you decorate. Repeat procedure, overlapping each successive row of leaves until former is covered. Let icing dry. Carefully loosen waxed paper from former and lift off icing tree.
- Allow cake to cool completely in back half of pan (at least 4 hours).
- Cover engine with tip 21 stars. Pipe tip 21 spiral "smoke" on smokestack (overpipe several times to add dimension).
- Push cookie "wheels" onto sides, and half cookies onto the front of cowcatcher. Pipe tip 21 stripe wheel shaft. Trim ends with tip 21 stars. Add tip 21 elongated shell smoke.
- Edge areas shown with chocolate chips. Pipe tip 17 shell borders on cake board. Add tip 352 leaves. Position Santa Candle. *Serves 12.*

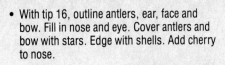

— CHRISTMAS —
Children Pleasers

CUPID'S TRIUMPH

- **8 in. Round Pans,** p. 168
- **Tips 3, 5, 21, 32,** p. 132-133
- **Wilton Red Icing Color,** p. 131
- **Harvest Cherub Separator Set, Frolicking Cherub,** p. 161
- **Buttercream Icing**
- **Flowers, greenery**

- Ice 2-layer cake smooth–top white, sides red. Edge top with crown border (tip 32 upright shell, tip 3 overlapping strings). Where shells and strings meet, add tip 3 dots.
- Pipe tip 5 bead hearts on border, randomly on cake top and on cherubs. Edge cake base with tip 21 shell border.
- To serve: Position tier on pillars. Arrange flowers and greenery on separator plate. Glue flower to Frolicking Cherub. Place cherub on cake top. *Serves 12.*

POPPY LOVE

- **Puffed Heart Pan,** p. 186
- **Tips 1, 3, 6, 8, 14, 103, 352,** p. 132-136
- **Flower Nail No. 7,** p. 138
- **Red-Red, Pink, Golden Yellow, Black, Moss Green Icing Colors,** p. 131
- **Rolled Fondant, Buttercream, Royal Icings**

- With royal icing, make 6 full poppies and 1 half bloom with tips 1, 6, 14, 103. Also make 15 tip 225 drop flowers with tip 3 dot centers.
- Ice cake with a thin layer of buttercream icing, then cover with rolled fondant.
- Write tip 3 message. Edge base with tip 8 "comma-motion" bead border.
- Attach flowers to cake top with dots of icing. Trim with tip 352 leaves. *Serves 12.*

MESSENGERS OF LOVE

- **Cookie Sheets,** p. 169
- **Sweetheart Cookie Cutter Set,** p. 119
- **Tip 3,** p. 132
- **Wilton Red Icing Color,** p. 131
- **Roll-Out Cookie Dough & Cookie Icing Recipes,** p. 109

- Roll out dough and cut out desired shapes. Remove dough from around each cookie. Bake per recipe instructions. Place on a rack to cool.
- Outline with tip 3 strings. Print tip 3 messages.

CHEERY CHERRY HEARTS

- **Heart Quartet Pan,** p. 186
- **Tip 21,** p. 133
- **Stabilized Whipped Cream**
- **Cherry pie filling (21 oz.) and cherry cake mix**

- Spoon on cherry pie filling. Edge hearts with tip 21 rosettes. *Serves 12.*

VALENTINE'S DAY

Lovely and Delicious

— V A L E N T I N E ' S   D A Y —

Heart's Desire

BROWNIE POINTS
- **Heart Minicake Pan, p. 186**
- **Tip 1, p. 132**
- **Candy Melts™– Light Cocoa, p. 115**
- **Decorator's Brush, p. 140**
- **Modeling Candy Recipe (½ recipe), p. 112**
- **Brownie mix, pecans, small rose leaves**
- Make desired number of roses out of modeling candy. Paint rose leaves with light cocoa Candy Melts. (See how to do on p. 112.)
- With tip 1, drizzle melted coating over tops of brownies. Ice sides of several with coating. Let set. Add roses and leaves or pecans. *Each serves 1.*

TRUE LOVE TRIO
- **Heart Mini-Tier Set, p. 187**
- **Tips 2, 4, 5, 12, 102, 103, 104, 352, p. 132-137**
- **Flower Nail No. 7, p. 138**
- **Pink, Wilton Red, Leaf Green Icing Colors, p. 131**
- **'90 Pattern Book (Scallop Heart Patterns), p. 121**
- **Piping Gel, p. 131**
- **12 in. Cake Circle, Fanci-Foil Wrap, p. 139**
- **Buttercream (stiffen or use Royal for roses) Icing**

- Make 11 full roses–5 with tip 102, 3 with tip 103, 3 with tip 104. Pipe 8 tip 103 half roses and 5 buds.
- Ice cakes smooth, largest on cake circle cut to fit, two smaller ones directly on plates. Place largest cake on foil-covered base.
- Using Scallop Heart Patterns, mark designs on cake tops. Cover marks with tip 2 tinted piping gel outlines.
- Edge tops with tip 5 bead borders. At bases, pipe triple bead borders with tips 4 and 5 (see Borders, p. 104).
- Place roses on cake tops. Trim with tip 352 leaves. Assemble tiers on pillars. *Serves 12.*

SWAN LAKE
- **Happiness Heart Pan Set, p. 186**
- **Tips 3, 4, 7, 18, 101, 103, p. 132-136**
- **Wilton Red, Pink Icing Colors, p. 131**
- **Buttercream Icing**

- Ice 2-layer cake smooth. Write message with tip 3.
- Pipe tip 3 outline water marks. Figure pipe tip 7 swans (see figure piping, p. 105).
- Pipe tip 4 outline vines on cake top. Trim with tip 101 petals and tip 3 dots.
- Pipe tips 18 and 103 Ruffly Swirled Shell Border (see Borders, p. 104).
- Edge base with tip 18 shell border. Add tip 4 dots. *Serves 12.*

TRUFFLED TREASURE
- **Heart Flan Pan, p. 187**
- **Candy Melts™ *– Pink, Green (1 bag each) and Light Cocoa (2 bags), p. 115**
- **Tip 1, p. 132**
- **Rosebuds & Roses Candy Mold, p. 116**
- **Candy Dipping Fork or Spoon, p. 114**
- **Truffle Recipe, p. 111**
- Prepare 22 luscious truffles according to recipe.
- Mold 19 rosebuds out of pink and green melted Candy Melts.
- Pour melted candy into Heart Flan and mold per instructions, p. 111. Use remaining coating for dipping.
- Dip truffles and place in refrigerator to set. With tip 1, drizzle each with melted coating. Let set.
- Place truffles and rose candies into heart and refrigerate. Bring to room temperature before serving.

*brand confectionery coating

54

Sweet Traditions

"EGGCEPTIONAL" BASKET

- 12 in. Round Pan, p. 168
- Egg Minicake Pan, p. 189
- Tips 2B, 3, 21, p. 132-137
- Sky Blue, Pink, Leaf Green, Violet, Orange, Lemon Yellow Icing Colors, p. 131
- Buttercream, Royal Icings
- Tinted coconut, jelly beans

- To tint coconut green, place it in a plastic sandwich bag. Dilute a small amount of icing color with water and pour into bag. Shake and knead bag until color is evenly distributed.
- Ice 2-layer cake smooth. Cover cake top with tinted coconut. Ice egg mini-cakes smooth on cake boards cut to fit. Place on top of cake. Print tip 3 names on eggs.
- Pipe tip 2B basketweave on sides. Edge cake top and base with tip 21 rope. Add jelly beans. *Serves 30.*

EASTER EGG BREAD CUPS

- Muffin Pan, p. 173
- Tip 2, p. 132
- 8-Icing Color Kit, p. 131
- Confectioners icing— powder sugar & milk
- 6 uncooked eggs, easy yeast dough coffee cake mix

- To tint eggs: Add Wilton icing color (amount varies with desired intensity) to hot water (enough to cover egg) and a teaspoon of vinegar. Dip eggs and let dry.
- Prepare coffee cake mix following directions on box up to shaping of dough.
- Divide dough in half. Shape each into a rectangle and cut into thirds. Divide each section in half. Roll into ropes and twist loosely twist together. Place dough around cup, cut, then pinch ends together. Place egg in the center (it will be hard-cooked when baked). Let dough rise again. Bake per directions on box.
- Remove from pan and let cool. Pipe tip 2 scallop designs around tops. *Each serves 1.*

FLUFFY

- Little Lamb Pan, p. 188
- Tips 18, 233, p. 132-133
- Violet, Lemon Yellow, Leaf Green Icing Colors, p. 131
- Icing Recipe: Buttercream
- Coconut, jelly beans

- Tint coconut per instructions under "Eggceptional" Basket cake.
- Ice face smooth. With tip 18 pipe star eyes, rosette nose and outline mouth.
- Cover inside of ears with tip 18 stars. Pipe tip 233 reverse shell motion fleece on head, ears and body.
- Cover cake board or serving plate with tinted coconut. Add jelly beans. *Serves 12.*

56

PECAN CAKE CROSS

- Cross Pan, p. 189
- Pecan Coffee Cake Recipe (p. 108)
- Prepare dough per recipe instructions. Divide into two rectangles. Cut one rectangle into 1 in. pieces and the other into 1½ in. pieces.
- Pour nut glaze into bottom of pan. With the cut edge down, cover glaze with large pieces only. Place smaller pieces with cut sides together around edges.
- Bake at 375° for 20 minutes. Invert onto serving platter immediately.

EASTER GOODY BASKETS

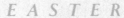

- Sunny Bunny Pan, p. 188
- Little Ducky Pan, p. 188
- Cookie Sheets, p. 172
- Tips 2B, 3, 4, 6, 17, 19, p. 132-137
- Pink, Violet, Golden Yellow, Leaf Green Icing Colors, p. 131
- '90 Pattern Book (Basket Panels), p. 121
- Easter Cutters: Basket, Mr. & Mrs. Bunny, p. 118
- Candy Melts™* – Spring Mix, Yellow, p. 115
- Egg Candy Molds, p. 117
- Rectangle Cake Board, Fanci-Foil Wrap, p. 139
- Roll-Out Cookie Dough Recipe (or favorite sugar cookie dough), p. 109
- Royal Icing
- Easter basket grass

- **For Bunny or Ducky:** Lightly spray pan with vegetable oil. Roll out dough on lightly floured surface to ⅜ in. thickness. Carefully transfer dough to inside of pan, then press into indentations. Smooth edges with finger (dough should not be up the sides). Pierce dough with a fork. Bake for 17 to 20 minutes or until edges begin to pull away from sides of the pan. Turn out onto a rack to cool.

- **For side panels of basket** (each has different size pieces): Roll dough out on lightly floured cookie sheet. Using Basket Panels Patterns, cut (a pizza cutter works great) 4 side panels and 2 back brace panels. Bake and cool.

- **Make basket treats!** Cookies: Cut and bake cookies. When cool, outline with tip 3. Fill in with tip 17 zigzags. Let icing dry. Candy: Melt Candy Melts and mold eggs. Let set.

- **To decorate Bunny:** Ice "feet" smooth. Outline details with tip 4. Pipe in background areas and features (smooth with finger dipped in cornstarch). Cover bunny and bow with tip 17 stars. Add tip 4 lashes and whiskers. Pipe tip 4 beads on "feet."

- **To decorate Ducky:** Outline features with tip 4. Build up bill with tip 6 (shape with fingers dipped in cornstarch). Pipe in eyes and mouth with tip 4 (smooth with cornstarch). Cover face and body with tip 17 stars. Pipe tip 17 pull-out stars on wings. Add tip 17 swirl curl and outline bow. Pipe tip 4 outline brows and lashes.

- **To assemble & decorate:** Let Bunny or Ducky cookies dry completely. Cut a 10 in. square for Bunny, 12 in. square for Ducky from cake board. Cover with foil. For added support, ice back of cookie onto a cake board cut to fit. With tip 6 generously pipe icing onto bottom and side edges of panels. Use a jar or can to support panels until icing dries. Attach back braces. Let dry. Ice inside of back panel and position bunny or ducky cookie. Cover side panels with tip 2B basketweave. Edge top with tip 19 rope border.

- Fill with "grass," candy or cookies. Let all decorated cookies dry completely!

*brand confectionery coating

BUNNY HOP

- 11 x 15 in. Sheet Pan, p. 169
- Tips 3, 14, 17, 70, 349, p. 132-134
- Lemon Yellow, Pink, Leaf Green, Violet Icing Colors, p. 131
- Mr. Bunny Cookie Cutter, p. 118
- Alphabet Candy Molds, p. 116
- Candy Melts™* –1 bag each Yellow and Spring Mix, p. 115
- Buttercream Icing

- Melt and mold letters out of Candy Melts.

- Ice cake white with green grass area on top. Use Mr. Bunny Cookie Cutter to imprint bunny. With toothpick, mark bunny tracks. Outline bunny and tracks with tip 3 strings. Fill in bunny with tip 14 stars.

- Spell out message with candy letters. Add tip 14 rosettes between words.

- Edge top with tip 17 shell border, base with tip 70 shell-motion leaf border. Trim border and cover "grass" with tip 14 rosettes. Add tip 349 leaves to rosettes on "grass." *Serves 20.*

*brand confectionery coating

EASTER

Pastel Pals

ROSE CAMEO

- 9 x 13 in. Sheet Pans, p. 169
- Tips 4, 12, 17, 21, 102, 103, 352, p. 132-136
- Flower Nail No. 7, p. 138
- Terra Cotta, Creamy Peach, Icing Colors, p. 131
- Oval Cookie Cutter Set, p. 119
- Buttercream Icing

- For roses, spatula-stripe bag with terra cotta and peach icing. Make roses with tips 12 and 103 – 1 full and 4 medium (only 2 rows of petals).
- Ice 2-layer cake smooth. With 6 in. oval cutter, mark oval on cake top. Also mark sides at top into 2 in. intervals.
- Edge oval shape on cake top with tip 102 ruffles. Pipe tip 4 beads around oval. Write tip 4 message.
- Pipe tip 4 outline stems. Add tip 103 spatula-striped rosebuds and half roses to spray. Trim with tip 4 calyxes and sepals. Add roses and trim with tip 352 leaves. Pipe tip 103 ribbon bow.
- Connect marks on side with tip 4 overlapping drop strings. Edge cake top with tip 17 shell border. Pipe tip 21 C-motion shells at base. Trim with tip 102 ruffles. *Serves 28.*

HE'S OUT-OF-THIS-WORLD

- Shining Star Pan, p. 174
- Tips 16, 18, 32, p. 133
- Brown*, Creamy Peach, Terra Cotta Icing Colors, p. 131
- Buttercream Icing

- Ice cake smooth. Write "Dad" with tip 18.
- Pipe tip 32 upright shells on cake top and sides. Trim with tip 16 stars. Edge base with tip 18 shell border. *Serves 12.*

*Or substitute chocolate.

DOWN-TO-EARTH DAD

- 12 in. Hexagon Pans, p. 171
- Tips 1, 2, 3, 5, 13, 16, 81, 104, 132, 349, 352, p. 132-137
- Flower Nail No. 7, p. 138
- Ivory, Terra Cotta, Teal, Brown, Creamy Peach Icing Colors, p. 131
- '90 Pattern Book, (Father Pattern) p. 121
- Buttercream, Royal Icing

- Make 4 tips 5 and 104 daisies; 4 tips 1, 5, 16 bachelor buttons; 3 tips 1, 5, 81 chrysanthemums.

- Ice 2-layer cake smooth. With toothpick, mark Father pattern in center. Outline script with tip 3.
- Dot mark scallops on top ½ in. from edge, approximately ¾ in. wide. Connect dots with tip 2 strings.
- Arrange flowers on cake. Pipe tips 3 and 349 ferns (see p. 104). Trim flowers with tip 352 leaves.
- Edge cake top with tip 132 C-motion shell border. Pipe two rows of tip 2 scallops using shells as a guide.
- Edge base with tip 132 shells. Outline shells with tip 13 zigzag scallops. *Serves 28.*

PEARLY TREASURE

- Dessert Shell Pan, p. 179
- Tips 12, 103, 352, p. 132-136
- Flower Nail No. 7, p. 138
- Terra Cotta, Teal, Ivory Icing Colors, p. 131
- Cake Board, Fanci-Foil Wrap, p. 139
- Poured Fondant, Buttercream (stiffen for flowers) Icings

- Place cake on a rack over a drip pan; cover with poured fondant icing (see p. 94). Let set.
- Make 15 tips 12 and 103 roses and 35 tip 103 sweet peas.
- Arrange flowers on top and at base. Pipe tip 352 leaves. *Serves 12.*

Parent Pleasers

Proudly We Hail

GLORY DAY

- 11 x 15 in. Sheet Pan, p. 169
- Tips 3, 5, 12, 32, 104, 125, 352, p. 132-137
- Flower Nail No. 7, p. 138
- Violet, Pink, Leaf Green Icing Colors, p. 131
- Glad Grad Girl, p. 143
- Buttercream Icing
- With tips 12 and 104, make 4 full roses, 8 with only two rows of petals and 8 half roses.
- Ice 2-layer cake smooth with a marbelized effect (gently swirl a small amount of pink icing into white icing).
- Write script message with tip 3.
- Edge top with tip 32 upright shells. Connect tails with tip 3 overlapping drop strings. Around tops of shells, pipe tip 3 beads. Trim tails with tip 3 dots.
- Edge base with tip 125 ruffle. Trim with tip 5 bead border.
- Arrange roses and pipe tip 104 rosebuds. Trim with tip 352 leaves. Position Glad Grad Girl. *Serves 40.*

HEAD OF THE CLASS

- 4-Pc. Oval Pan Set (use 10¾ & 16 in. pans) p. 171
- Tips 2, 3, 4, 16, 32, 364, p. 132-137
- Pink Icing Color, p. 131
- '90 Pattern Book (Silhouette Pattern), p. 121
- Color Flow Mix, p. 131*
- Oval Cutter Set, p. 119
- 11½ in. Oval Separator Plates (2 needed), p. 166
- 5 in. Grecian Pillars (4 needed), p. 165
- Crystal-Look Bowl, p. 163
- Cake Boards, p. 139
- Dowel Rods, p. 165
- Buttercream, Color Flow Icings
- Roses, greenery, craft stick
- With tip 2, make Silhouette Pattern out of Color Flow (see p. 108). When dry, attach a craft stick to back with royal icing.

*Timesaving idea: Cut out of posterboard and attach to card board backing.
- When ordering floral arrangements, bring Crystal-Look Bowl (the two parts are used as individual vases).
- Ice and prepare 2-layer cakes for pillar tier construction (see p. 106).
- With oval cutter (use large enough size to accommodate name), imprint oval on center front of bottom tier. With a toothpick, mark sides of top tier at 2 in. intervals (alternating height) and bottom tier at 3 in. intervals. Write name in oval with tip 3. Edge oval with tip 16 C-motion shells.
- Edge top of tiers with tip 364 shell borders. At bases, pipe Pretty Pillar Border (see p. 104) with tips 4, 16, 32 and 364.
- To serve: Place arrangement on separator plate of bottom tier. Position top tier on pillars. Add flowers and push in color flow piece. *Serves 66.*

Congratulations Marc

For Our Favorite Grad in the U.S.A. James

Worthy of Honor

SYMBOLS OF SUCCESS

- 16 in. Round Pans, p. 168
- Tips 3, 14, 17, 32, p. 132-133
- Royal Blue Icing Colors, p. 131
- Candy Melts ™* – Light Cocoa, Yellow, p. 115
- Graduation Candy Mold Set, p. 116
- 9-pc. Pattern Press Set, Decorator's Brush, Cake Dividing Set, p. 140
- Successful Grad, p. 143
- Buttercream Icing

- To mold candy: "Paint" tassels of caps, diploma bow and tassels with yellow candy. Let set. Fill molds with cocoa coating. Let set and unmold. (See Candy Making, p. 110.)
- Ice 2-layer cake smooth. With Cake Dividing Set, divide top into 8th. With pattern press, imprint petal shapes. Outline with tip 17 C-scrolls.
- Write tip 3 script message with decorative build-up on capital letters (see p. 104).
- Pipe tip 32 upright shells at base. Connect tops with tip 3 drop strings and trim with tip 17 rosettes. At base of shells, pipe tip 14 zigzags. Edge cake top with tip 17 reverse shell border. *Serves 60.*

ALL-AMERICAN GRAD

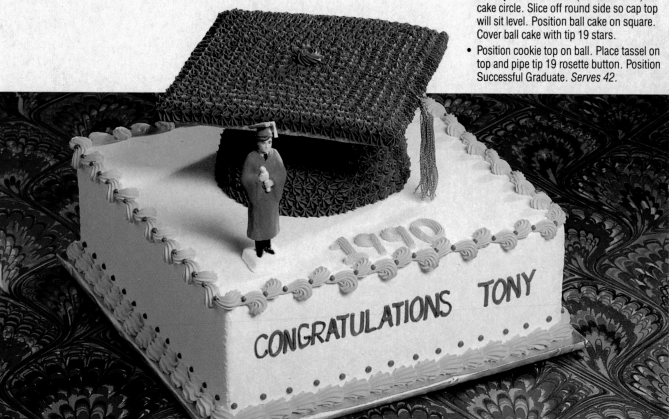

- USA Pan, p. 177.
- Tips 3, 21, 66, 102, 106, p. 132-137
- Flower Nail No. 7, p. 138
- Golden Yellow, Royal Blue, Leaf Green Icing Colors, p. 131
- Flower Formers, p. 140
- Cake Board, Fanci-Foil Wrap, p. 139
- Glad Grad, p. 143
- Buttercream, Royal Icings

- With royal icing, make 12 daisies using tip 102. Pipe centers with tip 3. Place on flower formers to dry.
- Make 10 tip 106 drop flowers with tip 3 dot centers.
- Ice top of cake smooth. Write tip 3 message. Pipe in "Great Lakes" with tip 3 (smooth with finger dipped in cornstarch).
- Cover cake sides with tip 21 stars. Arrange flowers and trim with tip 66 leaves. Position Glad Grad. *Serves 12.*

HAT'S OFF!

- 12 in. Square Pans, p. 169
- Ball Pan Set, p. 184
- Tips 3, 19, 21, 301, 132-133
- Golden Yellow, Royal Blue Icing Colors, p. 131
- Message Pattern Press, p. 121
- Successful Grad, p. 143
- 6 in. Cake Circle, Cake Board, Fanci-Foil Wrap, p. 139
- Dowel Rods, p. 165
- Roll-Out Cookie Dough Recipe, p. 109
- Buttercream, Royal Icings
- Tassle

- For top of cap, cut an 8 in. square out of cookie dough. Bake and cool. Using royal icing, cover top of cookie with tip 19 stars. Also "paint" Successful Grad's cap and gown with thinned royal icing. Let both dry.
- Ice 2-layer cake smooth. Push dowel rods into top where cap will go. With pattern press, imprint message on side. With toothpick, name and date. Print tip 301 message. Outline date with tip 19.
- Edge cake top with tip 19 reverse shell border; base with tip 21 shell border. Trim top border and sides with tip 3 dots.
- For cap: Place half ball (flat side down) on cake circle. Slice off round side so cap top will sit level. Position ball cake on square. Cover ball cake with tip 19 stars.
- Position cookie top on ball. Place tassel on top and pipe tip 19 rosette button. Position Successful Graduate. *Serves 42.*

GOO-GOO GOOSE

- Country Goose Pan, p. 179
- Tips 1A, 2, 3, 16, 102, 124, p. 132-136
- Peach, Teal, Burgundy, Ivory Icing Colors, p. 131
- 15-pc. Decorator Pattern Press Set, p. 140
- Buttercream Icing
- **For Goose:** Ice cap and shawl smooth. Imprint areas with C-scroll pattern press. Outline cap, beak, head, neck and shawl with tip 3 strings.
- Pipe in beak with tip 3 (smooth with finger dipped in cornstarch). Outline C-scrolls with tip 2. Trim with tip 2 dots and tip 16 rosettes.
- Cover face, neck and background on top and sides with tip 16 stars. Add tip 3 outline eyelid, lashes and mouth.
- **For Gosling:** Pipe tip 1A ball face (flatten with finger dipped in cornstarch). Outline wing with tip 3. Fill in with tip 16 pull-out stars. With tip 2, outline eyelids, lashes, bow and beak. Pipe tip 102 ruffle around face.
- Edge cap and shawl with spatula-striped ruffles – tip 102 on cap, tip 124 on shawl. *Serves 12.*

Adorables

LITTLE LOVEY

- Panda Pan, p. 181
- Tips 2, 4, 102, 362, p. 132-136
- Ivory, Teal, Creamy Peach Icing Colors, p. 131
- Buttercream Icing
- Ice bib and bottoms of paws smooth. Outline facial features and bib with tip 4 strings.
- Pipe in inside of ears, eyes and snout with tip 4 (smooth with finger dipped in cornstarch). Add tip 4 dot eyeballs and nose with tip 4 (flatten with finger dipped in cornstarch). Pipe 2 dot highlights on eyeballs.
- Cover head, body and paws with tip 362 stars. Print tip 2 dot message. Edge bib with tip 102 ruffles. Trim edges with tip 2 beads. *Serves 16.*

HOPES & DREAMS

- 12 in. Hexagon Pans, p. 171
- Tips 2, 16, p. 132-133
- Creamy Peach Icing Color, p. 131
- Crystal Clear Booties, p. 145
- Buttercream Icing
- Silk flowers, 1¼ yds. of grease-resistant ribbon for cake; ¾ yd. satin ribbon for booties
- Ice 2-layer cake smooth. Write tip 2 message.
- Place ribbon around sides. Edge top with tip 16 fleur-de-lis border; base with tip 16 shell border.
- Lace ribbon through booties. Arrange flowers and position booties. *Serves 28.*

C H R I S T E N I N G
Baby Cakes

PRETTY JOYOUS

- 4-Pc. Oval Pan Set (10¾ x 7⅞ in. used), p. 167
- Tips 2, 3, 5, 7, 65s, 103, 104, 129, 190, p. 132-136
- Pink, Royal Blue, Leaf Green Icing Colors, p. 131
- '90 Pattern Book (Scalloped Oval Pattern), p. 121
- Buttercream Icing

- Ice 2-layer cake smooth. With toothpick, mark Scalloped Oval Pattern on cake top. Mark 2 in. intervals 1½ ins. above base on sides.

- Write tip 2 message. Pipe bead borders—tip 5 on top, tip 7 at base. Pipe double rows of ruffles—tip 103 on top, tip 104 at base. Edge ruffles with tip 3 beads.

- Pipe tip 2 outline stems. Pipe tip 190 (large) and tip 129 drop flower on top and sides. Add tip 3 dot centers. Trim with tip 655 leaves. *Serves 35.*

PRECIOUS HEART

- Heart Mini-Tier Set, p. 187
- Tips 1D, 3, 6, 16, 102, 352, p. 132-137
- Pink, Leaf Green Icing Colors, p. 131
- Flower Nail No. 7, p. 138
- Sleeping Angel, p. 145
- Cake Boards, Tuk 'N Ruffle, Fanci-Foil Wrap, p. 139
- Buttercream Icing

- Using tips 6 and 102, with stiffened buttercream icing, make 24 roses—12 7-petal, 12 5-petal. Also make 24 tip 102 sweet peas.

- Ice cakes smooth (top tiers on cake boards cut to fit and plates; bottom tier on Tuk 'N Ruffle-trimmed, foil-covered board).
- With toothpick, mark 1 in. intervals on sides of top tier; 1¼ in. on center and bottom tiers. Connect marks with tip 3 overlapping drop strings.
- Write tip 3 message on center tier. Edge cake tops with tip 1D ribbed stripes. Pipe tip 16 shells at bases and around pillars.
- Pipe tip 102 rosebuds on top tier. Arrange flowers on center and bottom tiers. Trim with tip 352 leaves. Position tiers on pillars and add Sleeping Angel. *Serves 12.*

"SON-SHINE"

- Round Mini-Tier Set, p. 167
- Tips 3, 6, 16, 17, 102, 352, p. 132-136
- Flower Nail No. 7, p. 138
- Royal Blue, Leaf Green Icing Colors, p. 131
- Sleeping Angels, Shining Cross, p. 145
- 6 & 8 Cake Circles, Fanci-Foil Wrap, Tuk 'N Ruffle, p. 139
- Buttercream Icing

- Use stiffened buttercream, make 24 tips 6 and 102 roses.
- Ice cakes smooth. Write tip 3 message on side of center tier. Edge cake tops with tip 16 reverse shell borders. Pipe tip 17 shell borders at bases and around pillars. Trim with tip 3 zigzags.
- Position Sleeping Angel on center tier. Pipe tip 102 rosebuds. Mound icing on top tier and position cross. Arrange roses on top and bottom tier. Trim roses and rosebuds with tip 352 leaves. Assemble tiers on pillars. *Serves 12.*

GUARDIAN ANGEL

- 11 x 15 in. Sheet Pans, p. 169
- Tips 3, 6, 14, 16, 225, 352, p. 132-136
- Golden Yellow, Royal Blue, Leaf Green, Brown Icing Colors, p. 131
- '90 Pattern Book (Angel/Baby Patterns), p. 121
- Buttercream, Royal Icings

- Make 75 tip 225 drop flowers with tip 3 dot centers with royal icing.
- Ice 2-layer cake smooth. With toothpick, mark Angel/Baby Pattern and scallop "frame" on cake top. Cover scallop marks with tip 14.
- Outline angel and baby with tip 3. Print tip 3 message. Pipe in faces with tip 6; hands with tip 3 (smooth with finger dipped in cornstarch). Outline facial features with tip 3. Fill in halo, wings, gown, pillow and blanket with tip 14 stars.
- With tip 16, edge, cake top with shells; base with zigzag puffs. Pipe tip 16 zigzag puff clouds. Add flowers to top and at base. Trim with tip 352 leaves. *Serves 40.*

Blessings upon Patrick Anthony

PRAISE HER

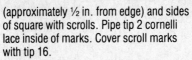

- 8 in. Round Pans, p. 168
- 12 in. Square Pans, p. 169
- Tips 2, 4, 16, 18, 103, p. 132-136
- Flower Nail No. 7, p. 138
- Golden Yellow Icing Color, p. 131
- '90 Pattern Book (Communion Girl Pattern), p. 121
- Edible Glitter, Flower Formers, p. 130
- 1¼ in. Green Artificial Leaves, p. 146
- 15-Pc. Decorator Pattern Press Set, p. 140
- Color Flow Mix, p. 131
- Dowel Rods, p. 165
- Tuk 'N Ruffle, Fanci-Foil Wrap, Cake Boards, p. 139
- Buttercream, Color Flow, Royal Icings

- With color flow icing and tip 2, outline Communion Girl and flow in with thinned icing (see p. 108). Let dry.
- With royal icing, make 35 (be sure to allow for breakage) tip 103 daisies with tip 4 dot centers. Pat center with edible glitter and let dry on flower formers.
- Ice and prepare 2-layer cakes for stacked assembly (see p. 106). With C-scroll pattern press, imprint top and sides of round

(approximately ½ in. from edge) and sides of square with scrolls. Pipe tip 2 cornelli lace inside of marks. Cover scroll marks with tip 16.

- Edge bases; top and corners of square with tip 18 shell borders. Arrange daisies and add artificial leaves. Push dowel rods into cake top and position color flow Communion Girl*. *Serves 52.*

*Note: Since buttercream icing will break down color flow, either position piece on cake shortly before serving or place on a piece of plastic wrap.

CROWNING GLORY

- Cross Pan, p. 189
- 3, 12, 16, 103, 224, 352, p. 132-136
- Flower Nail No. 7, p. 138
- Kelly Green, Golden Yellow, Creamy Peach Icing Colors, p. 131
- Buttercream, Royal Icings

- Make 6 roses with tips 12 and 103—three each with 5 and 7 petals. With royal icing, make 8 tip 224 drop flowers with tip 3 dot centers.
- Ice cake smooth. Cover top with tip 3 latticework. Edge top, beveled sides and base with tip 16 shell borders.
- Allow latticework to set, then print tip 16 name. Arrange flowers and trim with tip 352 leaves. *Serves 12.*

TOUCHING TRIBUTE

- Two-Mix Book Pan, p. 177
- Tips 2, 12, 16, 67, 104, p. 132-136
- Flower Nail No. 7, p. 138
- Creamy Peach, Ivory, Copper, Kelly Green Icing Colors, p. 131
- '90 Pattern Book (Praying Hands Pattern), p. 121
- Color Flow Mix, p. 131
- Buttercream, Color Flow Icings

- Make 8 roses—four each 7-petals and 5-petal with tips 12 and 104.
- With color flow icing, outline Praying Hands Pattern with tip 2 and flow in with thinned icing. Let dry.
- Print and write tip 2 message.
- Edge tops with tip 16 side-by-side elongated shells. Trim ends with tip 16 stars. Edge base with tip 16 shell border.
- Arrange roses on corners. Pipe tip 104 half roses and rosebuds. Trim with tip 67 leaves. Position praying hands (refer to hint about color flow under "Bless Him". *Serves 24.*

BLESS HIM

- 14 in. Round Pans, p. 168
- Tips 2, 3, 12, 16, 18, 21, 67, 104, p. 132-136
- Flower Nail No. 7, p. 138
- Golden Yellow, Kelly Green, Black, Copper, Royal Blue, Brown Icing Colors, p. 131
- '90 Pattern Book (Communion Boy Pattern), p. 121
- Color Flow Mix, p. 131
- Cake Dividing Set, p. 140
- 16 in. Cake Circle, Fanci-Foil Wrap, p. 139
- Buttercream, Color Flow Icings

- Make 9 tips 12 and 104 two-tone roses.
- With color flow icing and tip 2, outline Communion Boy and flow in with thinned icing. Let dry.
- Ice 2-layer cake smooth. Using Cake Dividing Set, divide sides into 20ths (use 10 divisions twice) approximately 1¼ in. from top. Connect marks with tip 16 double garlands. Trim with tip 16 upright shells and tip 3 dots.
- Write tip 2 message. Position Communion Boy*.
- Pipe shell border on top with tip 18 and at base with tip 21. Trim with tip 3 dots. Edge base shells with tip 3 zigzags.
- Arrange roses and pipe tip 104 half roses and rosebuds. Trim with tip 3 calyxes and sepals. Add tip 67 leaves. *Serves 44.*

*Note: Since buttercream icing will break down color flow, position on a piece of plastic wrap cut to fit, sugar cubes or mini marshmallows.

Blessings

Gods
Blessings
on this
Holy Day
Nancy
Jean

CRAIG

Jonathan's
First
Communion
May 6, 1990

Congratulations
David

October 6, 1990

—B A R & B A T M I T Z V A H—
Blessings

TRIBUTARY TABLETS

- **4-Pc. Oval Pan Set (3 largest are used), p. 167**
- **Tips 2, 3, 12, 14, 16, 67, 102, 104, 225, p. 132-136**
- **Flower Nail No. 7, p. 138**
- **Pink, Golden Yellow Icing Colors, p. 131**
- **'90 Pattern Book (Tablets Patterns), p. 121**
- **Dowel Rods, p. 165**
- **Color Flow Mix, p. 131**
- **Rectangle Cake Boards, Fanci-Foil Wrap, p. 139**
- **Buttercream, Color Flow Icings**
- **14 candles**
- With color flow icing, outline Tablets Patterns with tip 2, then flow in. Let dry. Add tip 2 numbers. Let set.
- With stiffened buttercream (or royal) icing, make 22 tips 12 and 104 roses; 41 tip 225 drop flowers with tip 3 dot centers.

- Prepare 2-layer cakes (for stacked construction. Mark message areas on side— 5½ in. on top, 6 in. on center and 7 in. on bottom. Also mark intervals, 3 in. wide x 1¼ in. deep, on sides. Print tip 3 script message on sides.
- Connect marks on sides with tip 16 zigzag garlands. Overpipe with tip 3 triple drop strings. Edge tops and bases with shell borders—tip 14 at tops, tip 16 at bases. Trim shells at bases with tip 14 zigzags.
- Position flowers. Pipe tip 102 rosebuds. Trim with tip 67 leaves. Push dowel rods into cake top and position color flow tablets*. Pipe tip 16 rosettes and push in candles. *Serves 144.*

SCROLL OF HONOR

- **12 x 18 in. Sheet Pan, p. 169**
- **Jelly Roll Pan, p. 172**
- **Tips 1, 3, 5, 12, 16, 18, 102, 103, 301, 352, p. 132-136**

- **Flower Nail No. 7, 138**
- **Royal Blue, Golden Yellow, Leaf Green Icing Colors, p. 131**
- **'90 Pattern Book (Hebrew Star Pattern), p. 121**
- **Flower Formers, p. 130**
- **Dowel Rods, p. 165**
- **Cake Boards, Fanci-Foil Wrap, p. 139**
- **Buttercream, Royal Icings**

- Using royal icing, make 10 tip 103 and 8 tip 102 daisies. Add tip 3 dot centers. Dry on flower formers. With tips 1, 5 and 16, make 10 bachelor buttons. To make scroll handles (4 are needed): Fit decorating bag with tip 12. Push dowel rod into open end, squeeze bag and pull out. Pipe tip 12 dots on end. Push uniced end of dowel rod into a styrofoam block to dry.
- Ice sheet cake smooth. Immediately after baking jelly roll, cut in half lengthwise (5½ x 15½ in. halves). Roll immediately per recipe instructions. When cool, fill and trim to fit width of sheet. Position "scroll" cakes on sheet and ice.
- Mark Hebrew Star Pattern and outline with tip 3. Fill in with tip 16 stars. Print tip 301 message. Edge top and bases of scrolls with tip 18 shell borders. On ends of scrolls, down corners and at base, pipe tip 18 swirled shell borders.
- Push in scroll handles. Arrange flowers with trim with tip 352 leaves. *Serves 43.*

Hearts Desire

THE SHOWER CAKE

- **12 in. Heart Pans, p. 187**
- **Tips 3, 12, 16, 102, 103, 125, 349, p. 132-136**
- **Flower Nail No. 7, p. 138**
- **Kelly Green Icing Color, p. 131**
- **Buttercream Icing**
- Make 8 roses—4 with tips 12 and 102; 4 with tips 12 and 103.
- Ice 2-layer heart smooth. Write tip 3 message with decorative build-up on letters. With toothpick, mark garland guide, 2½ ins. wide, 1¾ ins. deep.
- Pipe tip 16 zigzag garlands. Overpipe with tip 3 triple drop strings.
- Edge top and base with tip 16 shells. Pipe tip 125 spatula-striped ruffles. Edge ruffles with tip 4 zigzags.

- Arrange roses and pipe tip 3 vines. Add tip 102 half roses and rosebuds. Pipe tip 16 rosette blooms on spray and sides. Trim flowers with tip 349 leaves. *Serves 32.*

THE WEDDING TIERS

- **Heart Pan Set (6, 9, & 15 in. used), p. 187**
- **Tips 4, 16, 125, 349, p. 132-136**
- **Kelly Green, Sky Blue Icing Color, p. 131**
- **15-Pc. Decorator Pattern Press Set, p. 140**
- **11 in. Heart Separator Plates, p. 166**
- **7 in. Corinthian Pillars, p. 164**
- **Cake Boards, Fanci-Foil Wrap, p. 139**
- **Dowel Rods, p. 165**
- **Happy Hearts, p. 156**
- **Buttercream Icing**
- **Fresh flowers**

- Prepare and ice 2-layer cakes for stacked and pillar construction (see p. 106).
- With a toothpick, dot mark garland guides, 2½ ins. wide, 1¼ ins. deep, on sides of 6 and 15 in. hearts. With C-scroll pattern press to imprint sides of 9 in. heart. Space scrolls approximately ¾ in. apart.
- Pipe tip 16 zigzag garlands. Overpipe with tip 3 triple drop strings. Cover scroll marks with tip 16. Trim scrolls with tip 16 side shells.
- Edge separator plate with tip 16 C-motion shells. Pipe tip 16 shells, then add tip 125 ruffles to tops and bases (double on 15 in.). Edge ruffles with tip 3 zigzags.
- Pipe tip 16 rosettes flowers on sides. Trim with tip 349 leaves.
- At reception, assemble tiers on pillars. Arrange fresh flowers on plate. Position Happy Hearts. *Serves 100.*

Chapel of Love

THE SHOWER CAKE
- 12 x 18 in. Sheet Pan, p. 169
- 6 in. Square Pans, p. 169
- Tips 2C, 2D, 3, 16, 131, 224, 352, p. 132-137
- Royal Blue, Golden Yellow, Leaf Green Icing Colors, p. 131
- '90 Pattern Book (Chapel Scroll A & B Patterns), p. 121
- Cathedral Kit, p. 162
- Old Fashioned Fence, p. 159
- 2 in. Filigree Bells (3 needed), p. 158
- 7 in. Square Separator Plates (2 needed), p. 166
- Cake Boards, Fanci-Foil Wrap, Tuk 'n Ruffle, p. 139
- Dowel Rods p. 165
- Buttercream, Royal Icings
- Nylon thread

- Make 125 royal icing drop flowers in assorted sizes with tips 2C, 2D, 131 and 224. Add tip 3 dot centers. Let dry. Attach flowers to bells with royal icing. Let dry. Tie thread to bells.
- Assemble Steeple and Archway from Cathedral Kit. Edge seams and archway opening with tip 16 royal icing shells. Let dry.
- Ice 1-layer sheet cake smooth on foil-covered, Tuk 'n Ruffle trimmed cake board. Dowel rod where Archway will go and position 7 in. separator plate. Ice 2-layer square on cake board cut to fit and 7 in. separator plate. With toothpick, mark Chapel Scroll Patterns on sides—A on 6 in.; B on Sheet. Outline scroll designs with tip 16.
- Edge tops and bases of both cakes with tip 16 shell borders. Pipe tip 16 scallops around separator plate.
- Write tip 3 message on cake top. Add Archway and position cake supports onto separator plate. Attach bells to bottom of 6 in. cake plate with glue or tape. Position cake and Steeple.

- Place Old-Fashioned Fence. Add flowers to sides and top. Trim with tip 352 leaves. *Serves 54.*

THE WEDDING TIERS
- 6 & 10 in. Square Pans, p. 169
- 12 x 18 in. Sheet Pan, p. 169
- Tips 2C, 2D, 3, 16, 131, 224, 352, p. 132-137
- Royal Blue, Golden Yellow, Leaf Green Icing Colors, p. 131
- '90 Pattern Book (Chapel Scroll A & B Patterns), p. 121
- Cathedral Kit, p. 162
- Tiny Kneeling Cherubs (8 needed), p. 161
- 2 in. Filigree Bells (3 needed) p. 158
- Cake Boards, White Tuk 'n Ruffle, Fanci-Foil Wrap, p. 139
- Dowel Rods, p. 165
- 7 in. Square Separator Plates (2 needed), p. 166
- Side-By-Side Porcelain Couple, p. 149
- Buttercream, Royal Icings
- Plywood for base, nylon thread, glue

- Make 250 drop flowers in assorted sizes with tips 2C, 2D, 224 and 131. Add tip 3 dot centers.
- Assemble Chapel with window, archway and steeple. Edge seams and archway opening with tip 16 royal icing shells. Tie thread to bells, then attach drop flowers to sides with dot of icing. Let icing dry.
- Prepare iced cakes for stacked construction. On foil-covered, Tuk 'n Ruffle-trimmed plywood base, position two 1-layer 12 x 18 in. sheet cakes side-by-side. Dowel rod sheet, then place 1-layer 12 x 18 in. on top so back sides are perpendicular. Add dowel rods. Center 2-layer 10 in. square on top and dowel rod. Place 2-layer 6 in. cake on cake board cut to fit atop separator plate.
- With toothpick, mark Scroll Patterns on cake sides—A on 6 and 10 in.;B on sheet cakes. Outline scroll designs with tip 16 scrolls. Edge tops and bases of each tier with tip 16 shell border. Outline separator plate on 10 in. cake with tip 16 scallops.
- Arrange flowers on tops and sides. Trim with tip 352 leaves.
- At reception, position cake supports into separator plate on 10 in. cake. Before placing 6 in. cake, tape or glue bells to bottom of plate. Add 6 in. cake and Steeple. Position Chapel and add Porcelain Couple. Place Tiny Kneeling Cherubs in corners. *Serves 212.*

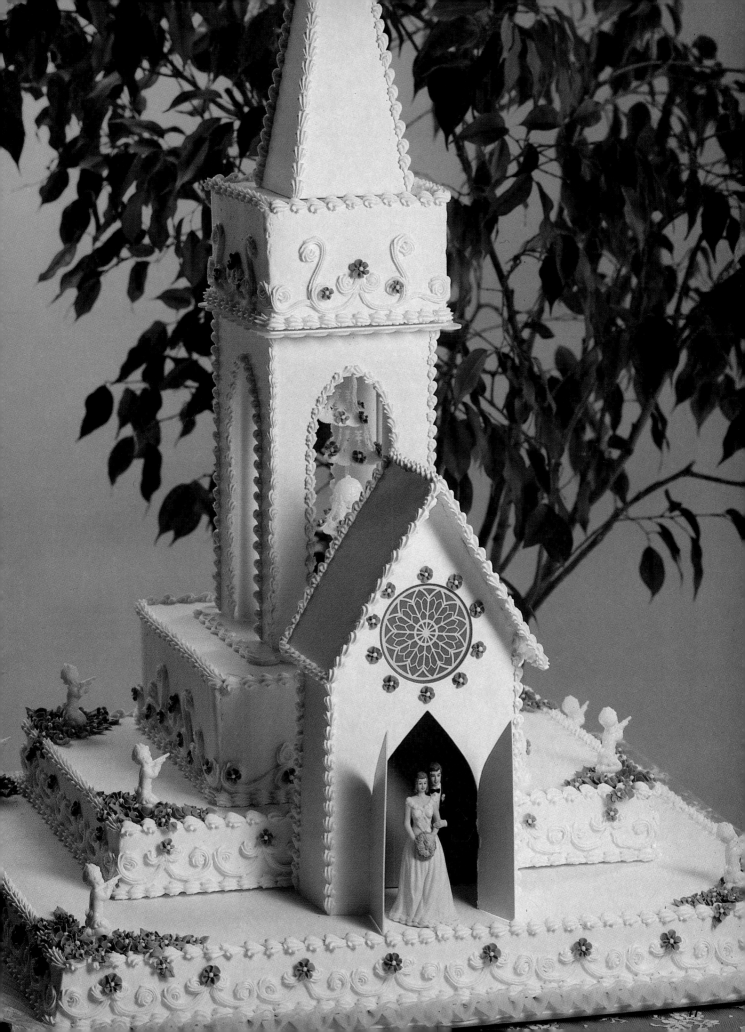

Striking Black & White

THE SHOWER CAKE

- Two-Mix Round Tier Set, p. 167
- Tips 3, 18, 86 or 87, p. 132-136
- Black Icing Color, p. 131
- Floating Tier Cake Stand, Crystal-Clear Dividing Set Plates—10 & 14 in. (optional), p. 162
- 8, 10, 14 in. Cake Circles & Doilies, p. 139
- Cake Dividing Set, p. 140
- Petite Double Rings, p. 156

- Buttercream, Royal Icings
- Ribbon trims, assortment of fancy pastries
- With royal icing, edge base of Petite Double Rings with tip 3 beads. Let dry.
- Ice 2-layer cakes smooth on cake circles. Position atop doily-trimmed plates. Using Cake Dividing Set, dot mark top tier into 6ths, center and bottom tier into 8ths. Connect marks with tip 86 or 87 ruffle garlands. Trim with tip 3 double drop strings.

- With tip 18, edge tops with reverse shell borders; bases with shells.
- At shower, tie ribbons on stand and position cakes. Add Petite Double Rings to top tier. Place pastries on and around tiers. *Cakes serve 48.*

THE WEDDING TIERS

- 7, 10, 14 in. Round Pans, p. 168
- Tips 3, 12, 16, 21, 32, 67, 104, p. 132-136
- Flower Nail No. 7, p. 138
- Black Icing Color, p. 131
- Two Crystal-Clear Cake Dividing Set Plates—8 & 12 in.; Twist Legs—7½ in. set, 9 in. set, p. 162
- Super Strong Cake Stand, p. 164
- 6, 8, 12 in. Cake Circles, p. 139
- Buttercream, Royal Icings
- Sophistication, p. 150
- Make 35 tips 12 and 104 roses.
- To prepare 2-layer cakes for push-in leg construction, see p. 106.
- Edge cake tops with tip 32 crown shell borders. On top and bottom tiers, trim crown shells with tip 16 inverted fleur-de-lis and tip 3 dots. On center tier, connect crown shells with tip 3 overlapping drop strings. Add tip 16 stars.
- Edge bases with upright shell borders—tip 21 on top tier, tip 32 on remaining cakes. Pipe tip 16 zigzags around shells on bottom tier. Add tip 3 overlapping drop strings to borders. Note: We suggest using royal icing for all black decorations to prevent color from bleeding into white.
- Place small mounds of icing in center of 10 in. and 14 in. cakes. Arrange roses on mounds. Pipe tip 67 leaves.
- At reception, assemble tiers on twist legs. Position Sophistication. *Serves 116.*

THE SHOWER CAKE

- Viennese Swirl Pan, p. 174
- 12 in. Round Pan, p. 168
- Tips 3, 16, 18, 21, p. 132-133
- Creamy Peach Icing Color, p. 131
- 13 in. Crystal-Look Plates,
- 7 in. Crystal-Look Pillars, p. 163
- 12 in. Cake Circle, p. 139
- Dowel Rods, p. 165
- Buttercream, Poured Fondant Icings
- Petite Spring Song, p. 156
- Fresh flowers

- Cover Viennese Swirl with fondant icing per recipe directions on p. 94. Ice one-layer round smooth atop cake circle and separator plate. Dowel rod and stack cakes together.
- Pipe tip 16 V-shells around center of fondant cake. Trim with tip 3 dots.
- Edge base of fondant cake with tip 18 scrolls and shells. Edge top of round cake with tip 18 V-shells. Add tip 3 dots. Pipe tip 21 comma-motion shells at base of round cake.
- At shower, assemble tiers on pillars. Position Spring Song. Arrange fresh flowers. *Serves 30.*

THE WEDDING TIERS

- 6, 8, 10 in. Round Pans, p. 168
- 12 x 18 in. Sheet Pan, p. 169
- Tips 3, 14, 18, 21, 67, 102, 103, 104, 506, p. 132-137
- 1¼ & 1⅝ in. Lily Nail Set (1¼ in. & 1⅝ in. used), p. 138
- Creamy Peach, Moss Green Icing Colors, p. 131
- 9 in. Crystal-Look Separator Plate, Crystal Bridge and Stairway Set (2 sets needed) Kolor-Flo Fountain, Fountain Cascade Set, p. 163

- Edible Glitter, Pearl Stamens (2 pkgs. needed), p. 130
- Rectangle Cake Boards, 6, 8 & 10 in. Cake Circles, White Tuk 'n Ruffle, Fanci- Foil Wrap, p. 139
- Dowel Rods, p. 165
- Porcelain Dancing Couple, p. 149
- Hearts A Flutter Ornament, p. 154
- Buttercream, Royal Icings
- Wide and narrow satin ribbon, flowers, greenery, 21 x 51 in. plywood for base
- Make 120 royal icing petunias—60 with tip 102 on 1¼ in. nail and 60 with tip 103 on larger nail. Add tip 14 star centers, stamens

Crystal Enchantment

and glitter. Tie bows out of narrow ribbon. Glue wide ribbon to Stairways; bows to railing.

- Prepare cakes for stacked construction. Cover plywood board with Fanci-Foil and add Tuk 'n Ruffle. Ice 4 sheet cakes smooth on cake boards. (At the reception, position cakes to measure 18 x 48 in. on plywood base and smooth icing where cakes meet. All decorating on these cakes will be done at reception.) Ice 2-layer round cakes smooth—one 6 in., two 8 in. and 10 in. Dowel rod cakes and where Kolor-Flo

Fountain will go. Stack 8 and 10 in. cakes together.

- Edge 6 in. cake top with tip 18 reverse shell border; base with tip 18 comma-motion border.
- Edge cake tops with pairs of V-shells—tip 18 on 8 in., tip 21 on 10 in. Connect points with tip 3 double drop strings. Trim with tip 3 dots. Edge bases of 8 and 10 in. rounds with tip 506 comma-motion shell border. Figure pipe tip 3 swan heads and necks on alternate shells at base. Trim "swans" with tip 104 ruffles.

- At reception, assemble cakes together. Position 9 in. plate where fountain will go. Add fountain with cascade. Cover plate with greenery. Edge half of sheet with C-motion shells and half with comma-motion shells—top with tip 21, base with tip 506. Figure pipe tip 3 swans in center of side and last shell from corner. Trim corners with tip 21 pairs of upright shells. Add tip 3 dots in centers. Assemble one set of stairs with platform and position on 8 in. cakes. Bridge cakes with remaining two stairways (no platform). Position Hearts A Flutter and Dancing Couple. *Serves 300.*

Romantic Fanfare

THE SHOWER CAKE

- 12 in. Round Pans, p. 168
- Tips 3, 14, 16, 32, 66, 102, 104, 352, p. 132-136
- Lily Nail Set, p. 138
- Teal Icing Color, p. 131
- 12 in. (4 needed), 16 in. (one needed) Tall Tier Plates, 7¾ in. Column, Top Column Cap Nut, 4-Arm Base Stand, p. 162
- Yellow Stamens, p. 130
- Cake Dividing Set, p. 140
- Romance & Ruffles, p. 153
- Buttercream, Royal Icings
- Assorted pastries

- With royal icing, make 20 tip 66 bluebells in 1¼ in. lily nail. Add yellow stamens. Let dry.
- Ice 2-layer cake smooth. Using Cake Dividing Set, dot mark sides into 12ths. Connect marks with tip 104 double rows of ruffles. Trim ruffles with tip 14 e-motion.
- Write tip 3 message. Edge top with tip 16 shells. At base, pipe tip 32 shell border. Trim with tip 102 ruffles.
- Arrange flowers (allow space for ornament) and trim with tip 352 leaves.
- To serve: Assemble column and plates onto 4-arm base stand. Position cake atop 16 in. plate. Add Romance & Ruffles. Place pastries on plates. *Cake serves 36.*

THE WEDDING TIERS

- 10, 14 in. Round Pans, p. 168
- Tips 14, 16, 66, p. 132-134
- Teal, Moss Green Icing Colors, p. 131
- Lily Nail Set, p. 138
- '90 Pattern Book (Scallop Tops A & B Patterns), p. 121
- Tall Tier Plates, 7¾ in. Column, Top Column Cap Nut, 4-Arm Base Stand, p. 162
- Tall Tier Stand—one 16 in. Plate, five 12 in. Plates, two 7¾ in. Columns, Top Column Cap Nut, Tall Tier 4-Arm Base, Cake Corer Tube, p. 162
- Yellow Stamens (2 pkgs.), p. 130
- Musicial Trio (2 sets needed), p. 161
- 14, 10 in. Cake Circles, p. 139
- Love's Fanfare, p. 151
- Buttercream, Royal Icings

- Make 200 tip 66 royal icing bluebells (three different shades) in 1¼ in. lily nail. Add yellow stamens. Let dry.
- Cut center holes in one 14 and 10 in. cake circle. Ice 2-layer cakes (five 10 in. and one 14 in. are used) smooth. Core out center of 14 in. cake and add column section.
- With toothpick, mark Scallop Top A on 10 in. cakes; Scallop Top B on 14 in. Cover marks with tip 14 scrolls.
- Pipe tip 14 colonial scrolls on sides of 10 in. cakes; tip 14 reverse colonial scroll on 14 in. side.
- Edge tops with tip 16 reverse shell borders. Pipe tip 16 shell borders at base of 14 in. and 10 in. side cakes (border will be added to 10 in. center tier after assembly).
- At reception: Place base bolt through 4-arm stand center and anchor bolt to 7¾ in. column. Position 10 in. side cakes on 4-arm base stand. Assemble 14 in. tier on column. Position 12 in. plate and anchor with column cap nut. Add 10 in. cake and edge base with tip 16 shell border. Position Musicial Trio figures on side cakes. Arrange flowers on tops and on bases of side cakes. Trim with tip 352 leaves. Position Love's Fanfare. *Serves 233.*

Dancing On Air

THE SHOWER CAKE

- 15 in. Hexagon Pan (sold in 4-Pc. Hexagon Pan Set), p. 167
- Tips 2D, 2, 3, 18, 129, 224, 352, p. 132-135
- Flower Nail No. 7, p. 138
- Pink Icing Color, p. 131
- Tuk 'N Ruffle, Fanci-Foil Wrap, p. 139
- Script Message Pattern Press Set, Flower Formers, p. 140
- Petite Bells of Joy, p. 156
- Buttercream, Royal Icings

- With royal icing, make 155 wild roses—40 with tip 2D, 45 with tip 129, 70 with tip 224. Add tip 2 dot centers. Dry on flower formers.
- Ice 2-layer cake smooth. Imprint Congratulations with pattern press. Outline and write names with tip 3.
- With tip 18, edge top with reverse shells; base with shell border.
- Position Petite Bells of Joy. Arrange flowers on top and sides. Trim with tip 352 leaves. *Serves 40.*

THE WEDDING TIERS

- 9, 12 in. Hexagon Pans, p. 167
- 16 in. Round Pans, p. 168
- Tips 2, 3, 16, 18, 86 or 87, 102, 104, 124, 349, p. 132-136
- Flower Nail No. 7, p. 138
- Pink Icing Color, p. 131
- Arched Tier Set, p. 161
- 4½ in. Arched Pillars, p. 164
- 11 in. Hexagon Separator Plates (2 needed), p. 166
- Kolor-Flo Fountain, Flower Holder Ring p. 163
- Heart Bowl Vase (3 needed), p. 159
- Dowel Rods, p. 165
- 10, 14 in. Cake Circles, Fanci-Foil Wrap, Tuk 'N Ruffle, p. 139
- Flower Formers, Cake Dividing Set, p. 140
- Bridal Waltz, p. 152
- Buttercream, Royal Icings
- Fresh flower arrangements (bring Heart Bowl Vases and Flower Holder Ring to florist)

- With royal icing, make 80 wild roses—60 with tip 102, 20 with tip 104. Add tip 2 dot centers. Let dry on flower formers.
- Ice 2-layer cakes (one 9 in. and three 12 in. hexagons; one 16 in. round). Place two 12 in. hexagons on Tuk 'N Ruffle-trimmed, foil-covered cake circles (cut to fit). Prepare remaining cakes for pillar and stacked construction (see p. 106).
- Using Cake Dividing Set, divide sides of round into 12ths. Edge bases with tip 18 shell borders. Pipe tip 18 scallops around hexagon separator plate.
- Pipe tip 124 ruffle garlands on 16 in. sides. Edge garlands with tip 16 zigzags. Pipe tip 86 or 87 garlands on 9 in. and rows of ruffles on sides of 12 in. hexagons.
- With tip 16, trim corners of hexagons—shells on 9 in.; zigzags on 12 in. cakes. Edge cake tops with tip 18 reverse shells.
- Arrange flowers on sides. On 12 in. sides, add tip 3 outline stems. Pipe tip 349 leaves.
- At reception: Place flower holder ring and fountain on plate. Assemble stacked tiers on pillars. Position hexagon side cakes and add floral arrangements to tops. Position top tier and Bridal Waltz. *Serves 250.*

Happy Anniversary

"FANSY"

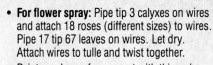

- 12 in. Round Pans, p. 170
- Tips 1, 3, 14, 16, 32, 67, 59s, 102, 103, 301, p. 132-136
- Flower Nail No. 7, p. 138
- Golden Yellow, Violet, Moss Green, Black Icing Colors, p. 131
- Decorator's Brush, Cake Dividing Set, p. 140
- Flower Formers, p. 130
- 10 in. Round Doily, p. 139
- Buttercream, Royal Icings

- To make fan: Fold doily in half and cut on fold. Accordian fold each half. Tape halves together.
- Using royal icing, make 10 pansies—3 with tip 102 and 7 with tip 103. "Paint" veins and pipe tip 1 string loop centers. Make 20 tip 59s violets with tip 1 dot centers (10 of each color).
- Ice 2-layer round cake smooth. Using Cake Dividing Set, with toothpick, mark sides into 10ths. At marks, pipe tip 16 fleur-de-lis. Pipe tip 3 overlapping drop strings from fleur-de-lis. Trim with tip 3 dots.
- Print tip 301 message. Edge top and base with tip 32 shell borders. Trim top shell with tip 102 ruffles; bottom shell with tip 14 zigzags.
- Position fan. Arrange flowers and trim with tip 67 leaves. *Serves 56.*

SWEET VIOLETS

- 8 in. Round Pans, p. 168
- 12 in. Square Pans, p. 169
- Tips 1, 3, 59s, 66, 199, 362, p. 132-137
- Flower Nail No. 9, p. 138
- Violet, Golden Yellow, Moss Green Icing Colors, p. 131
- '90 Pattern Book (Vines Patterns), p. 121
- 15 Pc. Pattern Press, Cake Dividing Set, p. 140
- Cake Boards, Tuk 'n Ruffle, Fanci-Foil Wrap, p. 139
- Dowel Rods, p. 165
- Large Double Wedding Rings, p. 158
- Buttercream, Royal Icings

- Make 150 royal icing violets with tip 59s. Dot centers with tip 1. Paint rings with thinned royal icing to match cake. Let dry.
- Prepare 2-layer cakes for stacked construction (see p. 106). Before positioning round cake, mark into 4ths using Cake Dividing Set. Imprint cake tops with C-Scroll pattern press. Mark Vine Patterns on sides.
- Outline vines and scrolls with tip 362. Edge bases with tip 199 bands. Pipe tip 362 columns on sides of each tier. Edge cake tops with tip 362 rope borders.
- Position rings on cake top. Overpipe vines with tip 3. Add flowers to tops, sides and rings (attach with dots of icing). Trim with tip 66 leaves. *Serves 97.*

IVORY TOWER

- Petal Pan Set, p. 167
- Tips 3, 6, 16, 18, 21, 65, 67, 101, 101s, 102, p. 132-136
- Flower Nail No. 7, p. 138
- Violet, Golden Yellow, Moss Green Icing Colors, p. 131
- '90 Pattern Book (Draped Stringwork Patterns), p. 121
- 7 in. Corinthian Pillars, p. 164
- 10 in. (2 needed), 16 in. (one needed) Round Separator Plates, p. 166
- Florist Tape, p. 130
- Petite Anniversary Years, p. 157
- 4⅝ in. Glazed Porcelain Couple, p. 149
- Dowel Rods, p. 165
- 9 & 14 in. Cake Circles, p. 139
- Buttercream, Royal Icings
- Tulle, florist wire

- Make roses and leaves on wires with royal icing. Using tip 6 for bases, make 75 tip 101 and 40 tip 101s roses.

- For flower spray: Pipe tip 3 calyxes on wires and attach 18 roses (different sizes) to wires. Pipe 17 tip 67 leaves on wires. Let dry. Attach wires to tulle and twist together.
- Paint numbers of ornament with thinned royal icing.
- To prepare one-layer 6 & 9 and 2-layer 15 in. cakes for stacked and pillar construction, see p. 106. Edge separator plate with tip 18 scallops.
- Mark Draped Stringwork Patterns on sides— A on 9 in. & B on 15 in. Connect marks with tip 3 double and triple drop string. Pipe tip 3 drop strings (1 in. deep) on 6 in. sides. Trim stringwork with tip 3 dots.
- Edge cake tops with C-scrolls—tip 16 on 6 in., tip 18 on 9 in. and tip 21 on 15 in. Pipe zigzag puff borders at bases—tip 18 on 6 and 9 in.; tip 21 at base of 15 in. Attach flowers to ornament and cakes; trim with tip 65 leaves.
- At party, tape flower sprays to separator plate and position couple. Assemble tiers on pillars. Add ornament. *Serves 90.*

RUFFLES 'N ROSES

- **12 in. Heart Pans,** p. 187
- **Tips 2, 12, 14, 66, 104, p. 132-136**
- **Flower Nail No. 7,** p. 138
- **Willow Green, Ivory, Rose Petal Icing Colors, p. 131**
- **'90 Pattern Book (Script Letters Patterns),** p. 121
- **Buttercream Icing**

- With stiffened buttercream (or royal icing) make 2 two-tone roses using tips 12 and 104.
- Ice 2-layer cake smooth. With toothpick, mark Script Letters Patterns. Write message with tip 2, adding decorative build-up on some letters.
- Edge cake top with tip 104 double ruffle. Trim center seam with tip 14 shells. At base, pipe tip 14 shells (to add dimension) Overpipe shells with tip 104 ruffle. Trim edge of ruffle with tip 14 shells.
- Pipe tip 2 vines. Add tip 104 half roses and rosebuds. Trim with tip 2 calyxes and sepals. Position roses. Pipe tip 66 leaves. *Serves 32.*

Romantic Roses

ROSE GARDEN

- **9 x 13 in. Sheet Pan,** p. 169
- **Ball Pan, p. 184**
- **Tips 2, 6, 12, 48, 68, 103, 125, p. 132-136**
- **Flower Nail No. 7,** p. 138
- **Willow Green, Ivory, Rose Petal Icing Colors, p. 131**
- **'90 Pattern Book (Script Letters Pattern),** p. 121
- **Dowel Rods, p. 165**
- **6 in. Cake Circle, p. 139**
- **Buttercream Icing**

- With stiffened buttercream (or royal) icing, make 50 two-tone roses with tips 12 and 103. Make 10 two-tone roses with tips 12 and 125.
- Ice sheet cake smooth. Lightly ice half ball cake on 6 in. cake circle. Cut and position dowel rods in sheet cake where ball cake will go. Place ball atop sheet. Cover ball cake with two shades of tip 68 leaves.
- With Script Letters Pattern, mark names on sheet. Write and add decorative build-up with tip 2. Pipe tip 48 ribbed stripe "trunk." Add tip 103 ribbon bow. Edge cake top with tip 6 bead border.
- Position roses on ball cake and at base of sheet. Trim roses at base with tip 68 leaves. *Serves 20.*

SATINY ROSE

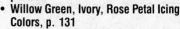

- **Viennese Swirl Pan,** p. 174
- **Tips 2A, 12, 67, 125, 127D, p. 132-136**
- **Flower Nails—No. 7 & 3 in., p. 138**
- **Ivory, Willow Green, Rose Petal Icing Colors, p. 131**
- **Poured Fondant, Buttercream Icings**

- With stiffened buttercream (or royal) icing, make 1 giant two-tone rose with tips 2A (for base) and tip 127D. Make 12 tips 12 and 125 two-tone roses.
- Lightly ice cake, then cover with poured fondant icing. Let set.
- Position roses and pipe tip 67 leaves at base. *Serves 12.*

Lovely Idea: Mold a beautiful bunch of rose-shaped candies with our Candy Melts™ * (p. 115) and Rose Candy Molds (p. 116).

*brand confectionery coating

The Secrets of Success

Baking Cakes

Beneath a beautifully decorated cake is a perfectly baked cake. Here's how to achieve baking success. **Note:** If you're baking with a Wilton shaped pan, follow the instructions included with your pan.

GREASE	FLOUR	SHAKE	PLACE RACK	REMOVE

• Preheat oven to temperature specified in recipe or on packaged mix.

• Thoroughly grease the inside of each pan with solid vegetable shortening or use a vegetable cooking spray. Use a pastry brush to spread the shortening evenly. Be sure sides, corners and all indentations are completely covered.

• Sprinkle flour inside of pan and shake back and forth so the flour covers all the greased surfaces. Tap out excess flour and if any shiny spots remain,

touch up with more shortening and flour. This step is essential in preventing your cake from sticking. If you prefer, the bottom of a simple geometric shaped pan (round, square, hexagon, etc.) may be lined with waxed paper after greasing. This eliminates flouring pan. Your cake will unmold easily, but with more crumbs.

• Bake the cake according to temperature and time specifications in recipe or on package instructions. Remove cake from oven and let cool 10 minutes

in pan on a cake rack. Larger cakes over 12-in. diameter may need to cool 15 minutes.

• So cake sits level and to prevent cracking, while in pan, cut away the raised center portion with serrated knife. To unmold cake, place cake rack against cake and turn both rack and pan over. Remove pan carefully. If pan will not release, return it to a warm oven (250°) for a few minutes, then repeat procedure. Cool cake completely, at least 1 hour. Brush off loose crumbs and frost.

Baking Hints

• If you like to plan ahead, do so. Your baked cake will stay up to three months wrapped in heavy-duty foil in the freezer. Always thaw cake completely before icing. Your cake will still be fresh and easy to ice because it will be firm.

• Wilton Bake-Even Cake Strips will help prevent crowns from forming on basic shaped cakes as they bake.

• Packaged, two-layer cake mixes usually yield 4 to 6 cups of batter, but formulas change, so always measure. Here's a handy guide: one 2-layer cake mix will make: two 8-in. round layers, one 10-in. round layer, one 9 x 13 x 2-in. sheet, one character cake, one Wonder Mold cake, one mini-tier cake.

• If you're in doubt as to how many cups of batter you need to fill a pan, measure the cups of water it will hold first and

use this number as a guide. Then, if you want a cake with high sides, fill the pan ⅔ full of batter. For slightly thinner cake layers, fill ½ full. Never fill cake pans more than ⅔ full. Even if the batter doesn't overflow, the cake will have a heavy texture.

• For 3-in. deep or 3-D pans, we recommend pound or pudding-added cake batters. Fill pan half full only.

• For 3-D cakes: When using the baking core, it's essential to be exact about baking time, as it's very difficult to test 3-D cakes for doneness. Be sure to preheat the oven. If your 3-D cake is to be given away or sold, after baking you can remove the baking core and insert crumpled aluminum foil into the opening for support.

Serve It Right!

Placing the cake on a sturdy yet attractive base is essential. Here are several very pretty ways to present your decorated masterpiece.

Shimmery Bases Are Easy To Make
Most of our cake ideas are shown on coordinating foil-covered boards. These surfaces are economical and convenient, especially when your decorated cake is to be given away. Stock up on our strong cake boards (round and rectangle shapes) and Fanci-Foil Wrap.

To make: Trace the shaped pan onto a Wilton cake board, ½ to 1 inch larger than pan. Cut out board with an artist's matte knife.

Trace board shape onto foil wrap, making outlines 3 to 4 inches larger than board. Cut out foil cover. Cut deep slits at several points around foil, leaving a ½ inch uncut so it folds neatly around board. Cover board with foil and tape securely to underside. Note: If the cake is heavy, use 2 or more boards for added serving support.

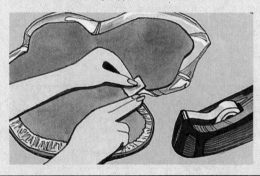

Lacy-Look Romantics
Show 'N Serve Boards combine the prettiness you love with the function you need.

Elegant Doilies have wide borders of lace that stand out beautifully from your decorated cakes.

Just For The Frill Of It!
Trim your cake boards with elegant Tuk 'n Ruffle. Here's how easy it is to surround your cakes with a frilly band of tulle and "lace." The cake board or plate under your iced cake should extend approximately 2 to 3 inches. Place dots of icing on board and press Tuk 'n Ruffle around cake base. Overlap ends 1 inch and cut.

Tastefully Torted

By simply cutting a cake into layers, you can enhance its taste and create impact! Classic and novelty shapes are easy to torte especially with our **New Cake Leveler!** It cuts perfectly-even layers on cakes up to 10 in. in diameter and adjusts to desired height.

Divide the cake horizontally into desired equal-sized layers (generally shaped into two, classic into as many as four). Follow directions for using our Cake Leveler on the package or use a serrated knife. Hold knife level at desired height and with a gentle sawing motion, rotate the cake against blade of knife.

• Provide support by sliding the sliced layer onto a cake board (for each layer follow this procedure).

Icing Consistency

Since proper consistency is the key to making decorator icing that will shape the petals of a flower, show the details of a border or cover the surface of a cake, it's important that you use the recommended icing and consistency for any technique. As a general rule, flowers require a stiff icing consistency, borders a medium-stiff consistency and writing or leaves a slightly thinned consistency. Icing that can peak to an inch or more is stiff, less than that is medium consistency. Icing that flows easily from a tip without running is a thin consistency. Every Wilton icing recipe is tested for taste and other important qualities. This chart will tell you each recipe's qualities, so you can determine which is the right one for your cake.

Icing	Recommended Uses	Tinting	Flavor & Consistency	Icing Storage	Special Features
Buttercream (Wilton Mix, Homemade or Wilton Decorator's Icing)	• Borders, writing • Roses, drop flowers & sweet peas • Figure piping • Icing cakes smooth	• Deep colors • Most colors deepen upon setting	• Sweet, buttery flavor • Thin-to-stiff consistency	• Refrigerate icing in an airtight container for 2 weeks	• Iced cake can be stored at room temperature for 2-3 days • Flowers remain soft enough to be cut with a knife
Snow-White Buttercream	• Borders, writing • Roses, drop flowers & sweet peas • Figure piping • Icing cakes smooth	• Deep colors • Most colors deepen upon setting • Gives true colors	• Sweet, almond flavor • Thin-to-stiff consistency	• Refrigerate icing in an airtight container for 2 weeks	• Iced cake may be stored for 2-3 days • Air-dried flowers have translucent look • Flowers remain soft to be cut with a knife • Good for wedding cakes • Tints true colors due to pure white color
Deluxe Buttercream (Use Wilton Icing Mix or Wilton Decorator's Icing)	• Borders, writing • Drop flowers & sweet peas • Figure piping • Icing cakes smooth	• Deep colors	• Rich, creamy flavor • Thin-to-stiff consistency	• Refrigerate icing in an airtight container for 2 weeks	• Texture remains soft on decorated cake • Iced cake may be stored at room temperature • All-purpose
Cream Cheese	• Basic borders, writing, stars, shells, drop flowers • Icing cake smooth	• Pastels	• Cream cheese • Thin-to-medium consistency	• Refrigerate icing in an airtight container for 1 week	• Iced cake must be refrigerated • Cream cheese flavor is especially good with spice cakes, carrot cakes, etc • All-purpose
Stabilized Whipped Cream	• Borders, writing • Icing cake smooth	• Pastels can be achieved • Paste colors are best to use	• Creamy, delicate sweetness • Light, thin-to-medium consistency	• Use immediately	• Iced cake must be refrigerated • Texture remains soft on decorated cake • Especially good on cakes decorated with fruits
French Buttercream	• Basic borders • Writing • Icing cake smooth	• Pastels can be achieved	• Tastes similar to vanilla ice cream • Consistency similar to whipped cream	• Use immediately	• Store iced cake in refrigerator • Texture remains soft on decorated cake • Cooked icing gives a special flavor, similar to vanilla ice cream
Quick-Pour Fondant Icing	• For icing cakes or cookies only	• Pastels	• Very sweet flavor • Pourable consistency	• Use immediately; excess fondant drippings can be reheated & poured again	• Dries to a shiny, smooth surface to coat petit fours and cookies • Seals in freshness
Rolled Fondant Icing	• For covering heavy pound or fruit cake	• Pastels • Rich, sweet flavor • Dough-like consistency	• Use immediately • Bring to room temperature before kneading	• Excess can be refrigerated 3 weeks	• Gives a perfectly smooth, velvety surface • Seals in freshness and moisture • Always decorate with royal icing
Royal	• Flower-making, figure piping, making flowers on wires • Decorating cookies & gingerbread houses	• Deep colors • Some colors may fade upon sitting in bright light	• Very sweet and hard • Thin-to-stiff consistency	• Store in airtight grease-free container at room temperature for 2 weeks	• Dries candy-hard for lasting decorations • Bowl & utensils must be grease free • Cover icing with damp cloth to prevent crusting

Decorator's Icing Recipes

Buttercream Icing

½ cup solid vegetable shortening
½ cup butter or margarine*
1 tsp. Clear Vanilla Extract (p. 131)
4 cups sifted confectioners sugar
    (approx. 1 lb.)
2 Tbsps. milk**

Cream butter and shortening with electric mixer. Add vanilla. Gradually add sugar, one cup at a time, beating well on medium speed. Scrape sides and bottom of bowl often. When all sugar has been mixed in, icing will appear dry. Add milk and beat at medium speed until light and fluffy. Keep icing covered with a damp cloth until ready to use. For best results, keep icing bowl in refrigerator when not in use. Refrigerated in an airtight container, this icing can be stored 2 weeks. Rewhip before using. YIELD: 3 cups

*Substitute all-vegetable shortening and ½ teaspoon Wilton Butter Extract (p. 131) for pure white icing and stiffer consistency.

**Add 3-4 Tbsps. light corn syrup per recipe to thin for icing cake.

Chocolate Buttercream

Add ¾ cup cocoa or three 1 oz. unsweetened chocolate squares, melted, and an additional 1 to 2 Tbsps. milk to recipe. Mix until well blended.

For a unique change of pace, add Wilton Candy Flavors (p. 115) in Rum, Orange or Cherry, in place of vanilla extract.

Snow-White Buttercream

⅔ cup water
4 Tbsps. Wilton Meringue Powder Mix
    (p. 131)
12 cups sifted confectioners sugar
    (approximately 3 lbs.)
1¼ cups solid shortening
¾ tsp. salt
½ tsp. almond extract (p. 131)
½ tsp. Clear Vanilla Extract (p. 131)
¼ tsp. Butter Extract (p. 131)

Combine water and meringue powder; whip at high speed until peaks form. Add 4 cups sugar, one cup at a time, beating after each addition at low speed. Alternately add shortening and remainder of sugar. Add salt and flavorings; beat at low speed until smooth.

YIELD: 7 cups.

Note: Recipe may be doubled or cut in half. If cut in half, yield is 2 ⅔ cups.

French Buttercream

⅔ cup sugar
¼ cup flour
¼ tsp. salt
¾ cup milk
1 cup cold butter; cut in several pieces
1 tsp. Clear Vanilla Extract (p. 131)

Place sugar, flour and salt in sauce pan and mix thoroughly; stir in milk. Cook over medium heat and stir constantly until very thick. Remove from heat and pour into a medium mixing bowl. Cool at room temperature. Add ½ cup butter at a time (cut into several pieces) and beat at medium-high speed until smooth. Add vanilla and beat well. Chill icing for a few minutes before decorating. Iced cake must be refrigerated until serving time.

YIELD: 2 cups

Stabilized Whipped Cream Icing

1 tsp. unflavored gelatin
4 tsps. cold water
1 cup heavy whipping cream (at least 24
    hours old and very cold)
¼ cup confectioners sugar
½ tsp. Clear Vanilla Extract (p. 131)

Combine gelatin and cold water in small saucepan. Let stand until thick. Place over low heat, stirring constantly just until gelatin dissolves. Remove from heat and cool slightly. Whip cream, sugar, and vanilla until slightly thickened. While beating slowly, gradually add gelatin to whipped cream mixture. Whip at high speed until stiff. YIELD: 2 cups. Cakes iced with whipped cream must be stored in the refrigerator.

Cream Cheese Icing

3-8 oz. packages slightly softened
    cream cheese
3 cups sifted confectioners sugar

Beat cream cheese until smooth. Add confectioners sugar and mix thoroughly. Beat at high speed until light and fluffy.

YIELD: 3½ cups

Frozen Non-Dairy Whipped Topping

Non-dairy whipped topping must be thawed in the refrigerator before coloring or using for decorating. Can be used for decorating techniques similar to stabilized whipped cream. Do not allow to set at room temperature, as it becomes too soft for decorating. After decorating, store cake in refrigerator.

Packaged Topping Mix

Whipped topping mix can be used for decorating similar to stabilized whipped cream. However, use immediately after preparing. Do not allow to set at room temperature as topping becomes too soft for well-defined decorations.

Wilton Creamy White Icing Mix (p. 131)

You'll love its creamy taste, luscious texture and convenience. Ideal for icing smooth and decorating. Just add butter and milk, the shortening's already in the mix. For chocolate icing: Mix icing according to package directions. Stir in 2-oz. melted, unsweetened baking chocolate. If too stiff, add a few drops of milk. For Deluxe Buttercream: Use 6 Tbsps. butter and ¼ cup whipping cream.

Ready-to-Spread Wilton Decorator's Icing (p. 131)

Ideal for all your decorating needs. Use for frosting, piping borders, flowers, writing and more. Just stir for proper decorating consistency. Tastes delicious, too.

Specialty Icing

ROYAL ICING

This smooth, hard-drying icing makes decorations that last. Ideal for making flowers, piping figures, overpiping and decorating cookies. Flowers and decorations made from royal icing will last for months, if stored properly, without softening. Royal icing decorations should be air dried. Allow several hours drying time for large decorations. Make sure bowl and utensils are grease free, since any trace of grease will cause royal icing to break down.

Royal icing dries quickly, so keep icing bowl covered with a damp cloth at all times. Store in air tight container. Rebeat at low speed before using.

Note: Royal icing is edible. Since it dries candy-hard, it is not recommended for icing your cakes. Use only for special effects you want to last.

For piping delicate stringwork, add 1 teaspoon of piping gel or light corn syrup to 1 cup icing.

Royal Meringue Recipe

3 level Tbsps. Wilton Meringue Powder
4 cups sifted confectioners sugar
  (approx. 1 lb)
6 Tbsps. water*

Beat all ingredients at low speed for 7 to 10 minutes (10 to 12 minutes at high speed for portable mixer) until icing forms peaks.
YIELD: 3 cups

*When using large counter top mixer or for stiffer icing, use 1 Tbsp. less water.

Royal Egg White Recipe

3 egg whites (room temperatures)
4 cups confectioners sugar (approx. 1 lb.)
½ tsp. cream of tartar

Beat all ingredients at high speed for 7 to 10 minutes. Use immediately. Rebeating will not restore texture.

YIELD: 2½ cups

QUICK-POUR FONDANT ICING

6 cups confectioners sugar
½ cup water
2 Tbsps. light corn syrup
1 tsp. almond extract (p. 131)
Wilton Icing Colors (p. 131)

Place sugar in a saucepan. Combine water and corn syrup. Add to sugar and stir until well mixed. Place over low heat. Don't allow temperature of fondant to exceed 100°. Remove from heat, stir in flavor and icing color. Optional: Cakes may be covered with a thin coating of buttercream icing or apricot glaze. Allow to set before covering with fondant. To cover, place cake or cookies on wire rack over a drip pan. Pour fondant into center and work towards edges. Touch up bare spots with a spatula. Let set. Excess fondant can be reheated. Even easier...use Wilton Candy Wafer/Fondant Center Mix (see pg. 114) Fondant Icing Recipe on label.

ROLLED FONDANT

This icing is rolled out and used as a covering for a pound or fruit cake which is traditionally first covered with a layer of marzipan to seal in flavor and moistness of the cake. It's characteristic of the Australian method of decorating. Traditionally cakes covered with rolled fondant are decorated with royal icing.

Rolled Fondant Recipe
1 Tbsp. unflavored gelatin
¼ cup cold water
½ cup Wilton Glucose (p. 131)
1 Tbsp. Wilton Glycerin (p. 131)
2 Tbsp. solid vegetable shortening
2 lbs. confectioners sugar
2-3 drops liquid food color and flavoring, as desired

Combine gelatin and cold water; let stand until thick. Place gelatin mixture in top of double boiler and heat until dissolved. Add glucose and glycerin, mix well. Stir in shortening and just before completely melted, remove from heat. Mixture should cool until lukewarm.

Next, place 1 lb. confectioners sugar in a bowl and make a well. Pour the lukewarm gelatin mixture into the well and stir with a wooden spoon mixing in sugar and adding more, a little at a time, until stickiness disappears. Knead in remaining sugar, icing color and flavoring. Knead until the fondant is smooth, pliable and does not stick to your hands. If fondant is too soft, add more sugar; if too stiff, add water (a drop at a time).

Use fondant immediately or store in airtight container in refrigerator. When ready to use, bring to room temperature and knead again until soft. This recipe yields enough to cover a 10 x 3-in. high cake.

TO ROLL FONDANT
Spray work surface and rolling pin with vegetable oil pan spray and dust with a mixture of confectioners sugar and cornstarch. Here are two ways to prepare cake for fondant. Coat with piping gel or apricot glaze, then cover with rolled marzipan. Coat again with piping gel or glaze. Add fondant. Or ice cake with buttercream icing, let dry, then cover with rolled fondant.

Roll out fondant into a circle twice the diameter of the cake you are covering. As you roll, lift and move the fondant to prevent it from sticking to the surface. Gently lift fondant over rolling pin and place over cake.

Smooth and shape fondant on cake, using palm of hand. If large air bubbles are trapped under fondant, prick with a pin and continue to smooth. Trim excess from base. A fondant-covered cake may be kept up to 2 months, when tightly wrapped and frozen.

Marzipan Recipe

1 cup almond paste
2 unbeaten egg whites
3 cups confectioners sugar
½ teaspoon vanilla or rum flavoring

In bowl, knead almond paste. Add egg white, mix well. Continue kneading as you add flavoring and sugar, 1 cup at a time, until marzipan feels like heavy pie dough.

Color Techniques

Color brings cake decorations to life; therefore it's essential that you learn how to tint icings to achieve different decorating effects. Wilton Icing Color is concentrated color in a creamy, rich base. It gives icing vivid or deep, rich color without changing icing consistency. See page 131 for a complete selection of quality Wilton Icing Colors. Icing Color kits are also available.

HOW TO TINT ICING

• Start with white icing and add the color a little at a time until you achieve the shade you desire. Use a toothpick to add icing color; (use more depending on amount of icing). Hint: Tint a small amount of icing first, then mix in with remainder of white icing. Colors intensify or darken in buttercream icings 1 to 2 hours after mixing, so keep this in mind when you're tinting icing. You can always add extra color to deepen the icing color, but it's difficult to lighten the color once it's tinted. Use White- White Icing Color to make your buttercream icing the purest snow-white!

• To mix deep or dark color icing (such as red for roses), you may need a larger amount of Wilton Icing Color. The color should still be added gradually, but use a clean small spatula each time to add the color. Wilton Red Color has no after-taste! It's ideal for decorating large areas. Red-Red or Christmas Red Color is still better to use in royal icing and for accent color, as each offers more color intensity. If you plan to use flavorings, make icing stiff consistency, then use enough flavoring to improve taste.

• Always mix enough of any one color icing. If you're going to decorate a cake with pink flowers and borders, color enough icing for both. It's difficult to duplicate an exact shade of any color. As you gain decorating experience, you will learn just how much of any one color icing you will need.

IMPORTANT HINTS

• Royal icing requires more base color than buttercream to achieve the same intensity.

• Use water, not milk, in buttercream icing recipe when using Violet Icing Color, otherwise the icing may turn blue.

• Substitute chocolate icing for dark brown colors. Use just 6 Tablespoons unsweetened cocoa powder, or 2 one-ounce squares, of melted unsweetened baking chocolate. 1 Tablespoon milk, and add to 1½ cups white icing.

• Add color to piping gel, color flow, gum paste, cookie dough, marzipan, cream cheese, sugar molds and even cake batter for striking decorating effects!

• To restore the consistency of Wilton Icing Colors that have dried out, add a few drops of Wilton Glycerin. Mix until proper consistency is reached.

• Use a clean toothpick or spatula to add Wilton Icing Colors each time, until you reach desired shade.

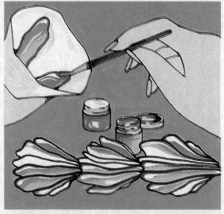

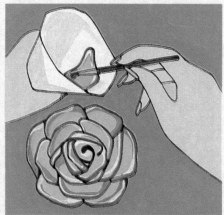

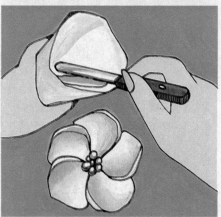

COLOR DRAMATICS

By applying one or more stripes of full strength icing color to the inside of a parchment paper bag or disposable bag (color will stain Featherweight Bag) you can squeeze out multicolored borders, flowers, even figure piped clowns.

BRUSH STRIPING

Striping is a method used to give multiple or deep color effects to icing. To do this, one or more colors are applied to the inside of the parchment paper bag with a brush. Then the bag is filled with white or pastel-colored icing and, as the icing is squeezed past the color, out comes the striped decorations!

SPATULA STRIPING

Use a spatula to stripe the inside of a decorating bag with Wilton pastel colored icing. Then fill the bag with white icing, or another shade of the same color as the striping, and squeeze out decorations with pastel contrasts. Use the above color techniques when figure piping for exciting results. It's fun to experiment with color! Try to achieve natural-looking flower colors by using the spatula striping method. (Roses look especially beautiful with this effect.)

The Perfectly Iced Cake

Think of your cake as the canvas that your beautiful icing decorations will be presented upon. So it's essential that it be smooth and free of crumbs. By following our 5-easy-steps icing method, we feel you'll get the results you want.

Leveling
There are two ways to remove the slight crown your baked cake will have. Cool cake for 10 minutes in the pan. Carefully slice off the raised center with a serrated knife or our Cake Leveler (p. 141). Or after cake is cooled completely as per directions on p. 90, invert so that its brown top crust is uppermost and trim away the crust for a flat surface (see pic. 1). Our Bake-Even Cake Strips will help prevent crowns from forming on basic shaped cakes (see p. 168 for details).

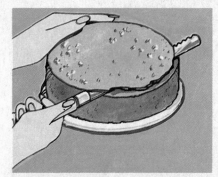

Filling Layers
Place one cake layer on a cake board or circle atop a cake stand or plate, top side up. **Hint:** To prevent cake from shifting, place a few strokes of icing on base surface before positioning cake. Fit bag with coupler and fill with icing. Make a dam by squeezing out a band of filling about 3/4-in. high around the top. With your spatula, spread icing, jam, pudding or other filling in center. Position top layer with bottom side up.

Icing The Top
Thin your buttercream icing with light corn syrup (approximately 2 teaspoons for each cup). The consistency is correct when your spatula glides over the icing. With large spatula, place mound of icing in center of top and spread across cake pushing excess down onto sides. Always keep spatula on the the iced surface. Pulling toward the cake surface will mix in crumbs. **Hint:** To keep your serving base free of icing, place 3-in. wide strips of waxed paper under each side of cake.

Icing The Sides
Cover the sides with excess icing from the top, adding more icing if necessary. Work from top down, forcing any loose crumbs to the cake base. Again, be sure spatula touches only icing. You'll find that an angled spatula is ideal for icing sides. When you're icing a curved side, hold the spatula upright against the side of the cake and, pressing lightly, turn cake stand slowly around with your free hand without lifting the spatula from the side surface. Return excess icing to bowl and repeat procedure until sides are smooth. For angled sides such as on a cross cake, do each straight side individually; hold spatula firmly to smooth.

Smooth Top
Place spatula flat on one edge of cake top and sweep it across to center of cake. Lift off, remove excess icing and repeat, starting from a new point on edge of cake top. Repeat procedure until entire top surface is smooth. To smooth center, apply an even pressure to spatula as you turn cake stand around in a full circle. Lift off spatula and any excess icing.

Sheet & Other Flat Surfaced Cakes
Use the same icing procedure as shown here for sheet cakes, heart, oval, square and other shaped cakes with flat surfaces.

To Ice Areas On Shaped Cakes
The sides of shaped cakes are usually the only areas iced smooth. Just place icing on side with your spatula and spread. After sides are covered, run spatula lightly over icing in the same direction. Sometimes small backgound areas or facial features on top are iced smooth. Use a small spatula or decorating tip (3 or 4) and squeeze icing onto area, then smooth with finger dipped in cornstarch.

The Cake Icer Tip Will Save You Time
If you haven't discovered this versatile tip (No. 789) you should! You'll love how quickly and easily you can cover flat-surfaced cakes with wide bands of icing. Just hold tip flat against cake surface, serrated side up, and squeeze out a ribbed band. Holding the smooth side up gives you a smooth band. To cover side, turn cake stand clockwise as you squeeze out a band of icing, wrapping it around the cake. When your cake is completely iced, use a fork to blend ribbed seams; a spatula to join smooth bands together.

Hints for cakes-to-go!
Use our Cake Pan Cover to protect sheet cakes in our 9 x 13-in. pan (p. 169). The Cake Saver is a great way to take cakes places (p. 168).

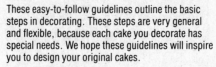

Let's Decorate!

Hints For Easier Icing:

• Thinning buttercream icing with light corn syrup makes consistency best for easy spreading.

• When icing small areas or sides of a shaped cake, be sure to ice a little past the area or edge or top to create a neat surface that can be outlined or covered with stars.

• To smooth the icing surface on 3-dimensional cakes such as the ball, egg, bear, lamb or bunny cakes, let buttercream icing crust slightly. Then place plastic wrap over the icing and smooth over the surface gently with your hands. Carefully remove wrap. For a textured surface, follow the same procedure using a cloth or paper towel.

• Canned icing works well for most decorating techniques and will withstand humidity better than buttercream. It must always be refrigerated before using (except when outlining or writing), to stiffen consistency. However, canned icing is not for flowers that require a stiff consistency like the rose, mum and lily.

• To make clean-up easier and quicker when decorating with buttercream icing, use a degreaser liquid soap to dissolve icing from tools. It is especially important to have grease-free utensils when using royal or color flow icings.

These easy-to-follow guidelines outline the basic steps in decorating. These steps are very general and flexible, because each cake you decorate has special needs. We hope these guidelines will inspire you to design your original cakes.

For Party-Perfect Cakes

• We suggest that flowers, candy, cookie or any special accent that's needed for your cake be made ahead of time, perhaps while your cake cools. It's smart to make extras of any fragile addition to allow for breakage. Before icing or decorating, place each cake on which you're working on a cake circle or board cut to fit. If a small cake is to be set atop a larger cake (see p. 2), it can be decorated on or off bottom cake. We usually recommend that you decorate both cakes first, then put them together. To transfer, let icing set (a slight crust will form and be more workable), then slip a wide spatula under cake and lift. Position cake and slowly pull spatula out (to prevent sticking, lightly dust spatula with cornstarch). If cake is large, support with free hand and redecorate areas that may get damaged.

• Now your cake is ready to mark. Use a toothpick, pattern press or cookie cutter to imprint design. Patterns for the cakes in our idea portion, which require some artistic ability, are included in the '90 Pattern Book (contains easy pattern transfer instructions). Geometric shaped cakes are often divided into 6ths, 8ths, 12ths, etc. You'll find dividing a round cake is quick 'n easy when you use our Cake Dividing Set (instructions included).

• After cake is clearly marked, generally the first step is to outline your design. Then instructions will probably say to pipe in small areas. Write or print message. Filling in areas with stars, zigzags, etc. will be next. Add borders. The icing on your cake should hold trims such as flowers, cookies, color flow and poster board but if your decoration doesn't seem secure enough, just add a few dots of icing. Heavier trims or accents that protrude out of cake should be attached to a craft stick or coffee stirrer with dots of royal icing and allowed to dry. Place flowers on cake and trim with leaves. Position Wilton cake tops or wedding ornaments.

Novelty Shaped Cakes

When decorating a cake that's basically covered with stars, here are the easy steps involved.
1. Ice sides and others areas per instructions smooth.
2. Outline details.
3. Pipe in facial features, small details, windows, doors, etc.
4. Cover areas with stars, stripes, zigzags or hair.
5. Add message.
6. Edge top and base with borders.
7 Attach flowers or trims.

Decorating Hints

• Tips from the same basic group that are close in size may be substituted for one another. The effect will be a slightly smaller or larger decoration.

• Use tip 20, 21 or the super fast Triple-Star Tip, when you're covering a large area with stars. You can also use zigzags or side-by-side stripes to fill in large areas.

• When using parchment bags, you can place a tip with a smaller opening over the tip you're using and tape it in place. This saves time changing bags and tips when you're using the same color icing.

• Stock up on the bags and tips in the sizes you use the most. Your decorating will go faster if several

are filled and ready to use. Close tips securely with with convenient Tip Covers.

• Overpiping: Outlining a piped decoration with the same technique will add dimension and make it stand out. Overpiping with a different technique in a contrasting color creates an eye-catching effect.

Three Essentials Of Decorating

1. Icing Consistency
Remember, if the consistency of your decorating icing isn't exactly right, your decorations won't be either. Follow the general guidelines on p. 92.

2. Bag Position
To hold the decorating bag correctly, grip the bag near the top with the twisted or folded end locked between your thumb and fingers. Guide the bag with your free hand.

Generally, there are two basic positions for decorating bag. The 90° angle with the bag straight up, perpendicular to the surface. And the 45° angle with the bag half-way between vertical and horizontal.

Pointing the back end of your decorating bag in the right direction is also important. Sometimes instructions will tell you to hold back end of bag pointing to the right or towards you.

Left-handed decorators do things differently. Hold the decorating bag in your left hand and guide the decorating tip with the fingers of your right hand. If the instructions say to hold the decorating bag over to the right, you should hold your decorating bag over to the left. A right-handed person will always decorate from left to right. A left-handed person should always decorate from right to left. The only exception to this rule is when you are writing or printing. When decorating a cake on a turntable, rotate the stand counterclockwise. For flower making on a flower nail, turn nail clockwise in right hand as you pipe petals using left hand.

3. Pressure Control
The size and uniformity of your icing design are directly affected by the amount of pressure you apply to the decorating bag and the steadiness of the pressure– how you squeeze and relax your grip on the decorating bag. Strive to apply pressure so consistently that you can move the bag in a free and easy glide while just the right amount of icing flows from the tip. Practice to achieve this control.

HEAVY	MEDIUM	LIGHT

The Techniques

The size and shape of the opening on a decorating tip identifies the basic group to which the tip belongs and determines the type of decorations the tip will produce.

PLAIN OR ROUND TIPS

Use to outline details, filling and piping in areas, printing and writing messages, figure piping, stringwork, beads, dots, balls, stems, vines, flower centers, lattice, cornelli lace. These tips are smooth and round– small plain tips include numbers 1,2,3,4; medium, 5,6,7,8,9,10,11,12; large, 1A, 2A. For fine stringwork, use 1S,1L,2L,0L,00L,000. For Philippine method flower making, oval tips 55 and 57. Writing tip 301 pipes fine, flat lines. See p. 132 for round tips.

Printing & Writing
Use a small round tip and thin icing consistency. **Hint:** With a toothpick or Message Pattern Presses draw guidelines to follow. With practice, you'll achieve control and soon be piping out messages free-handed.

To Print: Hold bag at 45° angle with tip resting lightly on surface with back of to the right for horizontal lines, toward you for vertical. With a steady, even pressure, squeeze out a straight line, lifting tip off surface to let icing string drop. Be sure to stop squeezing before you lift the tip to end the line so a tail doesn't form.

To Write: You must move your whole arm to write effectively with icing. Hold bag at a 45° angle with back of bag to the right. The tip should lightly touch the cake as you write.

To Outline:
Use thin icing consistency and bag at a 45° angle and touch tip (usually 3 or 4) to surface. Now raise the tip slightly and continue to squeeze. The icing will flow out of the tip while you direct it along the surface. To end an outline, stop squeezing, touch tip to surface and pull away.

To Pipe In: After area is outlined, squeeze out tip 3 or 4 zigzag motion strings to fill area. Immediately smooth over strings with finger tip or spatula dipped in cornstarch.

To Fill In: Follow same procedure as Pipe In, but thin icing before piping.

Dots
Use medium icing consistency. Hold bag at a 90° angle with tip slightly above surface. Squeeze and keep point of the tip in icing until dot is the size you want. Stop pressure, pull away; use tip to clean point away or smooth with finger dipped in cornstarch. To make large dots or balls, lift tip as you squeeze to allow greater icing build-up.

Beads
Use medium icing consistency. Hold bag at 45° angle with tip slightly above surface and end of bag pointing to the right. Squeeze and lift tip slightly so icing fans out into base. Relax pressure as you draw tip down and bring bead to point. Ideal for borders or piped in side-by-side rows to cover large areas.

For Hearts: Pipe two beads side by side and smooth together with finger dipped in cornstarch.

For Shamrocks: Pipe 3 bead hearts so points meet. Add tip 3 outline stem.

Cornelli Lace
With thin icing, use a 90° angle with tip slightly above surface. Pipe a continuous string of icing, curve it up, down and around until area is covered. Stop pressure; pull tip away. Make sure strings never touch or cross.

Drop Strings
Use stiff consistency icing that has been thinned with corn syrup. Icing is the right consistency if you can drop a loop of icing from your finger. With toothpick, mark horizontal intervals in desired widths. Hold bag at 45° angle to surface so that end of bag points slightly to the right. Touch tip to first marks and squeeze, holding bag in place momentarily so that icing sticks to surface.

Then pull tip straight out away from surface, allowing icing to drop into an arc. Stop pressure as you touch tip to second mark to end string.

Repeat procedure, attaching string to third mark and so on, forming row of drop strings. It's very important to let the string, not your hand, drop to form an arc. Try to keep your drop strings uniform in length and width.

For Double Drop Strings: Start at first mark again, squeeze bag. Let icing drop into a slightly shorter arc than arc in first row. Join end of string to end of corresponding string in first row and repeat procedure.

Always pipe longest drop strings first and add shorter ones. This technique is ideal for cake sides. Practice is important in making drop strings uniform.

Dropped Lattice Garlands: With stiff royal icing, connect garland marks with drop string guidelines. Cover strings with three rows of tip 16 zigzags (overpipe rows). Ease pressure at ends so icing doesn't build up too high. Drop a string guideline directly on top of zigzags. From cake to edge of zigzags, pipe tip 3 diagonal lines across area. From the opposite side, work strings in the other direction. Cover edges of lattice with tip 3 strings.

STAR TIPS
The star-shaped openings create the most popular decorations... stars, zigzags, shells, rosettes and more. The most often used star tips are numbers 13 through 22. Star tips range in size from small to extra large. For deep ribbed decorations, try tips 23-31, 132, 133 and 195. Large star tips include numbers 32, 96, 4B, 6B and 8B. Fine cut star tips are numbers 362, 363, 364, 172 and 199. For these techniques use medium icing consistency.

Stars
Hold bag at 90° angle with tip slightly above surface. Squeeze bag to form a star, then stop pressure and pull tip away. Increase or decrease pressure to change star size. An entire cake or just one area can be covered with stars made very close together so that no cake shows between stars. Use the triple-star or use large star tips to save time.

For Pull-Out Stars: Hold bag at 45° angle to surface. As you squeeze out icing, pull tip up and away from cake. When strand is long enough, stop pressure and pull tip away. Work from bottom to top of area to be covered with pull-out stars.

For Star Puffs: Use a large tip and hold tip in place to allow icing to build up.

For Star Flowers: Squeeze and keep tip in icing until star petals are formed. Stop pressure and pull tip away. Add tip 2 or 3 dot centers.

Ropes
Hold bag at 45° angle to surface with end of bag pointing over right shoulder. Touch tip to surface and squeezing bag, move tip down, up and around to the right forming a slight "s" curve. Stop pressure, pull tip away. Tuck tip under bottom arch of first "s" and repeat procedure. Continue joining "s" curves to form rope.

Zigzags

Hold bag at 45° angle to surface, so that end of bag points out to the right and fingers on the bag are facing you. Allow the tip to touch the surface lightly. Steadily squeeze and move hand in a tight side-to-side motion. To end, stop pressure and pull tip away. **Elongated Zigzags:** Follow procedure but keep an even pressure as you move hand in the desired length. Very large areas can be covered in this manner. **Relaxed Zigzags:** Simply relax pressure as you move bag along.

Zigzag Garlands

Hold bag as for basic zigzag procedure. Allow tip to touch the surface lightly and use light-to-heavy-to-light pressure to form curves of garland. To end, stop pressure, pull tip away. Practice for rhythmic pressure control so garlands are uniform.

Puffs

Hold bag at 45° angle to surface, finger tips on bag facing you. Touch tip to surface and use a light-to-heavy-to-light pressure and zigzag motion to form puff. Repeat procedure again and again as you move tip in a straight line to form row of puffs. To end row, stop pressure, pull tip away.

C, E & S-Motion (only "E" motion shown)

Hold bag at 45° angle to surface, finger tips on bag facing you. As you squeeze out icing, move tip down, up to the right and around as if writing the letter "c, e or s." Use a steady, even pressure as you repeat procedure. To end, stop pressure, pull tip away.

Shells

Hold bag at 45° angle with tip slightly above surface and end of bag pointing to the right. Squeeze with heavy pressure and slightly lift tip as icing builds and fans out into a full base. Relax pressure as you pull bag down to the right as you make the tail. Stop pressure completely, pull tip away. When you make the shells, always work to the right; starting each new shell slightly behind tail of previous shell.
For Elongated Shells: Extend tail while relaxing pressure, until desired length is achieved.
For Upright Shells: Hold bag at 90° angle to cake sides. Follow same procedure as elongated shells.

Note: Once you've mastered the motion of shell making, you can create unique borders with other tip groups such as leaf and ruffle.

Reverse Shells

Hold bag at 45° angle with tip slightly above surface. Squeeze to let icing fan out as if you were making a typical shell, then swing tip around to the left in a semi-circular motion as you relax pressure to form tail of a shell. Stop pressure, pull tip away. Repeat procedure, only this time, swing tip around to the right as you form tail of shell. Continue procedure alternating directions for a series of reverse shells.

Fleur-De-Lis

Make a shell. Keep bag at 45° angle and starting at the left of this shell, squeeze bag to fan icing into shell base. Then as you relax pressure to form tail, move tip up slightly around to the right, relaxing pressure, forming tail similar to reverse shells. Join to tail of the first shell. Repeat procedure to right side of first shell.

Scrolls

Hold bag at 45° angle to surface so that end of bag points to the right. Use tip 3 to draw an inverted "C" center and use circular motion to cover inverted "C." You may overpipe (go over lines) with tip 13 or any small star tip. Use a heavy pressure to feather the scroll, relaxing pressure as you taper end. Add side petals like reverse shells.

Reverse Scrolls

With tip 3 squeeze out an inverted "C" scroll. Then, starting at the top of this "C," squeeze and move tip down, up and around for a backward "C." Cover outlines with tip 13. Add reverse shell side petals.

Hint: Use our Scroll Pattern Presses to imprint an easy-to-follow guide on cake top or sides.

Rosettes

Hold bag at 90° angle with tip slightly above surface. Squeeze and move hand to the left, up and around in a circular motion to starting point. Stop pressure and pull tip away. For a fancy effect, trim center with a star.

For Spirals:

Follow rosettes technique. Starting at outer edge, move tip in a clockwise direction in a continuous circular motion decreasing size of circles until center is reached. Stop pressure and pull tip away.

Drop Flower Tips

These are the easiest flowers for a beginning decorator to do. The number of openings on the end of the tip determines the number of petals the flower will have. Each drop flower tip can produce two different flower varieties—plain or swirled. Swirled drop flowers cannot be made directly on cake. Some form center holes. Small tips include numbers 107, 108, 129, 217, 220, 224, 225; medium tips are 109, 131, 135, 140, 177, 190, 191, 193, 194, 195; for large flowers, tips 1B, 1C, 1E, 1G, 2C, 2D, 2E and 2F.

Drop Flowers

Icing consistency should be slightly stiffer. Hold bag at a 90° angle with tip touching surface and pipe as you would a star. For swirled flowers: Curve wrist around to the left and as you squeeze out icing, bring hand back to the right. Stop pressure, pull tip away. Add tip 2 or 3 dot centers.

LEAF TIPS

The v-shaped openings of these tips give leaves pointed ends. With any leaf tip you can make plain, ruffle or stand-up leaves. Make leaves with center veins from small 65s, 65-70, to large, 112-115 and 355. Other popular numbers are 71-76, 326, 349, 352.

Basic Leaf

Use thin icing consistency and hold bag at 45° angle to surface, back of bag facing you. Squeeze and hold tip in place to let icing fan out into base, then relax and stop pressure as you pull tip towards you and draw leaf to a point.

Stand Up Leaf

Hold bag at a 90° angle. Touch tip lightly to surface and squeeze, holding tip in place as icing fans out to form base. Relax and stop pressure as you pull tip straight up and away, creating stand-up leaf effect.

Holly Leaf: With tip 68, follow basic leaf method and use medium consistency royal icing to pipe desired size leaf. While icing is wet, pull out tiny points around edge with a dampened Decorator's Brush. Let dry on flower formers for a curved look.

Petal Tips

These tips have an opening that is wide at one end, narrow at the other. This teardrop-like shaped opening yields a variety of petals that form flowers like the rose, carnation, daisy, pansy and more (see pages 103-105). Petal tips can also make ribbons, drapes and swags; bows and streamers. Plain rose tips include numbers 101s, 101, 102, 103, 104, 124, 125, 126, 127 and giant roses, tip 127D. Swirled rose tips that make instant-curled petals are 97, 116, 118 and 119. Others include 59s, 59, 60, 61, 121, 122, 123, 62, 63, 64 and 150.

Ruffle

Use stiff icing consistency. Hold bag at a 45° angle to surface, finger tips on bag facing you. Touch wide end of tip to surface, angle narrow end out about ¼-in. away from surface. As you squeeze, move hand up and down slightly to ruffle the icing. **For Stand-Up Ruffle** just turn tip so wide end is at the top.

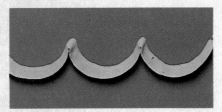

Swag/Drape

Use same procedure as for ruffle. As you squeeze, swing tip down and up to the right forming ribbon drape.

Bows

Creating bows with a petal tip is different from a round or star tip because of the shape of tip but otherwise the technique is the same. With tip 104 and medium icing consistency, hold bag at a 45° angle to surface. The wide end of the tip should point straight up. While squeezing, move the tip up and around to the starting point and continue around, making a second loop on the left. The two loops should form a figure 8. Still holding bag in the same position return to the center and squeeze out two streamers.

Stripe/Basketweave Tips

These are decorating tips with a smooth side for making smooth, wide icing stripes and/or one serrated side for making ribbed, wide icing stripes. When short ribbed horizontal stripes are interwoven in vertical rows the effect is that of a basketweave. Tips are 46 and 47. For smooth stripes, 44 and 45. For ribbed stripes, 48 and 327. Large ribbon tips include 1D, 2B and 789 (Cake Icer).

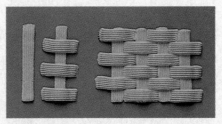

Basketweave

Use star or basketweave tips and medium consistency icing. For an interesting effect, use a round tip to make vertical lines.

• Hold bag at 45° angle to cake with serrated side of tip facing up (or use round tip). Touch tip lightly to surface and squeeze out a vertical line of icing.

• Next, hold bag at a 45° angle to surface, finger tips gripping bag facing you. Touch tip, serrated side facing up, to top left side of vertical line and squeeze out 3-in. horizontal bar. Add two more horizontal bars, each about a tip width apart, to cover vertical line and squeeze out 3-in. horizontal bar. Add two more horizontal bars, each about a tip width apart, to cover vertical line.

• With bag and tip at 45° angle, make another vertical line of icing to right of first one, overlapping ends of horizontal bars. Use same procedure as step two to cover this line with horizontal bars, working them in spaces of bars in first row.

• Repeat entire procedure, alternating vertical lines and horizontal bars, to create a basketweave effect. Other tips may be used for basketweave, but serrated tips 46-48 give icing a ribbed basket effect.

Stripes

• This versatile technique can be made with star and ribbon tips. They can be piped straight, curved or side-by-side to fill in an area. Hold decorating bag at 45° angle to surface. As you squeeze out icing with a steady, even pressure, move tip in vertical direction laying out a ribbed stripe of icing. When stripe is about half of desired length, swing tip around to the right or left. Stop pressure and pull tip up and away. When covering an area, stripes can be slightly overlapped for added dimension.

Ribbon Stripe Bow

• To make a bow with a basketweave tip as shown on our cover cake, hold bag at a 45° angle with the ribbed side of tip up. Start in center and move bag up and to the right. As you bring bag down to form loop, turn tip so that the ribbed side is now down. Repeat procedure for left loop. Pipe streamers with smooth or ribbed side up.

Flutes

• A pretty effect to add between rows of shells. Hold tip 104 at 45° angle so that wide end of tip is between two shells. Squeeze and move tip up slightly as icing fills in between shell. Stop pressure, lower tip, pull away.

Making a Rose

The flower nail (p. 138) is a decorating tool used to make the most popular flower of all, the rose. It is also used to make pretty flowers, like the violet, apple blossom and daisy. Flower nails come in a variety of sizes. No. 7 and No. 9 are the popular choices for small and average size blooms. Large flowers would use a 2 or 3-in. flower nail.

The key to making any flower on the nail is to coordinate the turning of the nail with the formation of a petal. The stem of the nail is held between your left thumb and forefinger, so you can turn the flat nailhead surface at the same time you're piping a flower with your right hand. Using the flower nail takes practice, but the beautiful results are well worth the effort!

Note: Left-handed decorators should use the nail opposite of above instructions.

Make all flowers on the nail with royal or stiffened buttercream icing (see p. 93-94)), and the tips specified for each flowers. Air dry flowers made in royal icing, and freeze buttercream flowers (buttercream roses can also be placed directly on iced cake) until firm at least 2 hours. Then, when you're ready to decorate, remove the frozen flowers, a few at a time, and position them on the cake. (Snow White Buttercream Icing flowers can be air dried.)

For each flower you make, attach a 2-in. square of waxed paper to the nail-head with a dot of icing. Make a flower; remove waxed paper and flower together. For more about rose making, order the **Wilton Celebrates The Rose,** p. 123.

Make The Rose Base

- Use tip 10 or 12. Hold the bag perpendicular at a 90° angle to nail with tip slightly above center of nailhead.
- Squeeze with a heavy pressure, keeping bottom of tip in icing until you've made a full, round base.
- Ease pressure as you raise tip up and away from nailhead, narrowing base to a dome head. The base is very important for successful rose-making. Be sure that it is secure to nail and can support all the petals. Practice until you feel comfortable with the technique.

The Center Bud

- Use tip 104. Hold bag at a 45° angle to nail with wide end of tip just below top of dome, and narrow end pointed in slightly. Back of bag should be pointed over your shoulder.
- Now you must do three things simultaneously…squeeze, pull tip up and out away from top of dome stretching icing into a ribbon band, as you turn the nail counterclockwise.
- Relax pressure as you bring band of icing down around dome, overlapping the point at which you started.

1st Row of 3 Petals

- Hold bag at 45° angle with end of bag pointed over your shoulder. Touch wide end of tip 104 to midpoint of bud base. Turn nail counterclockwise and move tip up and back down to midpoint of bud base forming first petal of rose.
- Start slightly behind end of 1st petal and squeeze out 2nd petal same as first.
- Start slightly behind end of 2nd petal and add a 3rd petal, ending this petal overlapping starting point of 1st petal. Now you have a full rosebud made on a nail to use just as you would a rosebud made on a flat surface (see p. 102).

2nd Row of 5 Petals

- Touch wide end of tip 104 slightly below center of a petal in 1st row, angle narrow end of tip out slightly more than you did for 1st row of petals. Squeeze and turn nail counterclockwise, moving tip up, then down to form 1st petal in second row.
- Start slightly behind this last petal and make a 2nd petal. Repeat this procedure for a total of 5 petals, ending last petal overlapping the 1st petal's starting point.

3rd Row of 7 Petals

- Touch wide end of tip 104 below center of petal in 2nd row, again angling narrow end of tip out a little more. Squeeze and turn nail counterclockwise and move tip up and down forming 1st petal. Repeat for a total of 7 petals.
- Slip waxed paper and completed rose off nail. Attach another square of waxed paper and start again. Have several squares of waxed paper cut

ahead of time so you can continue rose making without stopping. HINT: An easy way to place a buttercream icing rose directly on your cake is to slide open scissors under base of rose and gently lift flower off waxed paper square and flower nail. Position flower on cake by slowly closing scissors and pushing base of flower with stem end of flower nail. Practice & watch your talent grow!

Two-Tone Roses

Create a dramatic effect by making the center petals of your rose contrast with the outer petals. You'll need to pipe the base, center bud and 1st row of petals with one color. Then in your contrasting shade, add remaining petals.

Flowers

Flat Surface Flowers:
Rosebuds, Half Roses & Sweet Peas

These are flowers you can make right on a cake, or any other flat surface. To make all these, use tip 104 and royal or stiffened buttercream icing. Attach a sheet of waxed paper to the back of a cookie sheet with dots of icing or use Wilton Practice Board.

Make your practice flowers in horizontal rows and when you've filled the entire sheet, loosen the waxed paper with a spatula to remove it and start again.

When you're decorating a cake with lots of flat-surface flowers, make all the ones you need ahead of time using the same cookie sheet method. Air dry flowers made with Royal or Snow-White Buttercream. Freeze flowers made with buttercream until hard (at least 2 hours). Remove buttercream flowers with your spatula, a few at a time as you decorate, so they stay firm.

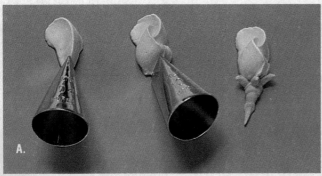

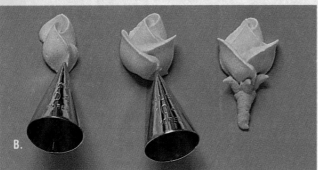

A. Rosebud
• Make base petal. Hold bag at a 45° angle so that the end of bag points over your right shoulder, finger tips gripping bag facing you. Touch wide end of tip 104 to surface, point narrow end to the right. Squeeze, move forward ¼-in.; hesitate so icing fans out, then move back as you stop pressure.
• Make overlapping center petal. Hold bag in same position as above with wide end of tip touching inside right edge of base petal, narrow end of tip pointing slightly up above base petal. Squeeze as icing catches inside edge of base petal and rolls into interlocking center bud. Stop pressure; touch large end back to surface and pull tip away.
• Make sepals and calyx directly on cake with tip 3 and thinned icing. Hold bag at a 45° angle to base of bud with end of bag pointing towards you. Touch tip to bud. Squeeze and pull tip up and away from flower, relaxing pressure as you draw calyx to a point. Add three tip 3 sepals.

B. Half Rose
• Make a rosebud without sepals and calyx. To make left petal: Hold bag at a 45° angle so the end of bag points to the right, finger tips gripping the bag should face you. Touch wide end of tip 104 to bottom left side of bud. Squeeze, move it up, around to the right and down, relaxing pressure.
• To make right petal: Hold bag in opposite position as for left petal. Touch wide end of tip to bottom right side of bud base. Squeeze, move up, around to the left and down to center of bud base. Stop pressure, pull tip away.
• Make sepals and calyxes with tip 3 and thinned icing. Follow same procedure as for step 3 of rosebud, starting at bottom center of half rose.

C. Sweet Pea
• Make center petal. Hold bag at a 45° angle to surface so that back end of bag points towards you. Touch wide end of the tip to surface with narrow end of tip straight up. Squeeze, raise tip slightly and let icing roll into center petal. Stop pressure, lower tip, pull away.
• Make side petals. Touch wide end of tip to bottom left edge of center rolled petal, point narrow end up and out to the left. Squeeze, lift tip slightly, stop pressure, lower tip, pull away. Repeat procedure for right petal, starting at bottom edge of center petal.
• Add calyx to flower base with tip 3 and thinned icing. Hold bag at 45° angle to surface so that end of bag points towards you. Insert tip into flower base and hold in place as you squeeze to build up pressure as you draw tip down, narrowing calyx to a point.

D. To Attach Flowers & Leaves To Wire Stems.
• **For flowers:** On waxed paper square, using royal icing, pipe a dot base with tip 4. Make 1/8-in. hook on one end of 4-in. florist wire and insert hook into base. With slightly moistened decorator's brush, smooth and taper icing on the wire. Push other end of wire into a piece of styrofoam to dry base. Remove waxed paper and attach flower with dots of icing. **For Leaves:** Pipe tip 3 royal icing dot on a waxed paper square and immediately push in hooked end of wire. Use tip 352 and royal icing to pipe a leaf directly on top of wire. Again, push into styrofoam to dry. Then remove waxed paper square. Entwine stems together.

Flower Nail Flowers

For best results, use royal icing to pipe these impressive blooms. To curve petals, dry on convexed or concaved flowers formers. Instructions will indicate the number of flowers needed, so make extras to allow for breakage.

Daisy

Use royal icing and tip 103. Dot center of nail with icing as guide for flower center. Hold bag at a 45° angle with tip almost parallel to nail surface, wide end of tip pointing to nail center, narrow end pointing out. Now, starting at any point near outer edge of nail, squeeze and move tip towards center icing dot. Stop pressure, pull tip away. Repeat procedure for a total of twelve or more petals.
• Add tip 4 yellow flower center and press to flatten. For pollen-like effect, dampen your finger, press in edible glitter, then flatten center.

Chrysanthemum

• Hold bag at 90° angle to nail and pipe tip 6 mound of icing on nail center. Use tip 79 and very stiff royal icing for short petal effect. Hold bag at a 45° angle to outer base edge of mound, with half-moon opening of tip 79 pointing up. Squeeze row of ½-in. long cupped base petals using pull-out star technique.
• Add second row of shorter petals atop and in between those in first row. Repeat procedure making each additional row of petals shorter than the previous row. When entire mound is covered, add a few stand-up petals to top and tip 1 center dots.

Bachelor Button.

• Like the chrysanthemum, start with a tip 7 dot base. Pipe a cluster of short pull-out dots in the center with tip 1. With tip 14, cover the rest of the mound with pull-out stars.

Daffodil And Jonquil

• Use tip 104 for daffodil or tip 103 for jonquil. Hold bag at a 45° angle to nail, with large end of tip touching nail, narrow end pointed out and almost parallel to nail surface. Squeeze and as you turn nail, move tip out about ½-in. and back to center of nail to form petal. Repeat procedure for five more petals. Dip fingers in cornstarch and pinch ends of petals to form points. Pipe row-upon-row of tip 2 string circles and top with tip 1 zigzag for center.

Narcissus

• Use tip 102 and same procedure as for daffodil to make six ¾-in. long petals. Add tip 1 coil center and tip 1 zigzag.

Apple Blossom

• Use tip 101 or 101s and hold bag at a 45° angle to flower nail with wide end of tip touching nail center, narrow end pointed out ⅛-in. away from nail surface.
• Squeeze bag and turn nail as you move tip ⅛-in. out from nail center and back, relaxing pressure as you return to starting point.
• Repeat procedure to make four more petals. Add five tip 1 dots for center.

Forget-Me Nots

• Very similar to the apple blossom. Use tip 101 and move tip out just ⅜-in. from center, curve around and return, letting the turn of the nail form petals. Dot center with tip 1. Use large flower nail No. 7 and pipe several at once!

Violet

• Use tip 59s and same procedure as for apple blossom to make three ¾-in. long petals and two ¼-in. base petals. Add two tip 1 center dots.

Pansy

• Fit two decorating bags with tip 104. Fill one with yellow icing, the other with violet. Hold bag with yellow icing at a 45° angle to nail center, squeeze and move tip out to edge of nail. Turn nail as you squeeze, relax pressure as you return to nail center. Repeat to form second yellow petal. Use same procedure to add two shorter yellow petals atop the first two.
• Now with bag of violet icing, squeeze out a base petal that equals the width of the yellow petals, using a back and forth hand motion for a ruffled effect.
• Use a decorator's brush to add veins of violet icing color after flower has air dried. Add tip 1 string loop center.

Wild Rose

• Use tip 103 and hold bag at a 45° angle. Touch nail with wide end of tip with narrow end just slightly above nail surface. Begin at center of nail and press out first petal, turning nail as you move tip out toward edge of nail, and return to center of nail as you stop squeezing. Repeat 4 more times. Pull out tiny stamens with tip 1.

Poppy

• Hold wide end of tip 103 down, narrow end pointed out at 45° angle. Starting in center, pipe out a large, rounded, ruffled petal. Jiggle hand as you move up and out to edge of nail and down again into a point. Make four petals around nail.
• Pipe a second row of smaller, cupped petals inside first row, starting first petal between piped petals.
• Pipe tip 6 dot center and tip 14 pull-out star stamens.
• **For half poppy:** With wide end of tip 103 touching center of nail, small end pointed out at a 45° angle, squeeze out a ruffle semicircle. Overpipe with another ruffle petal.

Lily Nail Flowers

The Wilton Lily Nail Set lets you make natural-looking flowers with bell-like shapes and cupped, turned-up petals. Different lily nail sizes relate to the size of flowers you can make. The larger the nail, the larger the flowers. Always use royal icing for flowers made on the lily nail since softer icing will not hold their deeply-cupped shapes. To make any flower on the lily nail, place an aluminum foil square in bottom half of nail. Press in top half to form a foil cup. Remove the top half. Lightly spray foil with vegetable oil spray. This makes it easier to remove from foil after icing has dried and reduces breakage. Pipe a flower on the foil cup and lift out flower and foil to dry.

Petunia

• Prepare 1 5/8-in. lily nail. Then with wide end of tip 102 held down, narrow end up, start piping icing deep inside nail.
• Move up to outer edge as you turn nail, jiggling hand slightly all the while to form ruffled petal edge, then go back to starting point.
• Pipe 5 separate petals in all. Add tip 14 green star center. Push in artificial stamens.

Bluebell

• Use 1¼ in. lily nail. With tip 66, pipe three ¾ in. long petals, pulling only to top of nail. Between these petals, add three more.
• Push in three short artificial stamens.

Borders & More

Ferns (p. 60)

Pipe tip 3 outline stem and frond. Then add tip 349 leaves on each side of stem.

Pretty Pillar Border (p. 62)

At guidemarks, pipe out an upright shell with tip 32. Allow shell to build up slightly at base. Pipe tip 352 shells to the following guidemark. Repeat procedure around cake. Connect pillars with tip 3 double drop strings. Add tip 16 rosettes.

Lettering With Decorative Build-Up

Using the small round indicated in instructions, on the down strokes of desired letters, hesitate an instant as you pipe, giving a short back and forth movement.

Ruffly Swirled Shells (p. 54)

With tip 18, squeeze to let icing fan out as if you were making a typical shell, then swing tip around to the left or right in a semicircular motion as you relax pressure to form tail of a shell. Stop pressure and pull tip away. The following shell should overpipe tail of previous shell slightly. Tuck tip 103 under shells and pipe ruffle around each.

Lattice

Lattice is piped from the center of design, outward. Use thinned icing and a tip 2 or 3, hold bag at a 45° angle at the top of design with tip slightly above cake. Squeeze out a diagonal line to the right, all the way to the edge of your design. On both sides of the first line, fill in more lines, evenly spaced and going in the same direction. Return to starting point in center and pipe diagonal lines to left.

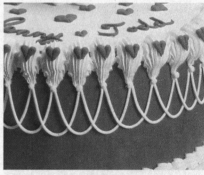

Overlapping Drop Strings

With toothpick, dot mark specified intervals on sides of your cake. Touch tip 3 to a mark, allow your string to skip the next mark and attach to the following on. Return to the mark that was skipped and drop string to connect the next mark. Be sure to keep depth of strings even.

Crown Border With Overlapping Drop Strings

Use tip 32 to make a row of side-by-side upright shells. Add overlapping drop strings with tip 4 following procedure above.

Triple Bead Border (p. 55)

With tip 5, pipe a line of icing around base. Pipe beads on the outer side of line. Then pipe the second row next of cake. Add third row in the center.

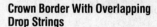

Pull-out Grass or Fur

Use tip 233 or 234 and medium icing consistency. Hold bag at a 90° angle. As you squeeze out icing, pull tip up and away from surface. When icing strand is long enough (about ½ in.), stop pressure and pull tip away.

Special Effects

Tinted coconut: Place shredded coconut in a plastic sandwich bag. Add a few drops of paste icing color, diluted slightly with water. Shake bag until color is evenly distributed.

Lace, Ribbons, Tulle, Flower Puffs & Fabric Leaves are easy to work with and look quite stunning. Here are a few hints to remember: Nylon lace will not absorb grease so it is the best choice. Be sure to use a waterproof, satiny ribbon for the same reason. Before attaching real trims, let icing crust a bit, then anchor in place with dots of icing.

Figure Piping

Medium icing consistency and pressure control are essential to successful figure piping. Most of the figure piping shown here can be done in buttercream icing directly on cake. If you're piping with buttercream icing, remember it doesn't hold its shape or resist humidity like royal icing does. More intricate shapes involving a pattern must be piped on waxed paper with royal icing. When dry, decoration can be positioned on cake. The swan, clown, ghost and turkey are just a few of the exciting creatures you will learn to pipe in our Basic Cake Decorating Course.

Basic Icing Build-Up Technique
Lightly touching tip to the surface, exert pressure as you lift the tip to let the form build up. It's essential that tip remains buried in the icing as it is squeezed out. When desired shape builds up, stop pressure as you bring the end of the tip to the surface. Smooth away ripples or unwanted points with finger dipped in cornstarch.

Clowns (p. 7)
Use brush-striped icing and tip 19.
Sitting: Hold tip at 90° angle and allow body to build up, then lift tip to desired height, easing pressure to taper at top. A piece of uncooked spaghetti or plastic straw can be pushed into icing for support. Pipe arms by inserting tip into body at shoulder, then squeezing as you bring tip straight down or curved around body.

On sides: Hold tip at a 45° and with medium pressure, squeeze out body. Pipe legs by inserting tip at body base and pulling out. Pull out arms in the same manner. Add Derby Clown heads.
Lying down: Hold tip at a 90° angle and build up a line of icing for body. Push tip into body and pull out arms and legs. Add head.

On all, use tip 3 to add dot hands, button and shoes. Trim costumes with tip 101 ruffles.

Turkey & Pumpkins (p. 42)
For Turkey: With tip 12 pipe center shell shaped feather. Continue to pipe shell shaped feathers on both sides to form a "fan." With tip 12 and heavy pressure, start at base and pipe an inverted shell shaped body. Ease pressure as you move upward. Lift and bring back down to form head. Pipe tip 12 curved shell wing on body. Add tip 3 dot eyes, pull-out beak and wattle. Edge tail feathers with tip 3 zigzags.

Swan (p. 55)
Use tip 7 and hold bag at a 90° angle. Squeeze out an icing dot for head, then ease off pressure as you move tip away to pull out bill. Touch tip to back of head and in one continuous motion, squeeze to pull out neck as you move tip in a question mark-like motion. Using tip 7, begin at the lower end of neck and with medium pressure, squeeze to build up icing for the body. As icing mounds up, lift tip slightly, then gradually decrease pressure as you move tip to the side tapering off to the tail. For wing, tuck tip into body and squeeze with steady pressure as you move tip away at a 90° angle, easing off pressure as you go. Repeat this procedure again to give wing a feathery effect.
Variation: The body of swan can also be done with a large shell tip as we did on p. 81.

Ghosts (p. 36 & 38)
Flying or reclining: With tip 12, pipe a ball shap for head and pull out a body, tapering off the en as you gradually decrease pressure. Tuck tip int body to pull out arms. Add tip 3 dot eyes.

On candlestick pillars: Hold tip 2A at 90° angle to pillar and squeeze out bulb-shaped head. Continue downward with heavy pressure to build body. Ease pressure and move bag in an S-motion to form tail. Tuck tip 12 into body and pull out arms. Outline facial features with tip 3.

For Pumpkins: With tip 8 and heavy pressure, pipe two quotation-motion marks that touch at top and bottom. Overpipe and fill space between with another pair. In center, pipe a straight oval shape line. Add tip 3 stem.

All About Tier Cakes

There are many methods of constructing tiered cakes. Here are some of the most popular:

To Prepare Cake For Assembly

Place base tier on a sturdy base plate or 3 or more thicknesses of corrugated cardboard. For heavy cakes, use masonite or plywood. Base can be covered with Fanci-Foil Wrap and trimmed with Tuk-N-Ruffle . Each tier in your cake must be on a cake circle or board cut to fit. Smear a few strokes of icing on boards to secure cake. Fill and ice layers before assembly.

To Dowel Rod Cakes For Pillar & Stacked Construction

Center a cake circle or plate one size smaller than the next tier on base tier and press it gently into icing to imprint an outline. Remove circle. Measure one dowel rod at the cake's lowest point within this circle. Using this dowel for measure, cut dowel rods (to fit this tier) the same size using pruning shears. If the next tier is 10-in. or less, push seven ¼-in. dowel rods into cake down to base within circle guide. Generally the larger and more numerous the upper tiers, the more dowels needed. Very large cakes need ½-in. dowels in base tier.

Stacked Construction

This method is often combined with pillar construction. Dowel rod bottom tier. Center a corrugated cake circle, one size smaller than the tier to be added, on top of the base tier. Position the following tier. Repeat procedure for each additional tier. To keep stacked tiers stable, sharpen one end of a dowel rod and push through all tiers and cardboard circles to base of bottom tier. To decorate, start at top and work down.

Pillar Construction

Dowel rod tiers. Optional: Snap pegs into separator plates to add support and prevent slipping (never substitute pegs for dowel rods). Position separator plates on supporting tiers, making sure that pillar projections on each tier will line up with pillars below. Mark center backs of cakes. Decorate cakes. At reception, align pillar projections and assemble cakes on pillars.

Fast & Easy Push-In Leg Construction

Dowel rods are not needed because legs attached to separator plates push right through the tiers down to the plate below.

Ice cakes on cake circles. To mark where legs will go, simply center separator plate for tier above (projections down) and gently press onto the tier. Lift plate off. Repeat this procedure for each tier (except top). Position upper tiers on separator plates. Decorate cakes.

To assemble: Insert legs into separator plates. Hold tier over base tier, making sure that legs line up with marks. Push straight down until legs touch cake board. Continue adding tiers in this way until cake is assembled.

Dowel Rod

Stacked

Mark Center Back

Pillar

Mark Where Legs Go

Push-In Leg

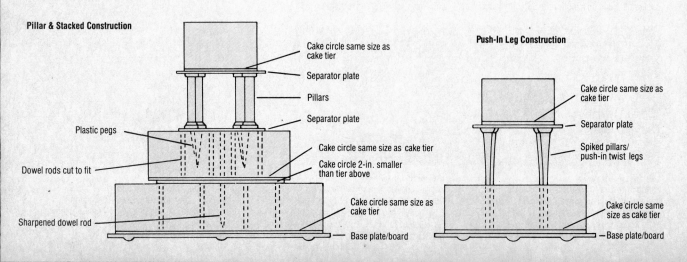

Pillar & Stacked Construction

- Cake circle same size as cake tier
- Separator plate
- Pillars
- Separator plate
- Cake circle same size as cake tier
- Cake circle 2-in. smaller than tier above
- Plastic pegs
- Dowel rods cut to fit
- Cake circle same size as cake tier
- Sharpened dowel rod
- Base plate/board

Push-In Leg Construction

- Cake circle same size as cake tier
- Separator plate
- Spiked pillars/ push-in twist legs
- Cake circle same size as cake tier
- Base plate/board

Hints for Assembling & Transporting Tiered Cakes

• Before placing separator plate or cake circle atop another tier, sprinkle a little confectioners sugar or coconut flakes to prevent plate or circle from sticking. Letting icing crust a bit before positioning plate on cake will also prevent sticking.

• You will have less crumbs when icing, if cakes are baked a day in advance.

• When filling or torting large layers, use less than you usually would. Your dam of icing should also be far enough from edge so filling doesn't form a bubble.

• The cake icer tip (789) is an invaluable timesaver in icing wedding tiers.

• The 16-in. bevel pan takes 1½ cake mixes. So your beveled sides bake properly, pull batter out from center to add depth to the sides.

• When transporting tiers, place cakes on damp towels or carpet foam and drive carefully.

• Some of the plates of the Tall Tier Stand will not sit level. Pack atop crumpled foil, tissue or towels when tranporting. To decorate, set plates on pan or bowl. The column cap nut of the Tall Tier Stand attaches under the top tier cake. Therefore, this cake must be positioned after assembling the Tall Tier Stand. Place top tier on a cake circle slightly larger than the cake to make positioning easier. Add base borders after assembling the top tier.

• To keep balance, cut cakes on the Tall Tier Stand from top tier down.

• To divide tiers, use the Cake Dividing Set . The Wheel Chart makes it easy to mark 2-in. interval on 6 to 18-in. diam. cakes. The triangle marker gives precise spacing for stringwork and garlands. The raised lines on separator plates can also be followed for easy dividing.

• When using Spiked Pillars , double cake boards or use separator plates to prevent the weight of tiers from causing the pillars to pierce through cake.

Wedding Cake Data

One cake mix yields 4 to 6 cups of batter. Pans are usually filled ½ to ⅔ full; 3-in. deep pans should be filled only ½ full. Batter amounts on this chart are for pans two-thirds full of batter. Icing amounts are very general and will vary with consistency, thickness applied and tips used. These amounts allow for top and base borders and a side ruffled border. For large cakes, always check for doneness after they have baked for one hour.

The charts to the right show how to cut popular shaped wedding tiers into pieces approximately 1-in. x 2-in. by two layers high (about 4-in.). Even if you prefer a larger serving size, the order of cutting is still the same.

Number of servings are intended as a guide only.

Pan Shape	Size	# Servings 2 Layer	Cups Batter/ 1 Layers 2"	Baking Temps	Baking Time	Approx. Cups Icing to Frost and Decorate
Oval	7¾ x 5¾"	13	2½	350°	25	3
	10¾ x 7⅞"	30	5½	350°	30	4
	13 x 9¾"	44	8	350°	30	5½
	16 x 12¾"	70	11	325°	30	7½
Round	6"	14	2	350°	25-30	3
	8"	25	3	350°	30-35	4
	10"	39	6	350°	35-40	5
	12"	56	7½	350°	35-40	6
	14"	77	10	325°	50-55	7¼
	16"	100	15	325°	55-60	8¾
	18"	127	17½	325°	60-65	10½
Round 3" Deep	8"	15	5	325°	60-65	2¾
	10"	24	8	325°	75-80	4¾
	12"	33	11	325°	75-80	5¾
	14"	45	15	325°	75-80	7
Petal	6"	8	1½	350°	25-30	3½
	9"	20	3½	350°	35-40	6
	12"	38	7	350°	35-40	7¾
	15"	62	12	325°	50-55	11
Hexagon	6"	12	1¾	350°	30-35	2¾
	9"	22	3½	350°	35-40	4¾
	12"	50	6	350°	40-45	5¾
	15"	72	11	325°	40-45	8¾
Heart	6"	11	1½	350°	25	2½
	9"	24	3½	350°	30	4½
	12"	48	8	350°	30	5¾
	15"	76	11½	325°	40	8¾
Square	6"	18	2	350°	25-30	3½
	8"	32	4	350°	35-40	4½
	10"	50	6	350°	35-40	6
	12"	72	10	350°	40-45	7½
	14"	98	13½	350°	45-50	9½
	16"	128	15½	350°	45-50	11
	18"	162	18	350°	50-55	13

Wedding Cake Cutting Guide

The first step in cutting is to remove the top tier, and then begin the cutting with the 2nd tier followed by 3rd, 4th and so on. The top tier is usually saved for the first anniversary so it is not figured into the serving amount.

Cutting guides for shapes not shown can be found in other Wilton publications. The diagrams below show how to cut popular shaped wedding tiers into pieces approximately 1-in. x 2-in. by two layers high (about 4-in.). Even if you prefer a larger serving size, the order of cutting is still the same.

To cut oval tiers, move in 2-in. from the outer edge and cut across. Then slice 1-in. pieces of cake. Now move in another 2-in. and slice again until the entire tier is cut.

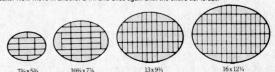

7¾ x 5¾   10¾ x 7⅞   13 x 9¾   16 x 12¾

To cut round tiers, move in two inches from the tier's outer edge; cut a circle and then slice 1-in. pieces within the circle. Now move in another 2-in., cut another circle, slice 1-in. pieces and so on until the tier is completely cut. The center core of each tier and the small top tier can be cut into halves, 4ths, 6ths and 8ths, depending on size.

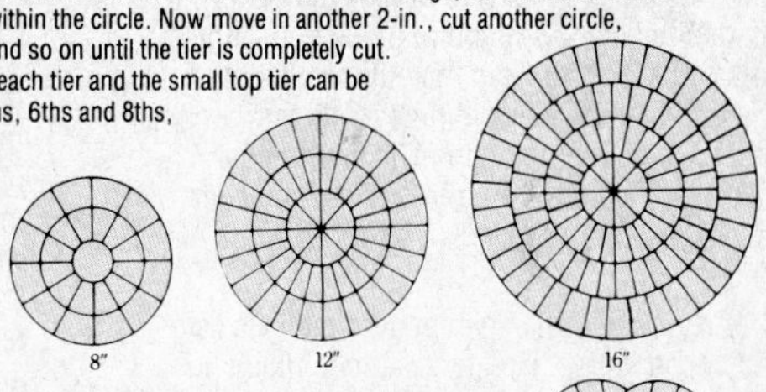

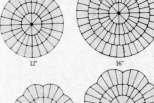

8"   12"   16"

Cut petal-shaped tiers similar to round tiers as diagram shows.

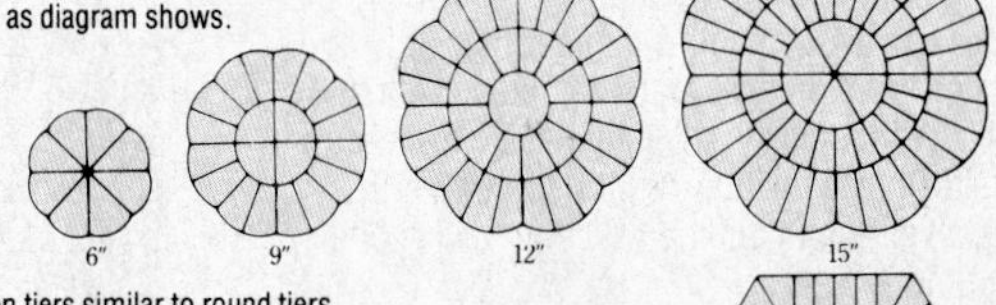

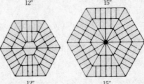

6"   9"   12"   15"

Cut hexagon tiers similar to round tiers.

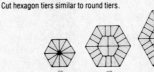

6"   9"   12"   15"

To cut heart-shaped tiers, divide the tiers vertically into halves, quarters, sixths or eights. Within rows, slice one inch pieces of cake.

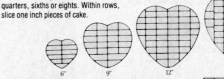

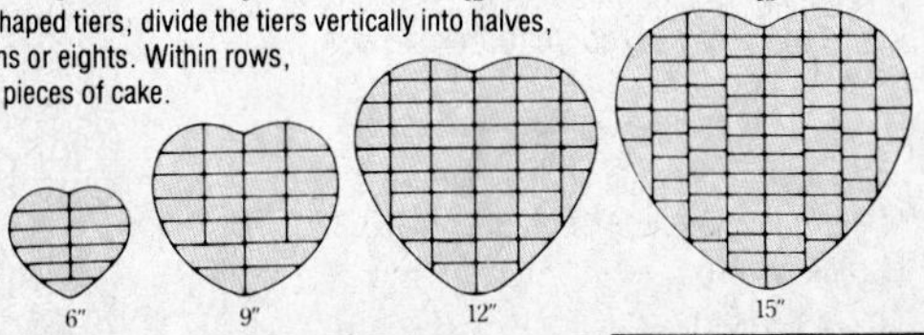

6"   9"   12"   15"

To cut square tiers, move in 2-in. from the outer edge and cut across. Then slice 1-in. pieces of cake. Now move in another 2-in. and slice again until the entire tier is cut.

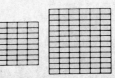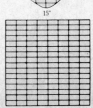

8"   12"   16"

Color Flow & More

Color Flow Icing Recipe
(Full-Strength for Outlining)
¼ cup water + 1 teaspoon
1 lb. sifted confectioners sugar (4 cups)
2 Tablespoons Wilton Color Flow Icing Mix

In an electric mixer, using grease-free utensils, blend all ingredients on low speed for 5 minutes. If using hand mixer, use high speed. Color Flow icing "crusts" quickly, so keep it covered with a damp cloth while using. Stir in desired icing color. In order to fill in an outlined area, this recipe must be thinned with a ½ teaspoon of water per ¼ cup of icing (just a few drops at a time as you near proper consistency.) Color Flow icing is ready for filling in outlines when a small amount dropped into the mixture takes a full count of ten to disappear. Use grease-free spoon or spatula to stir slowly.
Note: Color Flow designs take a long time to dry, so plan to do your Color Flow piece at least 2-3 days in advance.

Color Flow Technique
• Tape pattern and waxed paper overlay to your work surface. (The back of a cookie pan makes a great work surface.) For curved decorations, use flower formers. Use full-strength Color Flow icing and tip 2 or 3 to outline the pattern with desired colors. If you're going to use the same color icing to fill in the outlines, let the icing outlines dry a few minutes until they "crust." If you're going to fill in with icings that differ in colors from the outlines, then let outlines dry thoroughly (1-2 hours) before filling in.

• Soften icing for filling in pattern outlines as specified in recipe. Don't use a tip for filling in outlines; instead, cut a very small opening in end of parchment bag. Begin filling in along the edges of the outline first, squeezing gently and letting the icing flow up to the outline almost by itself. Work quickly, filling in design from the outside edges and in from top to bottom. If you have several outlined sections, fill in one at a time.

• If you're filling in a large area, have two half-full parchment bags ready, otherwise icing could "crust" before you finish filling in the pattern.

Hint: The back of a cookie pan makes a great work surface. For curved decorations, use flower formers. Since buttercream icing will break down color flow, either position color flow decoration on cake shortly before serving or place a piece of plastic wrap cut to fit on area first.

Piping Gel Hints: When piping delicate stringwork, we find that adding 1 teaspoon of piping gel to each cup of royal icing required will add elasticity to your strings. To paint plastic or porcelain bridesmaid's gown with royal icing, thin ½ cup royal icing with 1 Tablespoon water and add 1 teaspoon piping gel for shine.

Marshmallow Creme Flow-In
It stays very shiny, tastes great and is easy to cut through. These decorations will not dry hard as color flow will so they must be done directly on cake.

To Soften Marshmallow Creme
• **Pan Method:** Place about 1½ in. of water in a large skillet or electric pan. Depending upon design, set up to four jars (one for each color) of marshmallow creme into pan and bring water to a boil For faster heating, fill jars only halfway. Add icing color as as the creme softens, stir until color is well blended. Let water boil about 5 to 7 minutes, then stir until creme is smooth. When smooth, reduce heat but leave jars in water while you're decorating.

• **Microwave Method:** Place the desired amount of marshmallow creme in a bowl. Add desired paste color. Microwave on high power for about 10 to 12 seconds, then stir. If not softened (the total time depends on quantity being heated), microwave again for 7 to 8 seconds more. After heating, stir until color is completely blended. Caution: Marshmallow creme is very hot.

To decorate: Trace pattern on cake with a toothpick. Outline design with stiffened buttercream or royal (preferable because the heat of the marshmallow creme may soften buttercream) and tip 2. Let outlines dry for 10 minutes or more. Place marshmallow creme in parchment bag and flow in following color flow method. If marshmallow starts cooling and won't flow smoothly, simply microwave bags for about 7 or 8 seconds on high power. Any remaining creme in your bags can be stored in a zip-close bag and microwaved for 8 to 9 seconds.

Kaleidoscope Goodies
See page 44 for decorating instructions.

Crescent Coffee Cake Recipe
3 packages (8 ounces each) refrigerator crescent rolls
6 Tablespoons brown sugar
6 Tablespoons granulated sugar
1½ teaspoons cinnamon
6 Tablespoons raisins
Nut Glaze
(for bottom of pan)
¼ cup butter, divided
¼ cup brown sugar
1 Tablespoon light corn syrup
¼ cup chopped pecans
Preheat oven to 375° F.

Divide dough from each package into two rectangles. Press perforations together to form 4 x 12 rectangles. Combine sugars, cinnamon and raisins in a small bowl. Sprinkle sugar mixture evenly over dough rectangles, leaving one long edge plain.

Starting with the widest edge, roll up and press plain edge to seal roll. Cut into 1 in. pieces. Hint: To cut slide a strong thread or string under dough. Bring ends up and twist together tightly. This prevents flattening dough as knife would do.

For nut glaze, melt 1 Tablespoon butter and brush bottom and sides of pan. Heat remaining butter, sugar and syrup until melted; stirring to combine. Pour mixture evenly into prepared pan; sprinkle with pecans.

Place 1 in. pieces of dough (cut edges down for trees or see p. 57 for cross how-to's) into pan filling in all spaces. Bake at 375°F per specific times on p. 43 and p. 57. Invert onto serving platter. Decorate per instructions in the Idea section.

Grandma's Gingerbread Recipe
5 to 5½ cups all-purpose flour
1 tsp. baking soda
1 tsp. salt
2 tsp. ginger
2 tsp. cinnamon
1 tsp. nutmeg
1 tsp. cloves
1 cup shortening
1 cup sugar
1¼ cups unsulphured molasses
2 eggs, beaten

Thoroughly mix flour, soda, salt and spices.

Melt shortening in large saucepan. Cool slightly. Add sugar, molasses and eggs; mix well. Add four cups dry ingredients and mix well.

Turn mixture onto lightly floured surface. Knead in remaining dry ingredients by hand. Add a little more flour, if necessary, to make a firm dough. Roll out on a lightly floured surface to a ¼ in. thickness for cut-out cookies.

If you're not going to use your gingerbread right away, wrap dough in plastic and refrigerate. Refrigerated dough will keep for a week, but be sure to remove it 3 hours prior to rolling so it softens and is workable. 1 recipe of this gingerbread dough will yield 40 average-size cookies.

Kaleidoscope Icing Technique
Use color flow or thin royal to color flow consistency. Decorate one cookie at a time. With tip 2, flow in white icing. Immediately pipe lines or dots with tinted icing. With a straight pin, pull through icing lines (follow direction of arrows on patterns). Let dry.

Gum Paste & Cookie Recipes

This is a pliable mixture that we used to shape the calla lillies shown on p. 29. In addition to these beautiful blooms, gum paste can be shaped to many impressive, lasting decorations. Ingredients, molds and instruction books are available on p. 130.

Gum Paste Recipe

1 Tbsp. Wilton Gum-Tex™,
1 heaping Tbsp. Wilton Glucose
4 Tbsps. warm water
   (100°, test temperature with candy thermometer)
1 lb. confectioners sugar

In mixing bowl, mix Gum-Tex with ½ lb. confectioners sugar. In separate mixing bowl, mix water and glucose until thoroughly blended. Make a well in the center of the sugar mixture and add glucose mixture. Stir gradually until mixture becomes the consistency of children's playing dough. If mixture is too thin, add small amounts of confectioners sugar to achieve proper consistency. Place remaining confectioners sugar on work surface with dough-like mixture and knead until sugar is blended in. Place mixture in plastic bag and seal tightly, squeezing all air out of bag to prevent drying. Let gum paste set in bag for approximately 5 to 10 minutes. Remove gum paste and knead until it's pliable, non-sticky and a workable consistency. Gum paste is ready to use when it stretches without snapping.

To Store

Wrapped in a plastic bag inside an airtight container, your gum paste can be stored for several months. It handles best when it is several days old. When you are ready to use, rework it with your hands.

To Color

Add icing color in small amounts and knead gum paste until color is even all over. If you use liquid color, add a little more confectioners sugar to compensate for the extra liquid. Sugar added after color will make the gum paste lighter. Be sure you make enough of any one color you need, because like icings, colors are hard to match.

To Cut Out Or Mold

Dust work surface with cornstarch. To roll out gum paste, take a small piece, work it with your hands and place it over the cornstarch-covered area. Dust your hands and rolling pin with cornstarch and roll out gum paste to desired thickness. Roll out one piece at a time and cover remaining gum paste to prevent drying.

To Make Calla Lily

STEP I: Make Stamen—roll gum paste between palms of your hands to ¼-in. thickness. Cut into 1 3/4-in. pieces. Take a 6-in. length of wire and hook (fold over) one end ¼-in. Dip hook end of wire into elongated piece of gum paste. Brush stamen with egg white and roll in yellow-tinted sugar (use a small amount of icing color). Push wire into styrofoam block to dry.

STEP II: Cut Out Petal—lightly wipe work surface with solid vegetable shortening and roll out gum paste to 1/16-in. thickness. With Petal Pattern and an artist knife, cut out petal. Smooth outside edge on top half of petal with your finger. Then place the petal, point forward, in palm of hand. Lay pointed stick down center of petal. Overlap round side of petal over pointed stick. Add egg white to top of overlapped petal and on inside of the bottom half of the lip side of petal. Press firmly and remove stick.

STEP III: Curl & Chalk Petal—place petal over a tree former (dusted with cornstarch) and gently fold the petal edges back. Let the petal remain on former to dry. Grate non-toxic chalk and mix with cornstarch. Using an art brush, paint from the inner throat to the point with dry grated chalk.

STEP IV: Add Stamen & Calyx—add egg white to bottom of stamen and insert wire end into the flower. Pull the wire through until the stamen is in place. Roll out green-tinted gum paste. Cut a small circle (use small carnation cutter). Elongate sides of circle by rolling pointed stick from side to side to form oval shape. Brush egg white over all of oval, place calla lily on top of oval and wrap around calla lily and wire. Let dry.

Roll-Out Cookies

1 cup butter
1 cup sugar
1 large egg
2 tsp. baking powder
1 tsp. vanilla
2¾ cups flour

Preheat oven to 400°. In a large bowl, cream butter and sugar with an electric mixer. Beat in eggs and vanilla. Add baking powder and flour, one cup at a time, mixing after each addition. The dough will be very stiff; blend last flour in by hand. Do not chill dough. **Note:** Dough can be tinted with Icing Color. Add small amounts until desired color is reached. **For chocolate cookies:** Stir in 3 ounces melted, unsweetened chocolate (if dough becomes too stiff, add water, a teaspoon at a time).

Divide dough into 2 balls. On a floured surface, roll each ball into a circle approximately 12 inches in diameter and 1/8 in. thick. Dip cutters in flour before each use. Bake cookies on top rack of oven for 6-7 minutes, or until cookies are lightly browned.

Cookie Icing Recipe

This icing dries to a shiny, hard finish and tastes good, too. Great to use for icing or to outline and fill in with a tip 2 or 3.

1 cup sifted confectioners sugar
2 tsps. milk
2 tsps. light corn syrup

Place sugar and milk in bowl. Stir until mixed thoroughly. Add corn syrup and mix well. For filling in areas, use thinned icing (add small amounts of light corn syrup until desired consistency is reached.)

Basic Candy Making

Wilton Candy Melts™ brand confectionery coating take the guesswork out of making candy at home. They melt easily, right to the ideal consistency for molding and dipping, and have a creamy, rich flavor. For a change of taste, they can be flavored with Wilton Candy Flavors. See our complete collection of candy making products (p. 114-117). For more about candy making, order the Let's Make Candy book or the Complete Wilton Book of Candy (p. 124). Our CandyMaking Home Study Course tells all (p. 128).

Candy Melts Are So Easy To Use

For melting, molding and dipping directions, simply refer to the back of the Candy Melts package. Remember that constant stirring is very important to insure even heating, when using the double boiler method. Here's a no-mess way of melting in microwave: Fill an uncut disposable decorating bag half-full of Candy Melts. Microwave 1 minute at half power; knead candy. Repeat at 30-second intervals until candy is completely melted. Then cut the tip and squeeze melted coating out into candy molds.

To Flavor: The creamy, rich taste can be enhanced by adding approximately ¼ teaspoon Wilton oil-based Candy Flavor (p. 115) to 1 lb. of melted Candy Melts. Never use alcohol based flavorings; they will cause coatings to harden.

To Color: Add Wilton Candy Colors (p. 114) to melted Candy Melts a little at a time. Mix thoroughly before adding more color. Colors tend to deepen as they're mixed. Pastel colored candies are most appetizing, so keep this in mind when tinting. **Decorating with Candy Melts:** To 1 cup of melted coating, add ¼ teaspoon light corn syrup. Mix well. More corn syrup may be added until coating is a piping consistency, smooth and slightly stiff. Mix well. Fill disposable or parchment bag with candy and snip end off bag (size opening of a 2 or 3). Work quickly and pipe decorations on candy. Allow coating to set until firm.

To Mold Stand-Up Candy Delights

Cut Wilton 3-D mold (see p. 117) in half along dotted line and snap together. Stand inverted. Fill mold with melted coating and gently tap mold to release air bubbles. To make hollow candy: Place filled mold in refrigerator for about 5-10 minutes to harden the outside of the mold. Pour out excess. Return mold to refrigerator to harden completely. Unmold. To seal the bottom, cover cookie sheet with waxed paper. Pour a pool of melted Candy Melts that's larger than the opening. Position hollowed candy on top of pool. Let set. Trim excess coating away with a sharp knife. For solid, stand-up candy: Fill as for hollow method and refrigerate until firm (approx. 1½ hours). Unmold and trim excess.

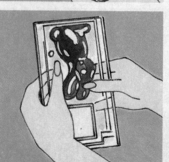

Shimmery Hard Candy Recipe

2 cups granulated sugar
⅔ cup water
¼ teaspoon cream of tartar
Icing color
1 teaspoon candy flavor
Candy thermometer

Combine water, sugar and cream of tartar in heavy saucepan and bring to a boil over high heat, stirring constantly. When it begins to boil, insert candy thermometer and stop stirring. Continue cooking over high heat, occasionally wiping sides of pan and thermometer with wet pastry brush. It will take 12 to 15 minutes for candy to cook, but check thermometer often. When candy reaches 300° remove from heat. Let stand a minute or two until bubbles disappear. Stir in icing color and flavoring.

To mold candy: With a pastry brush, coat hard candy molds with non-stick vegetable oil spray. Pour candy into molds and let harden at room temperature (do not refrigerate). Note: Hard candy can only be molded in hard candy molds.

Tempting Truffles Recipe

One 14 oz. package Candy Melts
½ cup whipping cream

Coarsely chop Candy Melts; set aside.

Conventional method: Place cream in a small saucepan over medium heat and bring to a boil, remove from heat; add chopped coating and cover pan. Let stand approximately 5 minutes or until coating has melted. Stir until smooth and creamy. Refrigate until firm. Roll into round centers.

Microwave Method: Put cream in a 1 quart glass measure and microwave on high about 1½ minutes or until cream comes to a boil. Remove from microwave. Add Candy Melts; cover and let stand about 5 minutes or until coating is melted. Stir until smooth and creamy. Refrigerate until firm. Roll in centers.

To decorate: Dip into melted candy. Let set. Drizzle with contrasting color. Variations: Roll in chopped nuts, coconut, confectioners sugar, chocolate sprinkles or cocoa.

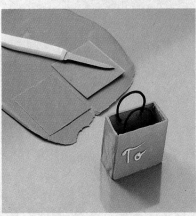

To Mold Multi-Color Candy

"Painting" Method: Use a decorator's brush dipped in melted Candy Melts. Paint features or details desired. Let set. Fill mold. Refrigerate until set. Unmold.

"Layering" Method: Pour melted coating into dry molds to desired height. Refrigerate until partially set. Pour contrasting color melted coating to desired height. Refrigerate until partially set. Repeat until desired numbers of layers are formed. Let candy harden in refrigerator. Unmold. Wilton Classic Candy Molds are available in a wonderful variety of unique and traditional shapes. Their generous depth makes painting and layering fun and easy. See page 116 for our outstanding Classic Candy Molds selection.

To Mold Marble-Look Candy

Arrange Candy Melts (two or three colors) in a single layer in the top of double boiler, alternating colors. For microwave oven or electric skillet, arrange the candy wafers in a flat, shallow dish. Melt coating, but do not stir. When completely melted, test frequently, candy wafers will not lose their shape; draw a spoon through coating several times to swirl the colors together. Don't stir or overmix or color will become muddy. Now, spoon into molds. Refrigerate until firm.

To Mold Candy Plaques

Molding a section or the entire pan out of Candy Melts is easy and impressive.

- Pour melted coating into center of pan. Tap pan gently on counter to break up bubbles and spread coating evenly over bottom (approximately ¼ in. thick). For control, use a decorating bag fitted with tip 2 or a cut disposable bag.
- Place pan in refrigerator for approximately 5 to 10 minutes (check occasionally, if coating becomes too hard it will crack). Unmold onto hand or soft towel (tap pan gently, if nesessary).
- **For multi-color effect:** Paint desired areas with a decorator's brush. Let set. Pour in melted coating to fill remaining area.

Candy Cut-Outs

Following the same procedure as for making a candy plaque, pour candy into center of 6 or 8 in. square pan.

- Place coating on work surface and with a sharp knife, score into desired shapes. Snap into pieces.
- **For bags** (p. 24): Cut side pieces and join together with melted candy. Attach licorice handles with dots of coating. **On charge plates:** Cut shapes and attach candy wafers for dots with melted coating. Print messages on with melted candy.

Confectionery Artistry

Created expressly for Wilton by Elaine Gonzalaz, these fun and fancy ideas (shown on pages 34-35) will make your creations the topic of conversation. Working with our delicious Candy Melts*™ will save you time and insure success!

Modeling With Candy Melts

This edible candy "clay" is so versatile. You can shape it into a breathtaking rose or an amusing party blower. Enjoy discovering the easy-to-make, impressive-to-see decorating possibilites.

Candy Clay

Melt 10 oz. Candy Melts (40 wafers), add ⅓ cup light corn syrup. Mix only until blended.

Shape mixture into a 6 in. squre of waxed paper and let set at room temperature until dry.

Wrap well and store at room temperature until needed. Clay handles best if hardened overnight. To use, knead a small portion at a time. If it gets too soft, set aside at room temperature, or refrigerate briefly. Store in a well-sealed container for several weeks.

Ganche Glaze Recipe

14 oz. package of Candy Melts (p. 115)
1 cup whipping cream

Finely chop wafers (use food processor). Heat whipping cream just to boiling point (do not boil) in a sauce pan. Add chopped wafers and stir until smooth and glossy. If mixture is too thin to pour, wait a few minutes until cool. To cover, place cake on a wire rack over a drip pan. Pour glaze into center and work towards edges. **For piping and filling:** Allow mixture to cool so it sets, then whip. It can now be used to ice cakes, pipe borders, scrolls and even roses.

MODELING A ROSE

Start with the base and mold a cone that's approximately 1½-in. high from a 3/4-in. diameter ball of modeling candy. Next, make petals. Flatten 3/8-in. ball of modeling candy into a circle that's about ¼-in. thick on one side and about the diameter of a dime. Make several petals this size.

• Wrap first petal around the point of the cone to form a bud. Now press three more petals around the base of the bud.

• Gently pinch edges of petals. Make five more petals using slightly larger balls of modeling candy. Flatten, then thin edge with finger and cup petals. Press petals under first rows of petals. Continue adding petals, placing them in between and slightly lower than previous row. For a fuller flower, continue adding petals in this manner.

TO MAKE CANDY LEAVES

On the back of clean, thoroughly dried, grape or rose leaves, paint on melted Candy Melts with a soft pastry or decorator's brush. Pull out pointed or curved edges to resemble certain kinds of leaves such as the "oak" leaves on our Inspiration cake. Let coating set and when completely dry, carefully peel off candy.

*brand confectionery coating

To Make Party Time Gear on Exclamation

- **To mold party hat:** Make a cone shape mold out of freezer paper (shiny side should be on inside) Note: A guide to exact size is included in '90 Pattern Book. Melt approximately 1¼ bags of Candy Melts. Place hat mold in a bowl filled with dried beans or unshelled peanuts (be sure sides aren't indented). Pour candy up to the top. Place in refrigerator for 3 to 5 minutes. Watch for a solid rim, approximately ¼ in. wide, to form. Check occasionally. When set to desired thickness, pour out excess candy. Let set completely in refrigerator. If sides are too thin, repeat procedure. Remove freezer paper and decorate. If it is necessary to level bottom edge of hat, simply run over a warm hot tray or cookie sheet.

- **For party blower:** Roll candy clay into a 1 in. diameter, 4 in. long tube. With a rolling pin, flatten out about 3 in. of tube. Roll up flattened portion. Pinch other end to narrow so it will fit onto mouth piece. Roll, then cut a piece of white candy clay into a 3 in. x 2 in. diameter rectangle for mouth piece. Overlap long sides for form a tube. Insert two drinking straws to shape and stand on end. Gently push pieces together and let set.
- **For ribbons, fringe, confetti:** Roll candy clay into log shapes, approximately ¼ inch in diameter. With a rolling pin, flatten candy down to form strips. Press red strip around base of candy party hat. With a craft knife, cut edge for a fringed effect. Add another strip and repeat procedure. Cut a strip, then wrap around point of hat.
- **For bow:** Form a figure-8 and allow ends to extend. Pinch center and cover with a small strip. and let dry. For ribbons: Place brown strips on top and down sides of cake (smooth ends of strips together). For streamers: Wrap strips around drinking straws and let dry. For confetti: Cut strips into squares.
- Decorate hat and blower with melted candy. Attach pieces of confetti with dots of candy.

To Make Fascination Lacework Pieces

- **For Heart and Lace Collar:** (we suggest collar be made in two pieces to prevent breakage). Trace pattern and place on a heavy board or piece of glass, cover with waxed paper and tape securely.
- Fill a parchment or disposable bag with melted Candy Melts. Cut a very small opening in end (approximately the size of a tip 3). Cover outer lines of Heart and Collar. Flow in heart (to smooth surface, skim area with end of bag immediately). Complete lace pattern design, then overpipe the lace pattern on collar and heart for strength. Overpipe edges with bead borders. To prevent sticking or curling, immediately run a spatula under pieces to prevent them from sticking to waxed paper.
- **For Scallops:** Trace Scallop Patterns following the same procedure on separate pieces of waxed paper (12 are used, so make approximately 15 to allow for breakage). Outline then fill in with lace design. Overpipe edges with beads. Carefully slide scallop (still on waxed paper) onto the concaved side of flower former. Let set 10 to 15 minutes.

Engraving Technique on Dedication

- Place Dogwood pattern on top of molded candy. Use a sharp point and just enough pressure to trace design. Remove pattern.
- Half-fill parchment decorating bag with tempered chocolate; cut small opening, equivalent to tip 2.
- Pipe over design with gentle pressure. To fill in areas, allow outline to dry slightly before flowing in. Let set completely.

Candy Making

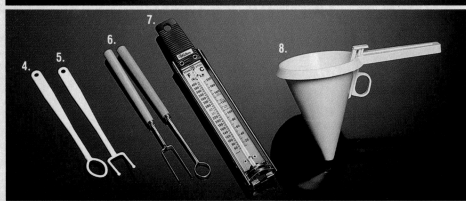

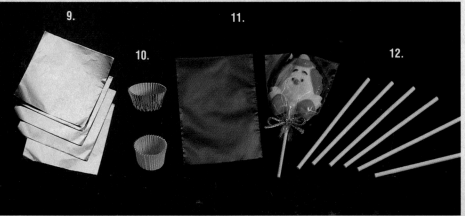

Discover the fun and ease of making candy the Wilton way!

CANDY COLORS
Rich, concentrated oil-based color that blends beautifully into Wilton Candy Melts.

1. CANDY COLORS KIT
Contains red, green, yellow and orange ¼ oz. jars. Convenient and economical.
1913-V-1299 $3.99 kit

2. THE COMPLETE WILTON BOOK OF CANDY.
Create candy that rivals the fanciest store-bought kinds. Filled with delicious recipes, step-by-step instructions and more. Full-color photographs are a treat to see. Soft-cover.
902-V-1243. $10.99 each

3. NEW! LET'S MAKE CANDY
A step-by-step guide to candy making.
A little treasury of candy making ideas and techniques for beginning and experienced candy makers. Basic candy making techniques such as molding, and dipping, plus specialty ideas, such as candy clay and candi-pan are clearly explained. Soft cover; 44 pages, 5½ x 8½ in.
902-V-2100 $1.99 each

ESSENTIAL CANDY MAKING TOOLS

4. CANDY DIPPING SPOON
White plastic, 7¾ in. long.
1904-V-714 $1.99 each

5. CANDY DIPPING FORK
White plastic, 7¾ in. long.
1904-V-749 $1.99 each

6. 2-PC. DIPPING SET
Sturdy metal with wooden handles. 9 in. long.
1904-V-925 $7.99 set

7. CANDY THERMOMETER
Proper scale for hard candy, nougat, more.
1904-V-1168 $13.99 each

8. EASY-POUR FUNNEL
Push button controls the flow. 5 x 4 in. wide; nylon.
1904-V-552 $3.99 each

9. FANCY CANDY WRAPPERS
Gold foil to protect and fancy up your candy. 125 sheets, each 3 x 3 in.
1912-V-2290 $2.99 pack

10. CANDY CUPS
Crisply pleated cups, just like professionals use. Choose gold foil or white glassine-coated paper. 1 in. diameter. Packs of 100.
GOLD FOIL 1912-V-1227 $3.99 pack
WHITE 1912-V-1243   99¢ pack

11. LOLLIPOP BAGS
Plastic bags for lollipops and other candies. 3 x 4 in. 50 bags in a pack.
1912-V-2347 $2.29 pack

12. LOLLIPOP STICKS
Sturdy paper sticks are easy to add to candy molds. 4½ in. long. 50 sticks per pack.
1912-V-1006 $1.29 pack

Plastic dipping fork and spoon made in Hong Kong. Thermometer made in Japan. Dipping set made in Japan.

Candy Making

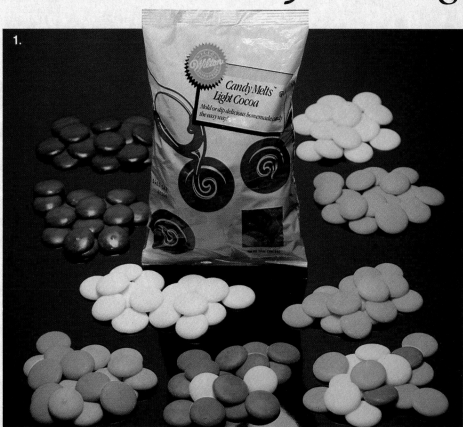

1. CANDY MELTS™ *
brand confectionery coating. Creamy, easy-to-melt wafers are ideal for all your candy making needs—molding, dipping and coating. Delicious taste that can be varied with our Candy Flavors. 14 oz. bag. Certified Kosher **$2.50 each**
WHITE 1911-V-498
LIGHT COCOA (All natural, cocoa flavor.)
1911-V-544
DARK COCOA (All natural, cocoa flavor.)
1911-V-358
PINK 1911-V-447
YELLOW 1911-V-463
GREEN 1911-V-404
CHRISTMAS MIX (Red, Green, Yellow.)
(Available 9/1-12/15/89)
1911-V-1625
SPRING MIX (Pink, Lavender, Blue.)
(Available 12/1/89-5/31/90)
1911-V-1637
FALL MIX (Orange, Yellow, Green.)
(Available 8/1-10/31/89)
1911-V-1619

2. CANDY FILLINGS
Delicious tasting and ready to use.
CARAMEL 16 oz.
1911-V-1400 $4.49 each
COCONUT 16 oz.
1911-V-1028 $4.49 each
NOUGAT 10 oz.
1911-V-1488 $4.49 each

3. 4-PC. CANDY FLAVOR SET
Cinnamon, Cherry, Creme De Menthe and Peppermint. ¼ oz. bottles.
1913-V-1029 $3.99 set

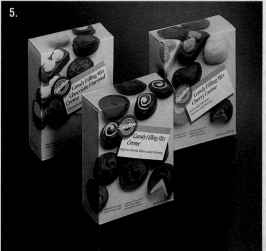

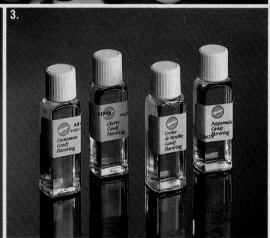

4. CANDY WAFER & FONDANT MIX
Makes satiny smooth candies or icing for cakes. 16 oz.
1911-V-1427 $3.99 each

5. CANDY CENTER MIXES
Creates creamy centers that can be dipped or molded for classic favorites. 9 oz. **$2.49 each**
CREME CENTER MIX 1911-V-1901
CHOCOLATE FLAVORED 1911-V-1903
CHERRY 1911-V-1905

PLEASE NOTE: All prices, certain products and services reflect the U.S.A. domestic market and do not apply in Australia and Canada.

Candy Molds

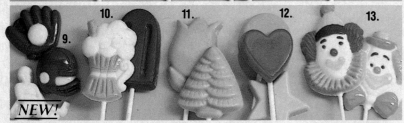

NEW!

NEW!

For Hard Candy

1. TEDDY BEARS & GUMBALL MACHINES
8 molds; 2 designs.
2114-V-4232 **$1.49 each**

2. BEARS
4 cute designs. Perfect for lollipops.
2114-V-4055 **$1.89 each**

3. PANDA MOLD
Clear plastic. About 3½ in. high.
2114-V-1463 **$1.99 each**

4. ALUMINUM PANDA MOLD
Ideal for baking or molding a delightful treat. Sides clip together, base opens for easy filling. 5 x 5 in. Instructions, base and clips included.
518-V-489 **$4.99 each**

5. DINOSAURS
9 molds; 4 designs per sheet.
2114-V-8888 **$1.49 each**

6. GARFIELD
4 lollipop designs per sheet.
2114-V-1816 **$1.89 each**
© 1984. United Features Syndicate, Inc.

7. ANIMALS
5 lollipops per sheet.
2114-V-3008 **$1.49 each**

8. FUNNY FACES LOLLIPOP SET
Mix and match facial features to make amusing pop art. Great for parties.
2114-V-7535 **$2.99 set**

9. NEW! SPORTS
Baseball, hockey, football, basketball designs—8 molds on sheet.
2114-V-1102 **$1.49 each**

10. TREATS
5 lollipops per sheet.
2114-V-3006 **$1.49 each**

11. LOLLIPOPS I
5 molds; 5 designs.
2114-V-882 **$1.89 each**

12. LOLLIPOPS II
5 molds; 5 designs on sheet.
2114-V-90861 **$1.89 each**

13. CLOWNS
4 zany lollipop designs.
2114-V-4110 **$1.49 each**

14. NEW! ROSES 'N BUDS
10 molds on sheet; 2 designs; 2 lolipops.
2114-V-1101 **$1.49 each**

15. ROSES
10 molds; 2 designs on sheet.
2114-V-1511 **$1.89 each**

16. LEAVES
10 molds; 2 designs on sheet.
2114-V-629 **$1.49 each**

17. FANCY CHOCOLATES I
12 molds; 2 designs.
2114-V-1269 **$1.89 each**

18. FANCY CHOCOLATES V
10 molds, 3 designs on sheet.
2114-V-4242 **$1.89 each**

19. CORDIAL GLASSES
6 molds; 1 design on sheet.
2114-V-1242 **$1.49 each**

20. RIPPLES
11 molds; 3 designs on sheet.
2114-V-2524 **$1.49 each**

21. MINT DISCS
12 molds; 1 design on sheet; ¼ in. deep.
2114-V-1226 **$1.89 each**

22. ACCORDIAN RUFFLES
10 molds; 1 design on sheet.
2114-V-1013 **$1.89 each**

23. ROUNDS
8 molds; 2 designs on sheet.
2114-V-90466 **$1.89 each**

24. BON BONS
12 molds; 1 design on sheet.
2114-V-1072 **$1.89 each**

25. LARGE BON BONS
8 molds; 1 design.
2114-V-2656 **$1.49 each**

26. HALLOWEEN
5 different designs.
2115-V-324 **$1.99 each**

27. HOLIDAY LOLLIPOPS
5 designs on sheet.
2115-V-358 **$1.99 each**

28. HEARTS
15 molds on sheet.
2115-V-322 **$1.99 each**

29. GARFIELD
Zany! 4 lollipops; 4 designs on sheet.
2115-V-360 **$1.99 each**
© 1984 United Features Syndicate, Inc.

30. ANIMALS
4 lollipops on sheet.
2115-V-350 **$1.99 each**

31. CLOWNS
5 lollipops on sheet.
2115-V-344 **$1.99 each**

32. STARS
16 molds on sheet.
2115-V-336 **$1.99 each**

33. TREATS
Yummy! 5 lollipops on sheet.
2115-V-352 **$1.99 each**

34. VARIETY LOLLIPOPS II
5 on sheet.
2115-V-338 **$1.99 each**

Candy Molds

1. NUMBERS
18 molds per sheet.
2114-V-2912 **$1.49 set**

2. ALPHABET SET
Capital letters; two of each vowel.
2114-V-2910 **$2.99 set**

3. SCRIPT WORDS I
Best, Wishes, Congratulations.
2114-V-2914 **$1.49 set**

4. SCRIPT WORDS II
Happy, Birthday, Anniversary.
2114-V-2915 **$1.49 set**

5. 3-D PUMPKIN
About 3 in. high.
2114-V-1447 **$1.99 each**

6. JACK-O-LANTERNS
2½ in. wide. 3 jolly-faced molds on sheet.
2114-V-91056 **$1.89 each**

7. PUMPKIN
12 identical smiling molds.
2114-V-90740 **$1.89 each**

8. HALLOWEEN VARIETY SET
2 sheets of molds.
2114-V-1031 **$2.99 set**

9. NEW! THANKSGIVING
3 traditional designs, including turkey lollipops.
2114-V-91128 **$1.89 each**

10. 3-D SANTA
About 4 in. tall.
2114-V-1374 **$1.99 each**

11. BELL
16 molds.
2114-V-1075 **$1.49 each**

12. CHRISTMAS TREES
12 molds on sheet.
2114-V-91099 **$1.89 each**

13. SNOWFLAKES
8 molds; 2 designs on sheet.
2114-V-90661 **$1.89 each**

14. CHRISTMAS II
10 molds, 9 joyful designs per sheet.
2114-V-94152 **$1.89 each**

15. CHRISTMAS CLASSICS II
Trees, trims & holiday friends.
2114-V-1225 **$2.99 set**

16. CHRISTMAS I
8 festive molds; 7 designs.
2114-V-94136 **$1.89 each**

17. CHRISTMAS CLASSICS
Santas, Sleigh, Reindeer and Toys.
2114-V-1224 **$2.99 set**

18. HEARTS I
12 molds, 3 designs on sheet.
2114-V-91030 **$1.89 each**

19. HEARTS II
8 molds; 2 designs on sheet.
2114-V-645 **$1.49 each**

20. HEARTS
15 classic molds on sheet.
2114-V-214 **$1.49 each**

21. NEW! BIT O' IRISH
10 St. Pat's day molds on sheet; 4 designs.
2114-V-91105 **$1.89 each**

22. 3-D LAMB
3¼ in. high.
2114-V-3229 **$1.99 each**

23. 3-D BUNNY
4½ in. high.
2114-V-1390 **$1.99 each**

24. EGG MOLD SET
2-pc. plastic molds. Includes one each: 5 x 4 in.; 4½ x 3 in.; 3 x 2 in.
1404-V-1040 **$3.99 each**

25. EASTER BUNNIES
12 cottontails per sheet.
2114-V-91200 **$1.89 each**

26. EGGS
Each 1 x 1½ in. long; 14 molds per sheet.
2114-V-90998 **$1.89 each**

27. EASTER VARIETY SET
2 sheets per set.
2114-V-3131 **$2.99 each**

28. BABY
4 designs, 10 molds per sheet.
2114-V-2816 **$1.49 each**

29. GRADUATION
4 designs, 11 molds per sheet.
2114-V-2818 **$1.49 each**

30. NEW! WEDDING
3 designs for bridal showers and weddings; 12 molds, including 2 lollipops, on sheet.
2114-V-1104 **$1.49 each**

31. NEW! 4TH OF JULY
Flags, bells, fireworks! 8 molds on sheet.
2114-V-1103 **$1.49 each**

NEW!

NEW!

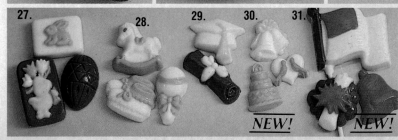

NEW! NEW!

Cookie Shapes

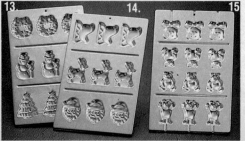

1. NEW! ROLL ALONG COOKIE CUTTERS. Easy and fun to use. Includes 18 interchangeable holiday designs. Cuts 6 different designs at once.
2104-V-2404 $6.99 each

2. SPRITZ COOKIE PRESS. Easy-squeeze trigger-action makes it fun to create delicious cookies. Includes 10 plastic disks in holiday cookie shapes. Gray/white plastic.
2104-V-2303 $10.99 each

3. NEW! HALLOWEEN COOKIE CANISTER SET. 10 super Halloween designs with plastic storage container.
2304-V-1031 $3.99 set

4. CHRISTMAS COOKIE CANISTER SET. 10 festive holiday shapes with reusable plastic storage container.
509-V-1225 $3.99 set

5. NEW! ZANY ZOO COOKIE CANISTER SET. 10 plastic cutters in adorable animal shapes with reusable plastic storage container.
509-9550 $3.99 set

6. 4-PC. HALLOWEEN COOKIE CUTTER SET. A frightfully fun assortment. Pumpkin, Cat, Witch, Ghost/Tombstone.
2304-V-994 $2.99 set

7. 4-PC. CHRISTMAS COOKIE CUTTER SET. Favorite holiday shapes—Angel, Santa, Wreath, Tree.
2304-V-995 $2.99 set

8. CHRISTMAS CUTTERS. 89¢ each
COTTAGE   509-V-1221
HOLLY   509-V-1222
REINDEER   509-V-1223
SNOWMAN   509-V-1224

9. HOLIDAY SHAPES SET. Santa, angel, tree, boy and girl—3⅝ to 6 in. high.
2304-V-105 $2.99 set

10. 4-PC. SWEETHEART COOKIE CUTTER SET. Romantic shapes.
2304-V-115 $2.99 set

11. NEW! 4-PC. EASTER COOKIE CUTTER SET. Easter treat shapes.
2304-V-110 $2.99 set
(Available 1/1/90)

12. GINGERBREAD FAMILY SET. Set includes two 5½ x 4 in. adults and two 2½ x 1½ in. children.
2304-V-121 $2.59 set

13-15. COOKIE MOLDS. Holiday and classic designs. Aluminum.
$7.99 each
13. WREATH/SNOWMAN/TREE
2306-V-112
14. SANTA/REINDEER/SLEIGH
2306-V-111
15. TEDDY BEARS   2306-V-116

Cookie Shapes

Cookie Cutters and Sets with plastic cutters. No sharp edges. Closed cutters make great toast stamps, too!

1. NEW! SPORTS SET.
Includes baseball, football, basketball, bowling, tennis.
2304-V-2101 $2.99 set

2. DINOSAURS SET.
Includes Brontosaurus, Tyrannosaurus, Pterodactyl and Stegosaurus.
2304-V-1990 $2.99 set

3. FARMYARD FRIENDS.
Goose, pig, lamb, rooster and cow will add country charm.
2304-432 $2.99 set

4. LOONEY TUNES™.
Crazy cut-ups—Bugs Bunny, Tweety, Porky Pig and Sylvester.
2304-V-404 $2.99 set

© 1988 Warner Bros, Inc. Wilton Enterprises Authorized User.

5. CHILDREN'S ALPHABET A TO Z SET.
Letter-perfect shapes—26 in all. 2½ in. wide, ⁵⁄₁₆ in. deep.
2304-V-104 $4.99 set

6. NUMBER SET.
Great for countless events. 2 x 1⅛ in.
2304-V-103 $4.99 set

7. ALPHABET SET.
Spells FUN for all. 26 letters, 2 x 1⅛ each
2304-V-102 $7.99 set

Use nesting cutters to mark shapes for patterns on cakes, too!

8. SESAME STREET.
Lovable favorites—Cookie Monster, Big Bird, Bert and Ernie.
2304-V-129 $2.99 set

Sesame Street and the Sesame Street Sign are the trademarks and servicemarks of Children's Television Workshop.

9. 6-PC. ROUND SET.
From 1½ to 4 in.
2304-V-113 $2.99 set

10. 6-PC. HEART SET.
From 1¼ to 4⅛ in.
2304-V-115 $2.99 set

11. 6-PC. OVAL SET.
From 3¼ to 7 in. long—2⅛ to 4¾ in. wide.
2304-V-388 $2.99 set

12. 6-PC. STAR SET.
From 1⅝ to 4⅝ in.
2304-V-111 $2.99 set

13. COOLING GRID.
Even the smallest shapes won't fall through. Chrome-plated steel. 10 x 16 in.
2305-V-128 $4.99 each

Plastic items made in Hong Kong. Cookie grid made in Taiwan. Molds made in Korea.

PLEASE NOTE: All prices, certain products and services reflect the U.S.A. domestic market and do not apply in Australia and Canada.

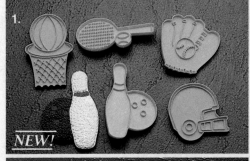
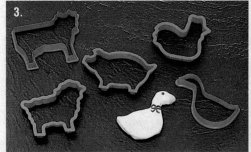

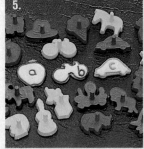

Publications

These treasuries of information and ideas will become permanent additions to your library.

THE WILTON WAY OF CAKE DECORATING –
A reference trilogy of techniques, tools, ideas, instructions and hints to help you master cake decorating. A must for anyone who decorates.

VOLUME ONE – THE BEAUTIFUL BASICS!
This valuable reference starts at the beginning and assumes no previous knowledge of cake decorating. Covers the a,b, c's of decorating the Wilton-American way in a stimulating manner. More than 600 full-color photos depict every type of decorated cake. Specialty techniques, such as Color Flow, Figure Piping, Sugar Molding and Marzipan modeling are easy to learn. Includes recipes. Hard cover; 328 color pages; 8½ x 11 in. Printed in Italy.
904-V-100 $29.99 each

VOLUME TWO – ALL ADVANCED TECHNIQUES!
A 328-page encyclopedia that features the world's most breathtaking cake decorating techniques. Filled with detailed, easy-to-follow descriptions of advanced Wilton-American and foreign techniques: English (Nirvana and over-piped), Australian, Continental, Mexican, Philippine and South African. Includes gum paste flowers and figures and the art of pulled sugar taught and demonstrated by Norman Wilton. Soft cover; 328 color pages; 8½ x 11 in. Printed in U.S.A.
904-V-119 $26.99

VOLUME THREE – THE USE OF DECORATING TIPS
A treasury of decorating tips (tubes). Tells all on what each tip is capable of creating, so decorating skills can be developed to their full potential. More than 400 color photos highlight over 40 gorgeous borders, scores of flowers and other decorative motifs. Exciting figure piped and gum paste creations are demonstrated and explained. Hard cover; 328 color pages; 8½ x 11 in. Printed in U.S.A.
ENGLISH VERSION
904-V-348 $29.99 each
VOLUME THREE – SPANISH VERSION (not shown)
Like the English version, this book is totally devoted to tips. In addition, it features a full chapter of beautiful quinceanos cakes and an easy-to-follow "pictorial dictionary."
904-V-1348 $34.99 each

Publications

NEW! 1990 YEARBOOK OF CAKE DECORATING

Order more! What an exciting way to introduce a friend or relative to the wonderful world of cake decorating. Soft cover; 192 pages. 8-7/8 x 11 in.
1701-V-900 $4.99 each

NEW! 1990 PATTERN BOOK

All the patterns needed to duplicate certain cakes in the 1990 Yearbook. A real timesaver for busy decorators. Soft cover. 8-7/8 x 11 in.
408-V-900 $3.99 each

DISCOVER THE FUN OF CAKE DECORATING

Here's the book that really demonstrates the fun and rewards of cake decorating. Over 100 irresistible cake ideas, from fast and easy sheet cakes to tall and towering wedding cakes, are depicted in glorious color with complete easy-to-follow, step-by-step instructions. Includes basic borders, fantastic flowers, fun figure piping, lovely color flow and more. Includes patterns and cake serving ideas. Hard cover; 184 color pages; 8-7/8 x 11 in.
904-V-206 $12.99 each

CAKE DECORATING – EASY AS 1-2-3

Shows and explains the basics of cake decorating in simple terms. Includes decorating techniques, uses of popular tips, easy-to-follow instructions for decorating 15 party and holiday cakes. Soft cover; 36 pages; full color; 5½ x 8½ in.
902-V-1792 $1.99 each

USES FOR DECORATING TIPS

Extremely valuable quick reference/idea book. Features five of the most popular decorating tip families and explains what each does. Tips are grouped by families so they're easy to find. Shows the versatility and range of many tips by depicting design variations. This informative book is a great gift for any decorator and a marvelous inspiration for a beginner. Full color; soft cover; 48 pages; 8½ x 11 in.
902-V-1375 $6.99 each

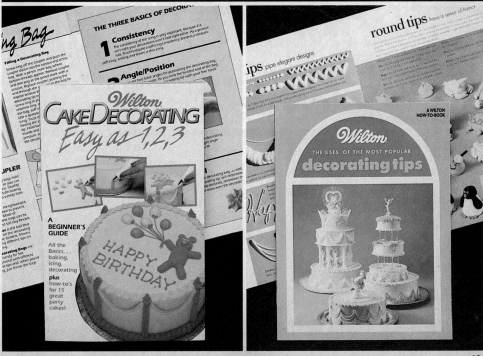

Publications

**NEW! WEDDING CAKES –
A WILTON ALBUM**
A magnificent treasury of wedding, shower and anniversary cakes–from classic to contemporary. Dozens of single and multi-tiered cakes, including a wonderful selection of Australian, Lambeth, Philippine, rolled fondant and cheese cakes, are depicted in glorious full color. Complete, easy-to-follow instructions, patterns, recipes and wedding cake data and cutting guide are also included. Soft cover; 82 color pages; 8¼ x 10¾ in.
908-V-100 $6.99 each

**CELEBRATE! WEDDING CAKES
BY WILTON**
From lavish cakes to serve hundreds to diminutive delights for intimate gatherings, this book has the cake to please every bride. Scores of designs use exciting decorating techniques including foreign methods, stairways and fountains. Instructions and patterns included. Hard cover; 192 color pages; 8¾ x 11 in.
916-V-847 $12.99 each

**BEAUTIFUL BRIDAL CAKES THE
WILTON WAY**
A marvelous selection of magnificent wedding cake ideas using the Wilton method of decorating plus continental, English, Australian and Philippine styles. Brides will love to go through this book, but will have a hard time choosing just one cake. Instructions and patterns included. Hard cover; 144 color pages; 8½ x 11 in.
908-V-117 $12.99 each

**THE WILTON BOOK OF WEDDING
CAKES**
More than a wedding cake book. Includes everything from gorgeous tiered wedding cakes to informal celebration cakes. A delightful selection of shower, engagement, bachelor party, rehearsal dinner and anniversary cakes, too! Hints on planning, choosing flowers, selecting music and more are included. Hard cover; 112 color pages; 8⅞ x 11 in.
908-V-109 $10.99 each

DRAMATIC TIER CAKES

Create your own tiered masterpieces with this complete Wilton guide. Learn the fundamentals of constructing and decorating lavish tier cakes, from the basics of building a cake to the safest way to transport wedding tiers to the reception. Includes uses of stairways and fountains, plus tested recipes, decorating descriptions and a complete selection of products needed to make the cakes shown. A must-have for any decorator. Soft cover; 80 color pages; 8½ x 11.
902-V-1725 $6.99

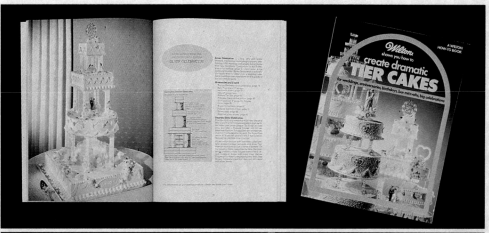

WILTON CELEBRATES THE ROSE

The book that tells all about the most popular icing flower. Includes easy-to-follow classic rose making directions plus a quick, impressive method. This valuable book also shows how to create petal-perfect candy flowers, how to model marzipan and gum paste roses, and how to stencil cakes. You'll adore the little treasury of rose-trimmed wedding cakes, using icing and fresh roses. Recipes and patterns included. Full-color; soft cover; 66 pages; 8½ x 11 in.
916-V-1218 $6.99 each

CELEBRATE WITH PARTY SPECTACULARS FROM A TO Z

Over 150 of the most unique creations. Delightful cakes children will adore, foreign decorating methods for you to explore, holiday treats galore… and more! Even how to model Candy Melts* into flowers and figures. Hard cover; 160 color pages; 8½ x 11 in.
916-V-936 $12.99 each

*brand confectionery coating

CELEBRATE! VI

A treasured annual for cake decorators and those who love decorated cakes! A multitude of impressive designs for weddings, showers, holidays and birthdays. Methods includes Australian, Philippine and English overpiped styles. Soft cover; 160 color pages; 8⅞ x 11¼ in.
916-V-618 $11.99 each

Publications

NEW! LET'S MAKE CANDY
A step-by-step guide to candy making.
A little treasury of candy making ideas and techniques for beginning and experienced candy makers. Basic candy making techniques such as molding, and dipping, plus specialty ideas, such as candy clay and candi-pan are clearly explained. Soft cover; 44 pages, 5½ x 8½ in.
902-V-2100 $1.99 each

THE COMPLETE WILTON BOOK OF CANDY
Discover how easy it is to make luscious molded and dipped chocolates, dessert shells, fudge, truffles, confectionery coating candies, marzipan, hard candies. These delicious candies are easy to make using our delicious recipes and helpful hints. Soft cover; full color; 176 pages; 7½ x 10½ in.
902-V-1243 $10.99 each

*confectionery coating

Publications

HOLIDAY

The complete book of Christmas cake, cookies, centerpieces, candy. See how easy and how much fun it is to fill your house with the smells and sights of this jolly holiday season. You'll find dozens of unusual festive ideas you'll love to make from gingerbread, cookie dough, cakes, candy and other confections...unique cookie baskets, gingerbread scenes, luscious specialty desserts, delightful holiday characters, a gallery of decorative cakes, trimmed ornaments and lots more! Make baking and decorating a family affair with these glorious designs that range from the whimsical to the magnificent...or surprise them all with your own special treat. Soft cover; 80 full color pages; 8½ x 11 in.
902-V-1225 $6.99 each

Video Library

These videos make it easy to learn on your own, right at home! Collect them all and soon you'll be showing off your cake decorating and candy making skills to family and friends.

CAKE DECORATING—EASY AS 1-2-3!
Zella Junkin, Director of the Wilton School, takes you through the basics. See how to level and frost a cake perfectly, make simple borders, flowers, leaves and more.
VHS. 901-V-115 $19.99 each

HOW TO MAKE ICING FLOWERS.
Learn how to make roses, Easter lilies, violets, pansies, daisies, poinsettias and more! Five lovely cake designs incorporate all the beautiful flowers included in this video.
VHS. 901-T-119 $19.99 each

HOW TO MAKE WEDDING CAKES.
Learn how to design and assemble dramatic types of tier cakes for weddings, showers, anniversaries and other special occasions. Hints for transporting and serving are also included.
VHS. 901-T-128 $19.99 each

CANDY MAKING-EASY AS 1, 2, 3!
Learn how to make truffles, candy novelties, dipped fruit, molded and filled candy. Melting candy in the microwave included.
VHS. 901-V-125 $19.99 each

Video Home Study Course

LESSON 1
Learn the fundamentals of baking and frosting shaped cakes, about icings, how to use decorating tools and more! Learn how to decorate 2 fun, shaped cakes.
Includes Lesson I 30-minute VHS video, Lesson Plan/Guide, Huggable Bear shaped pan, 10" Soft Touch decorating bag, 3 disposable decorating bags, 4 metal decorating tips, 2 quick-change couplers, practice board with practice sheets, 2 jars of icing color, heavy duty cake board, Trim 'N Turn cake stand, 1990 Wilton Yearbook of Cake Decorating.

LESSON 2
Learn how to torte, how to ice a cake smooth, how to make shells, drop flowers, leaves, figure pipe. Learn how to decorate 2 cakes and a clown cupcake, using figure piping and drop flowers.
Includes
Lesson II 30-minute VHS video, Lesson Plan/Guide, 9" Round Pan Set, 3 metal decorating tips, large angled spatula, 2 jars of icing color, 3 disposable decorating bags, 30 parchment sheets, 2 cake circles, Clown Heads cake tops.

Lesson 3
Learn how to make the rose and other icing flowers, how to make bows, and how to position flower sprays on cakes. Learn how to decorate 2 heart-shaped cakes with basket-weave and flowers.
Includes
Lesson III 30-minute VHS video, Lesson Plan/Guide, 9" Happiness Heart Pan Set, 3 metal decorating tips, #7 flower nail, 2 jars icing color, a container of meringue powder, 2 cake circles, a decorating comb and a Certificate of Completion.

IT'S FUN AND EASY... in just three enjoyable video lessons, you'll learn the basic skills of cake decorating. Then you'll see how great it is to delight family and friends with a decorated cake you made yourself. You get the video tapes and all the pans and tools you need to help you create six wonderful, decorated cakes for birthdays, holidays and any occasion you want to make special.

IT'S CONVENIENT... see actual decorating techniques demonstrated right in your own home. Learn, step-by-step, how to create these wonderful icing techniques yourself...then practice them on your practice board right in front of your TV. Start with the basics and build up to a beautiful rose. You'll love all the decorating fun and the ease of learning it with this great new video.

IT'S A TREAT... learn from the experts. Now you can learn all the secrets of experienced cake decorators. See and hear all the hints and tips that make decorating easy. You'll be surprised at how much you can learn and accomplish with this new Wilton Video Home Study Cake Decorating Course.

ENROLL IN THE WILTON VIDEO HOME STUDY COURSE NOW. The cost is only **$29.99*** per lesson...and the videos and all the pans and tools you receive are yours to keep. Don't delay! **Return the card on page 128-129** with your first payment of $29.99* to Wilton and we'll send you Lesson I. If you are not completely satisfied, you can return both the video and the materials within 30 days for a full refund or credit.

*plus $3.50 shipping and handling.

Learn how to decorate from the experts! Since 1929, when Dewey McKinley Wilton first opened the Wilton School, students have learned the fundamentals of decorating the Wilton Way. The Wilton Method of Cake Decorating stresses the essentials of decorating –beginning with a thorough understanding of the fundamentals. Students are then encouraged to express themselves creatively.

The Wilton School is approved by the Illinois State Board of Education under the provisions of the Illinois Private Business and Vocational Schools Act. All students receive individual instruction, supervision and guidance by expert instructors/decorators.

World renown, the Wilton School has greatly expanded its curriculum since the Wilton Method was first introduced 60 years ago. Today the basic Master Course is supplemented by courses in foreign methods, Lambeth, chocolate artistry, gum paste, pulled sugar, catering cakes and more. The following is a summary of courses we offer:

MASTER COURSE–2 weeks, 70 hours. Focuses on the fundamentals of cake decorating. Designed for the cake decorating shop owner, baker, caterer, chef or enthusiast.
TUITION: $500

INTRODUCTION TO GUM PASTE COURSE–12 hours –four afternoons during the Master Course. This mini-course teaches the art of making lovely gum paste flowers, bouquets and more.
TUITION: $125

GUM PASTE DOLL COURSE–5 days, 40 hours. Teaches the techniques of molding and modeling gum paste. Emphasis on gum paste dolls made with Wilton People Molds.
TUITION: $300

ADVANCED GUM PASTE/FOREIGN METHODS COURSE–2 weeks, 80 hours. Designed for the more serious decorator. Covers: Nirvana, the English method of cake decorating that uses color flow panels; South African and Australian Methods, which use delicate royal icing wings and are done on rolled fondant-covered cakes; gum paste flowers and arrangements. A demonstration on pulled sugar is also included. Previous decorating experience is required.
TUITION: $500

LAMBETH CONTINENTAL COURSE–2 weeks, 80 hours. Teaches intricate overpiping of borders on royal icing and rolled fondant- covered cakes. All students decorate cakes using a combination of over-piped borders. Previous decorating experience is required.
TUITION: $500

PULLED SUGAR COURSE–9 hours, 3 afternoons during Master Course. Learn how to use pulled sugar to cover a cake, make flowers, candy dishes, ribbons, bows and more
TUITION: $150

CHOCOLATE ARTISTRY WITH ELAINE GONZALEZ–5 days, 30 hours. Well-known chocolatier and author of *Chocolate Artistry* presents an in-depth course devoted exclusively to making and decorating candy. Professional techniques for creating fabulous candies from molded treats to delicious truffles.
TUITION: $300

CAKES FOR CATERING–5 days, 40 hours. Learn how to make and decorate cakes for parties. Class includes a baking workshop, which covers baking demonstrations, icings, and assembling and handling large cakes. Wedding cake making, assembling and transporting also included.
TUITION: $300

The Wilton School is located in Woodridge, Illinois (a suburb of Chicago). Course enrollment is limited. For more information, or to enroll, write to: School Secretary, Wilton School of Cake Decorating and Confectionary Art, 2240 W. 75th St., Woodridge, IL 60517. Or call 312-963-7100 for free brochure and schedule. You may charge your courses on VISA or MasterCard.

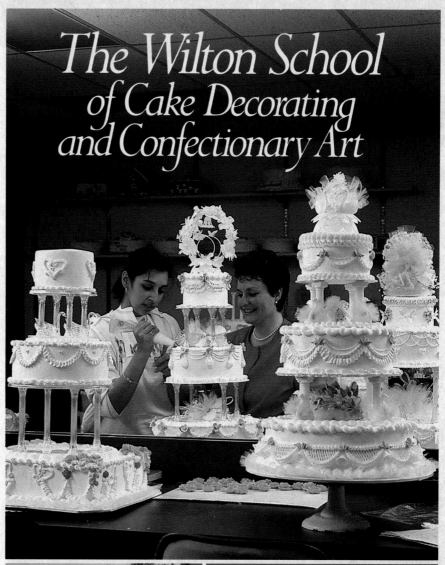

The Wilton School
of Cake Decorating
and Confectionary Art

Home Study Course
Candy Making

In just five easy lessons, you'll learn how to make and mold luscious candies that rival expensive store-bought delights.

You'll soon be impressing family and friends with your delicious homemade sweets and discovering that making candy is a real treat!

Step-by-step instructions, illustrations and photographs will take you from basic melting and molding techniques to advanced cooked candies. Special tools, supplies and ingredients are included.

TRY IT! RETURN COUPON AT RIGHT WITH YOUR PAYMENT AND WE'LL SEND LESSON 1 TO YOU!

LESSON 1

Melt and mold an assortment of candy treats in various shapes, flavors and colors. Make candy clusters and candies with nut centers. Combine creamy caramel, pecans and chocolaty coating to create chewy Caramel Turtles!

Lesson 1 includes:
Notebook Easel and Lesson Pages
3 pkgs. Candy Melts™ brand confectionery coating
3 Plastic Sheet Molds
Disposable Decorating Bags
Lollipop Sticks
Pink Candy Color
Peppermint Candy Flavor
Caramel Filling (16 oz. container).

LESSON 2

Shape and dip creme center candies! Learn to use Wilton Creme Center Mix to make vanilla, peppermint and peanut butter creme centers. It's easy to mold and dip these candies! Covered cherries are another tasty treat you'll learn to make.

Lesson 2 includes:
Lesson Pages
4 pkgs. Candy Melts™ brand confectionery coating
2 Plastic Sheet Molds
Panda 3-D Stand-Up Mold
Two Pkgs. Creme Center Mix
Disposable Decorating Bags
Plastic Dipping Spoon
Decorator's Brush
Candy Box, Liner, Label and Paper Candy Cups.

LESSON 3

Learn to turn plain candies into extraordinary treats by decorating with melted coating. Learn to make molded, layered and piped truffle candies—so very creamy and rich! Try your hand at making ice cream candies to thrill a sweet tooth!

Lesson 3 includes:
Lesson Pages
5 pkgs. Candy Melts™ brand confectionery coating
Heart Box 3-D Mold
Plastic Coupler and Decorating Tips
Disposable Decorating Bags
Green and Yellow Candy Colors
Lollipop Sticks
Lemon Candy Flavor
Foil Candy Cups.

LESSON 4

Mix and fix the most delicious candies! Mold candy cups to fill with liqueur or brandy. Learn how to make two cooked candies—light-as-air divinities and chewy nougats. Learn to shape an edible rose from special modeling candy recipe.

Lesson 4 includes:
Lesson Pages
3 pkgs. Candy Melts™ brand confectionery coating
Cordial Cup Plastic Sheet Mold
Candy Box and Liner
Professional Quality Candy Thermometer.

LESSON 5

Make some super, sensational sweets! Learn how to make chewy jellied candies and shimmering hard candies in hard candy molds. Make delicate mints and petit fours with their smooth and creamy fondant-like icing.

Lesson 5 includes:
Lesson Pages
1 pkg. Candy Melts™ brand confectionery coating
2 Hard Candy Molds
Nylon Candy Funnel
Candy Wafer & Fondant Mix
Disposable Decorating Bags
Lollipop Sticks

Home Study Course: Candy Making

$19.99 Per Lesson* Learn to make candy the fun Wilton way! Order Lesson 1 today! Just fill in and mail this card.

☐ Yes! Send me Lesson One of the Wilton Home Study Course of Candy Making for only $19.99 plus $3.50 for shipping and handling. I understand that if I'm not completely satisfied, I can return both the instruction manual and materials within 30 days for a full refund or credit. I understand that the other four lessons will be sent to me—one each month through Lesson 5—for the same low price of $19.99 plus $3.50 for shipping and handling. Any lesson can be returned within 30 days for a full refund or credit if I'm not completely satisfied.

Enclosed is a check or money order payable to Wilton Home Study Course or charge my Visa or Master Card account:

☐ Visa
Master Card
(Circle one)

_____ (card number)

_____ (Exp. date)

Name _____
(Please print)

Address _____

City _____ State _____ Zip _____

_____ (Signature)

Home Phone (_____) _____
area code

*Plus shipping & handling.

Dept. No. CH

VIDEO Home Study Course: Cake Decorating

$29.99 Per Lesson* ☐ Yes! Send me Lesson One of the Wilton Video Home Study Course of Cake Decorating for only $29.99 plus $3.50 for shipping and handling. I understand that if I'm not completely satisfied, I can return the video, instruction manual and materials within 30 days for a full refund or credit. I understand that the other two lessons will be sent to me—one each month through Lesson 3—for the same low price of $29.99 plus $3.50 for shipping and handling. Any lesson can be returned within 30 days for a full refund or credit if I'm not completely satisfied.

Enclosed is a check or money order payable to Wilton Home Study Course or charge my Visa or Master Card account:

☐ Visa
Master Card
(Circle one)

_____ (card number)

_____ (Exp. date)

Name _____
(Please print)

Address _____

City _____ State _____ Zip _____

_____ (Signature)

Home Phone (_____) _____
area code

*Plus shipping & handling.

Dept. No. CI

Attend Wilton Method Cake Decorating Classes

Convenient Wilton Method of Cake Decorating Classes are now being held in area department and craft stores and cake decorating specialty shops close to your home. You'll learn exciting basic decorating techniques in 4 easy lessons.* For a complete list of the classes nearest you, send us this coupon right away or call toll free 1-800-323-1717, Operator 440. (In Illinois, call 1-800-942-8881, Operator 440.)

. . . near your home. free information. Send or call:

Name _____
(Please Print)

Address _____

City _____ State _____ Zip _____

Daytime Phone No. (_____) _____
area code

Dept No. CJ

*Four 2 hour lessons include course book and personalized instruction. Class program available in continental United States only.

Home Study Course: Cake Decorating

$17.99 Per Lesson* Learn cake decorating the easy Wilton way! Order Lesson 1 today! Just fill in and mail this card.

☐ Yes! Send me Lesson One of the Wilton Home Study Course of Cake Decorating for only $17.99 plus $3.50 for shipping and handling. I understand that if I'm not completely satisfied, I can return both the instruction manual and materials within 30 days for a full refund or credit. I understand that the other four lessons will be sent to me—one each month through Lesson 5—for the same low price of $17.99 plus $3.50 for shipping and handling. Any lesson can be returned within 30 days for a full refund or credit if I'm not completely satisfied.

Enclosed is a check or money order payable to Wilton Home Study Course or charge my Visa or Master Card account:

☐ Visa
Master Card
(Circle one)

_____ (card number)

_____ (Exp. date)

Name _____
(Please print)

Address _____

City _____ State _____ Zip _____

_____ (Signature)

Home Phone (_____) _____
area code

*Plus shipping & handling.

Dept. No. CG

RETURN ADDRESS

Enclose in envelope provided on Order Form or call (312) 963-7100

Enclose in envelope provided on Order Form or call (312) 963-7100

Enclose in envelope provided on Order Form or call (312) 963-7100

Enclose in envelope provided on Order Form or call (312) 963-7100

BUSINESS REPLY MAIL

FIRST-CLASS MAIL   PERMIT NO. 305   DOWNERS GROVE, IL

POSTAGE WILL BE PAID BY ADDRESSEE

Wilton Enterprises, Inc.
2240 W. 75th Street
Woodridge, IL 60517

Attention: Retail CS, MS #9C

NO POSTAGE
NECESSARY
IF MAILED
IN THE
UNITED STATES

Home Study Course
Cake Decorating

Even if you've never tried cake decorating before, the Wilton Home Study Course will show you how to decorate beautiful cakes for every occasion. Easy-to-follow 5-lesson course includes the specialty tools you need plus the step-by-step instructions, illustrations and photographs that make it easy!

TRY IT! RETURN COUPON AT LEFT WITH YOUR PAYMENT AND WE'LL SEND LESSON 1 TO YOU!

LESSON 1
Discover the easy way to pipe buttercream icing stars, zigzag borders and more! Learn how to prepare and color icing for your decorating bag, the correct angle to use, and how to control the pressure for expert results. Make a ''Happy Birthday'' cake.

Lesson 1 includes:
Notebook Easel and Lesson Pages
Decorating Tips 4, 16 and 18
Quick-Change Plastic Coupler
Two Jars of Paste Icing Color
Shaped ''Happy Birthday'' Cake Pan
12″ Featherweight Decorating Bag
Pattern Sheets and Practice Board
Cardboard Cake Circle.

LESSON 2
Make royal icing drop flowers, star flowers and leaves. Mold a sugar basket. Create a blooming basket cake. Learn how to achieve special effects with color and floral sprays plus how to print or write personalized messages!

Lesson 2 includes:
Lesson Pages
Flower Basket Sugar Mold
Stainless Steel Angled Spatula
Decorating Tips 3, 20, 67 and 131
Two Jars of Paste Icing Color
Meringue Powder (4 oz. canister)
Pack of 50 Parchment Paper Triangles
Cardboard Cake Circle
Six Pattern Sheets

LESSON 3
Learn the proper techniques for making shells, rosebuds, sweet peas, ruffles, bows and more! Learn to make bouquets on a heart-shaped cake ideal for anniversaries, birthdays, Valentine's Day, weddings, showers.

Lesson 3 includes:
Lesson Pages
Two 9″ Heart-Shaped Aluminum Pans
Decorating Tips 22, 103 and 104
12″ Featherweight Decorating Bag
Quick-Change Plastic Coupler
Cardboard Cake Circle
Jar of Paste Icing Color.
Four Pattern Sheets

LESSON 4
Pipe daisies and chrysanthemums using a flower nail. Weave basketweave stripes. Create symmetrical cake designs, pipe rope borders and more. Use your new cake turntable to decorate a round cake.

Lesson 4 includes:
Lesson Pages
Trim 'N Turn Cake Stand
Decorating Tips 48 and 81
Cardboard Cake Circle
Flower Nails 7 and 9
Jar of Paste Icing Color
Wilton Cake Marker.
Six Pattern Sheets

LESSON 5
Shape a magnificent icing rose! Pipe stringwork and create a mini-tiered cake using the pans and separator set we'll send. After this lesson you'll qualify for your Wilton Certificate of Completion!

Lesson 5 includes:
Lesson Pages
Round Mini-Tier Kit (includes 3 cake pans, separator plates and columns)
Decorating Tips 2, 12, 87 and 102
Cardboard Cake Circle.
Four Pattern Sheets

Gum Paste

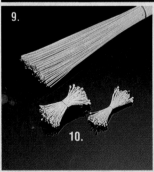

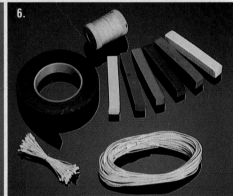

1. GUM PASTE FLOWERS KIT
Make lifelike, beautiful gum paste flowers. Create bouquets or single blooms for cakes, centerpieces, favors and more. Full color how-to book contains lots of ideas and step-by-step instructions. Kit includes 24 plastic cutters, 1 leaf mold, 3 wooden modeling tools and 2 squares of foam for modeling. 30-pc. kit.
1907-V-117 $14.99 kit

2. WILTON PEOPLE MOLDS
Create an entire gum paste family. Use as table or cake decorations, or as centerpieces. Includes 4 (man, woman, two children) 3-part molds and instruction book.
1906-V-5154 $16.99 set

3. GUM PASTE MIX
Easy to use! Just add water and knead. Results in a workable, pliable dough-like mixture to mold into beautiful flowers and figures. 1 lb. can.
707-V-124 $4.99 each

4. GLUCOSE
Essential ingredient for making gum paste. 24 oz. plastic jar.
707-V-109 $4.29 each

5. GUM-TEX™ KARAYA
Makes gum paste pliable, elastic, easy to shape. 6 oz. can.
707-V-117 $6.49 each

6. GUM PASTE ACCESSORY KIT
Includes 90' green florist tape, 30' fine florist wire, 20 pieces medium florist wire (18 in. long), 12-pc. chalk set and 144 yellow stamens.
1907-V-227 $10.99 kit

7. FLOWER FORMERS
Plastic stands used to dry icing leaves and flowers in a convex or concave shape. Set of nine (11 in. long) in three widths: 1½, 2, 2½ in.
417-V-9500 $5.99 set

8. TREE FORMERS
Use to make icing pine trees and to dry royal icing or gum paste decorations. Set of four, 6½ in. high.
417-V-1150 $1.99 set

9. FLORIST WIRE
Medium weight for a multitude of projects. 175 white wires (18 in. long) per pack.
409-V-622 $8.99 pack

10. STAMENS
Make flowers more realistic. 144 per pack.
PEARL WHITE
1005-V-102 $1.49 pack
YELLOW
1005-V-7875 $1.49 pack

11. MARZIPAN LEAVES
Adds a touch of realism to marzipan flowers. 100 pieces (4 designs) per pack.
1005-V-1000 $5.99 pack

12. EDIBLE GLITTER
Sprinkles sparkle on scores of things. ¼ oz. plastic jar.
WHITE
703-V-1204 $2.29 each

13. BAROQUE GUM PASTE MOLDS
Create lovely gum paste trims. Includes 12 classic super-flex molds, full-color idea/instruction booklet , plastic storage box.
1906-V-1299 $10.99 set

Icings and Flavorings

1. MERINGUE POWDER MIX
For royal icing, meringue, boiled icing.
8 oz. CAN. **702-V-6015** **$6.99 each**
4 oz. CAN. **702-V-6007** **$4.49 each**

2. CREAMY WHITE ICING MIX
Convenient mix that provides rich, homemade taste. Just add butter and milk. Ideal for frosting as well as decorating. Yields 2 cups.
710-V-112 **$1.99 each**

3. READY-TO-USE DECORATOR'S ICING
Perfect for decorating and frosting. Use for borders, flowers, writing, etc. Just stir and use! Delicious homemade taste! 16 oz.
710-V-117 **$1.99 each**

4. PIPING GEL
Clear gel. Can be tinted with paste color. Use for glazing, writing, more. 10 oz.
704-V-105 **$3.29 each**

5. COLOR FLOW MIX
Add water and confectioners sugar for smooth icing for color flow designs. 4 oz. can yields about ten 1½ cup batches.
701-V-47 **$6.99 each**

6. GLYCERIN
A few drops stirred into dried-out icing color restores consistency. 2 oz.*
708-V-14 **$1.99 each**

7. BUTTER EXTRACT
Gives a rich, buttery taste to icing, cakes, cookies. 2 oz.*
604-V-2040 **$1.69 each**

8. CLEAR VANILLA EXTRACT
Perfect for decorating because it won't change the color of your icing. 2 oz. Great for baking, too!*
604-V-2237 **$1.69 each**

9. ALMOND EXTRACT
Delicious almond flavor for icing, cookies, cakes. 2 oz.*
604-V-2126 **$1.69 each**

10. 10-ICING COLOR KIT
1 oz. jars of icing colors. Violet. Leaf Green, Royal Blue, Brown, Black, Pink, Watermelon, Moss Green, Orange and Lemon Yellow.
601-V-5569 **$12.99 kit**

11. 8-ICING COLOR KIT
½ oz. jars of colors. Christmas Red, Lemon Yellow, Leaf Green, Sky Blue, Brown, Orange, Pink, and Violet.
601-V-5577 **$8.99 kit**

12. WHITE-WHITE ICING COLOR
Just stir into icing to make icing made with butter or margarine white. Perfect for wedding cakes. 2 oz. plastic bottle.
603-V-1236 **$2.99 each**

13. 4-COLOR ICING KIT
(SOFT PASTEL COLORS) ½ oz. jars of paste colors. Petal Pink, Creamy Peach, Willow Green, Cornflower Blue.
601-V-5588 **$3.29 kit**

Color is vital to your decorating. With color you can add realism and vitality to all your character cakes, personalize special events cakes, highlight holiday cakes and add beauty and vibrance to all your cakes.

Wilton Icing Colors are concentrated in a rich, creamy base, are fast-mixing and easy to use, and will not change your icing consistency. Our extensive range of icing colors makes it convenient for you to achieve the colors you need and want.

WILTON ICING COLORS are available in 1 oz. jars at $1.39 each.* A variety of colors is available in convenient kits.

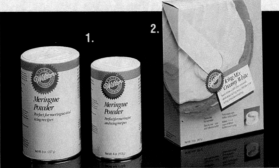

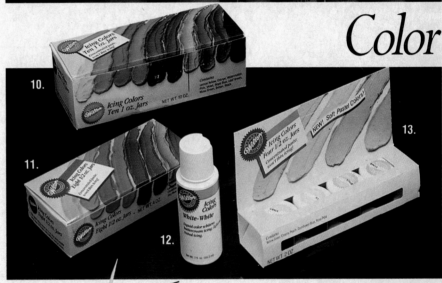

Color

DAFFODIL YELLOW*† 610-V-175	**IVORY** 610-V-208 *NEW!*	**ROSE PETAL PINK** 610-V-410	**WILLOW GREEN** 610-V-855
LEMON YELLOW 610-V-108	**TEAL** 610-V-207 *NEW!*	**CREAMY PEACH** 610-V-210	**CORNFLOWER BLUE** 610-V-710
GOLDEN YELLOW 610-V-159	**PINK** 610-V-256	**TERRA COTTA** 610-V-206 *NEW!*	**VIOLET** 610-V-604	**KELLY GREEN** 610-V-752
ORANGE 610-V-205	**CHRISTMAS RED** 610-V-302	**ROSE** 610-V-401	**BURGUNDY*** 610-V-698	**LEAF GREEN** 610-V-809
RED-RED* 610-V-906	**COPPER** 610-V-450	**ROYAL BLUE** 610-V-655	**MOSS GREEN** 610-V-851
RED* (no taste) 610-V-998	**BROWN**** 610-V-507	**SKY BLUE** 610-V-700	**BLACK**** 610-V-981

*Except Red-Red, Red (no taste) Daffodil Yellow, Burgundy, $1.99
**Brown & Black, $1.59. All Icing Colors are Certified Kosher
†Daffodil Yellow is an all-natural color. It does not contain Yellow #5. The color remains very pale.

*Certified Kosher

131

Decorating Tips Guide

Tip Openings and Techniques shown are actual size.

ROUND—outline, lettering, dots, balls, beads, stringwork, lattice, lacework.

Tip Opening   Techniques

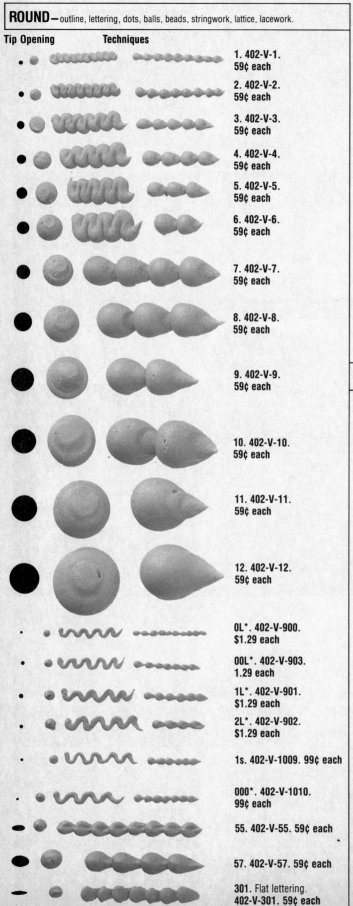

1. 402-V-1. 59¢ each

2. 402-V-2. 59¢ each

3. 402-V-3. 59¢ each

4. 402-V-4. 59¢ each

5. 402-V-5. 59¢ each

6. 402-V-6. 59¢ each

7. 402-V-7. 59¢ each

8. 402-V-8. 59¢ each

9. 402-V-9. 59¢ each

10. 402-V-10. 59¢ each

11. 402-V-11. 59¢ each

12. 402-V-12. 59¢ each

OL*. 402-V-900. $1.29 each

OOL*. 402-V-903. 1.29 each

1L*. 402-V-901. $1.29 each

2L*. 402-V-902. $1.29 each

1s. 402-V-1009. 99¢ each

000*. 402-V-1010. 99¢ each

55. 402-V-55. 59¢ each

57. 402-V-57. 59¢ each

301. Flat lettering. 402-V-301. 59¢ each

Tip Opening   Techniques

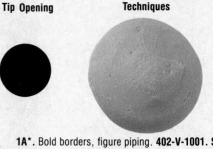

1A*. Bold borders, figure piping. 402-V-1001. $1.29 each

2A*. Smaller version of 1A. 402-V-2001. $1.09 each

230. For filling bismarcks & eclairs. 402-V-230. $1.89 each

MULTI-OPENING—rows and clusters of strings, beads, stars, scallops.

Tip Opening   Techniques

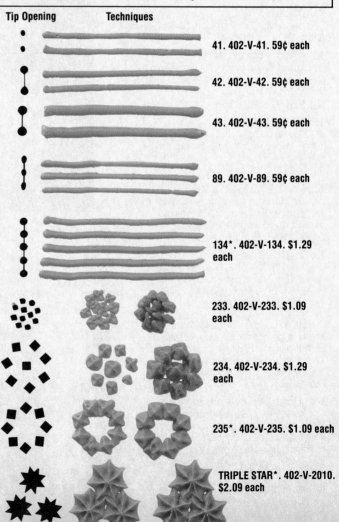

41. 402-V-41. 59¢ each

42. 402-V-42. 59¢ each

43. 402-V-43. 59¢ each

89. 402-V-89. 59¢ each

134*. 402-V-134. $1.29 each

233. 402-V-233. $1.09 each

234. 402-V-234. $1.29 each

235*. 402-V-235. $1.09 each

TRIPLE STAR*. 402-V-2010. $2.09 each

132

*Use with parchment bags only.

Tip Opening	Techniques		
★			13. 402-V-13. 59¢ each
★			14. 402-V-14. 59¢ each
★			15. 402-V-15. 59¢ each
✶			16. 402-V-16. 59¢ each
✸			17. 402-V-17. 59¢ each
✶			18. 402-V-18. 59¢ each
✶			19. 402-V-19. 59¢ each
✶			20. 402-V-20. 59¢ each
✶			21. 402-V-21. 59¢ each
✶			22. 402-V-22. 59¢ each
✶			32. 402-V-32. 59¢ each

Tip Opening	Techniques		
●			199. 402-V-199. $1.09 each
●			172*. 402-V-172. $1.09 each
●			362. 402-V-362. $1.09 each
●			363. 402-V-363. $1.09 each
●			364. 402-V-364. $1.09 each
★			2110. 402-V-2110. $1.09 each
✸			4B*. 402-V-4400. $1.09 each
✸			6B*. 402-V-6600. $1.09 each
✸			8B*. 402-V-8800. $1.29 each

Not shown: Deep-Cut Stellar Star Set. Includes tips 501, 502, 504, 506, 508.
401-V-502. $3.59 set
*Fits large coupler only.

133

CLOSED STAR—Create deeply grooved shells, stars and fleurs-de-lis.

LEAF

Tip Opening	Techniques	
✳		23. 402-V-23. 59¢ each
✳		24. 402-V-24. 59¢ each
✳		25. 402-V-25. 59¢ each
✳		26. 402-V-26. 59¢ each
✳		27. 402-V-27. 59¢ each
✳		28. 402-V-28. 59¢ each
✳		29. 402-V-29. 59¢ each
✳		30. 402-V-30. 59¢ each
✳		31. 402-V-31. 59¢ each
✳		33. 402-V-33. 59¢ each
✳		34. 402-V-34. 59¢ each
✳		35. 402-V-35. 59¢ each
✳		132. 402-V-132. 59¢ each
✳		133. 402-V-133. 59¢ each

Tip Opening	Techniques	
+		49. 402-V-49. 59¢ each
+		50. 402-V-50. 59¢ each
+		51. 402-V-51. 59¢ each
+		52. 402-V-52. 59¢ each
+		53. 402-V-53. 59¢ each
+		54. 402-V-54. 59¢ each

LEAF—so realistic! Ideal for shell-motion borders, too.

65S. 402-V-659. 99¢ each   65. 402-V-65. 59¢ each   66. 402-V-66. 59¢ each

67. 402-V-67. 59¢ each   68. 402-V-68. 59¢ each   69. 402-V-69. 59¢ each

70. 402-V-70. 59¢ each   71. 402-V-71. 59¢ each

72. 402-V-72. 59¢ each   73. 402-V-73. 59¢ each   74. 402-V-74. 59¢ each

75. 402-V-75. 59¢ each   76. 402-V-76. 59¢ each   349/352s. 402-V-349. 99¢ each

352. 402-V-352. 99¢ each   326. 402-V-326. 99¢ each   355. 402-V-355. 99¢ each

112*. 402-V-112. $1.09 each   113*. 402-V-113. $1.09 each

114*. 402-V-114. $1.09 each   115*. 402-V-115. $1.09 each

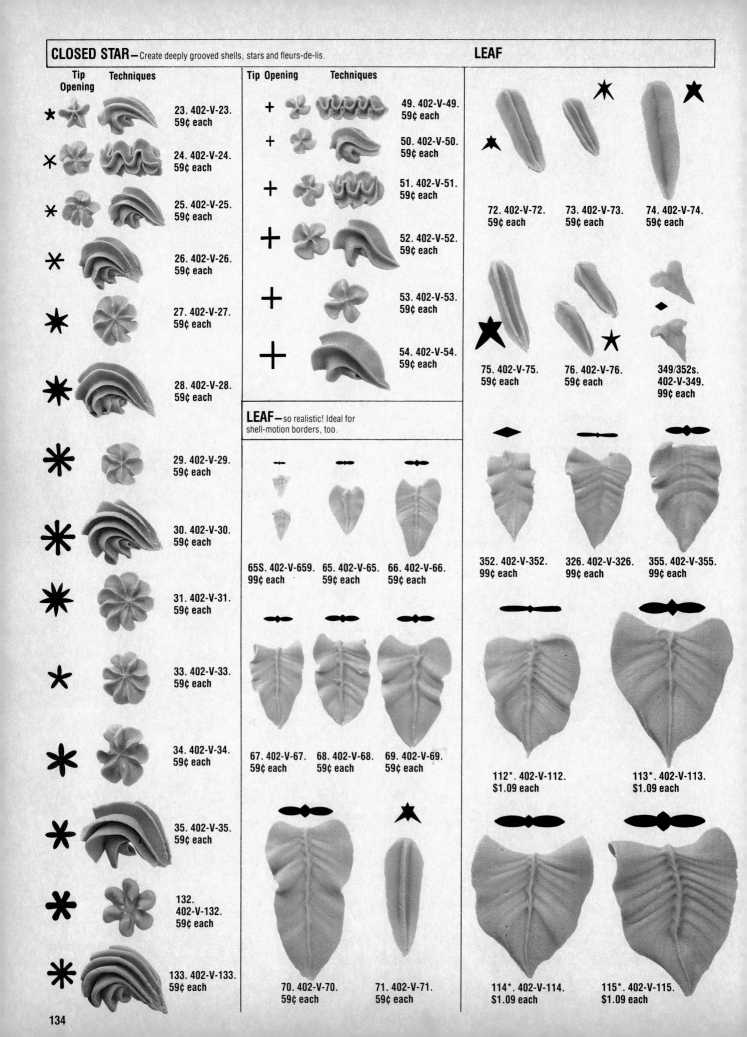

DROP FLOWER — small (106-225); medium (131-194); large (2C-1G) great for cookie dough, too.

Tip Opening   **Techniques**

106. 402-V-106. $1.09 each

107. 402-V-107. $1.09 each

108**. 402-V-108. $1.09 each

109**. 402-V-109. $1.29 each

129. 402-V-129. $1.09 each

217. 402-V-217. $1.09 each

220. 402-V-220. $1.09 each

224. 402-V-224. $1.09 each

225. 402-V-225. $1.09 each

131. 402-V-131. $1.09 each

177. 402-V-177. $1.09 each

Tip Opening

190**. 402-V-190. $1.29 each

191. 402-V-191. $1.09 each

193. 402-V-193. $1.09 each

194**. 402-V-194. $1.29 each

135**. 402-V-135. $1.29 each

140. 402-V-140. $1.29 each

195**. 402-V-195. $1.09 each

2C*. 402-V-2003. $1.09 each

2D*. 402-V-2004. $1.09 each

Tip Opening

2E*. 402-V-2005. $1.09 each

2F*. 402-V-2006. $1.09 each

1B*. 402-V-1002. $1.29 each

1C. 402-V-1003. $1.29 each

1E*. 402-V-1005. $1.29 each

1F*. 402-V-1006. $1.29 each

1G*. 402-V-1007. $1.29 each

* Fits large coupler only.
** use parchment bag only.

135

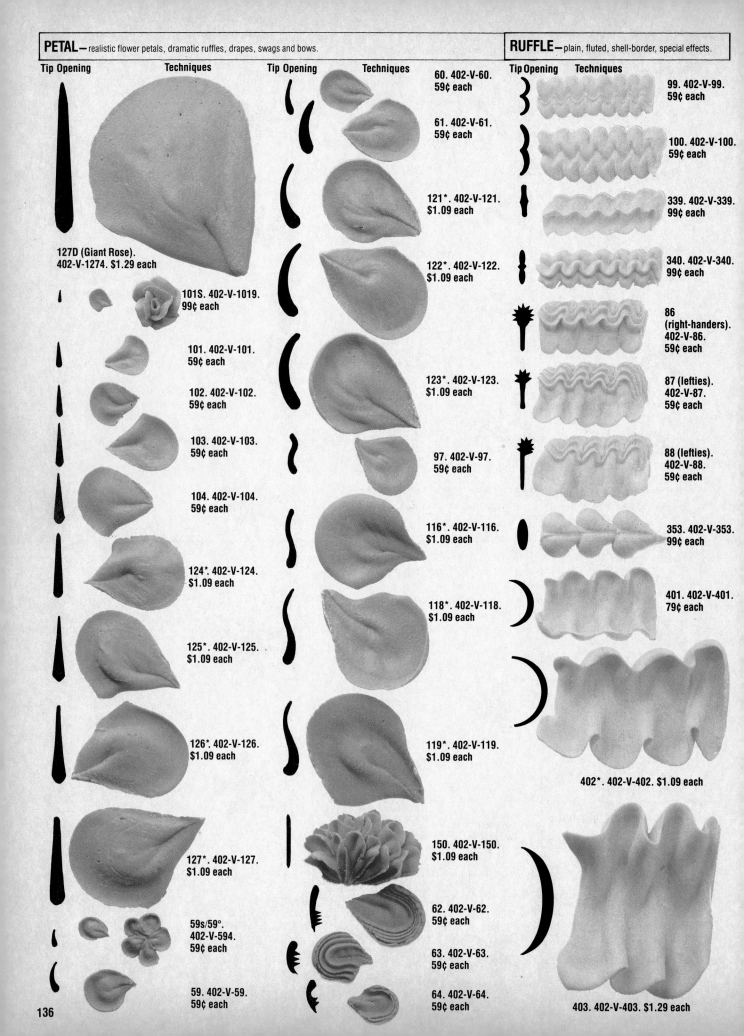

PETAL—realistic flower petals, dramatic ruffles, drapes, swags and bows.

Tip Opening   Techniques

127D (Giant Rose).
402-V-1274. $1.29 each

101S. 402-V-1019.
99¢ each

101. 402-V-101.
59¢ each

102. 402-V-102.
59¢ each

103. 402-V-103.
59¢ each

104. 402-V-104.
59¢ each

124*. 402-V-124.
$1.09 each

125*. 402-V-125.
$1.09 each

126*. 402-V-126.
$1.09 each

127*. 402-V-127.
$1.09 each

59s/59°.
402-V-594.
59¢ each

59. 402-V-59.
59¢ each

Tip Opening   Techniques

60. 402-V-60.
59¢ each

61. 402-V-61.
59¢ each

121*. 402-V-121.
$1.09 each

122*. 402-V-122.
$1.09 each

123*. 402-V-123.
$1.09 each

97. 402-V-97.
59¢ each

116*. 402-V-116.
$1.09 each

118*. 402-V-118.
$1.09 each

119*. 402-V-119.
$1.09 each

150. 402-V-150.
$1.09 each

62. 402-V-62.
59¢ each

63. 402-V-63.
59¢ each

64. 402-V-64.
59¢ each

RUFFLE—plain, fluted, shell-border, special effects.

Tip Opening   Techniques

99. 402-V-99.
59¢ each

100. 402-V-100.
59¢ each

339. 402-V-339.
99¢ each

340. 402-V-340.
99¢ each

86
(right-handers).
402-V-86.
59¢ each

87 (lefties).
402-V-87.
59¢ each

88 (lefties).
402-V-88.
59¢ each

353. 402-V-353.
99¢ each

401. 402-V-401.
79¢ each

402*. 402-V-402. $1.09 each

403. 402-V-403. $1.29 each

BASKETWEAVE — 44, 45 make smooth stripes; rest of basketweave tips make both smooth and ribbed stripes.

Tip Opening	Techniques

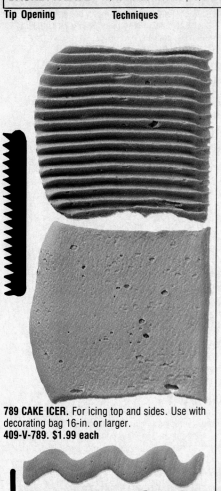

789 CAKE ICER. For icing top and sides. Use with decorating bag 16-in. or larger.
409-V-789. $1.99 each

44. 402-V-44. 59¢ each

45. 402-V-45. 59¢ each

46. 402-V-46. 59¢ each

47. 402-V-47. 59¢ each

Tip Opening	Techniques

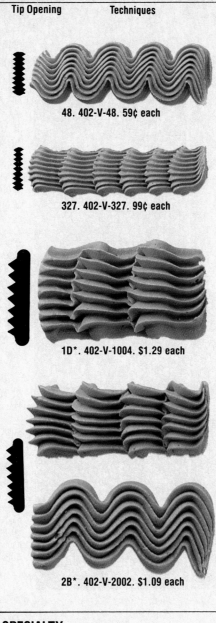

48. 402-V-48. 59¢ each

327. 402-V-327. 99¢ each

1D*. 402-V-1004. $1.29 each

2B*. 402-V-2002. $1.09 each

SPECIALTY — shells, ropes, heart, Christmas trees, ring candle holders!

320. 402-V-320. $1.09 each.

347. 402-V-347. $1.09 each.

96. 402-V-96. 59¢ each

98. 402-V-98. 59¢ each

Tip Opening	Techniques

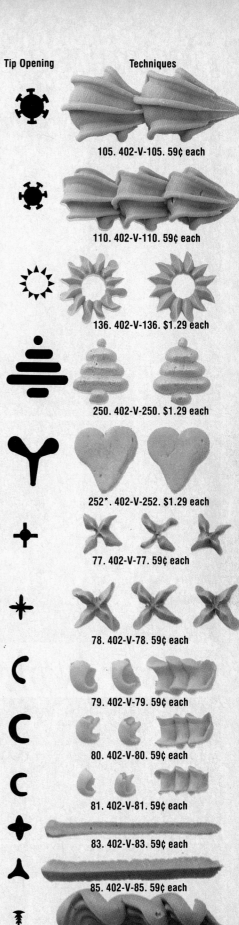

105. 402-V-105. 59¢ each

110. 402-V-110. 59¢ each

136. 402-V-136. $1.29 each

250. 402-V-250. $1.29 each

252*. 402-V-252. $1.29 each

77. 402-V-77. 59¢ each

78. 402-V-78. 59¢ each

79. 402-V-79. 59¢ each

80. 402-V-80. 59¢ each

81. 402-V-81. 59¢ each

83. 402-V-83. 59¢ each

85. 402-V-85. 59¢ each

95. 402-V-95. 59¢ each

*use with large coupler only.

Decorating Sets

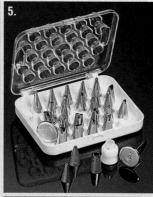

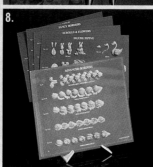

1. STARTER CAKE DECORATING SET
• 4 metal decorating tips • Instruction booklet • Six 12-in. disposable decorating bags. • Two tip couplers • Five liquid color packets.
2104-V-2530 $6.99 set

2. BASIC CAKE DECORATING SET
• 5 professional quality metal tips • Twelve 12-in. disposable bags • Two tip couplers • Flower nail no. 7 • Four ½-oz. icing colors • Instruction booket.
2104-V-2536 $9.99 set

3. DELUXE CAKE DECORATING SET
Contains 36 essentials! • 10 nickel-plated metal tips • Four ½-oz. icing colors • Plastic storage tray • Eighteen 12-in. disposable bags • Two tip couplers • No. 7 flower nail • Cake Decorating, Easy As 1,2,3 book.
2104-V-2540 $18.99 set

4. SUPREME CAKE DECORATING SET
52 tools in all! • 18 metal tips • Two tip couplers • Five ½-oz. icing colors • 8-in. angled spatula. No. 9 flower nail • Twenty-four disposable 12 in. bags • Cake Decorating Easy as 1,2,3 book • Storage tray.
2104-V-2546 $26.99 set

5. DELUXE TIP SET
• 26 decorating tips • 2 flower nails • Tip coupler • Tipsaver plastic box.
2104-V-6666 $18.99 set

6. MASTER TIP SET
• 52 metal tips • Tipsaver box • Two flower nails • Two couplers.
2104-V-7778 $34.99 set

7. TOOL CADDY
You can take it with you and keep it all beautifully organized. (Tools not included.) Holds 38 tips, 10 icing color jars, couplers, spatulas, books and more. Lightweight, stain-resistant molded polyethylene. 16⅝ x 11½ x 3 in.
2104-V-2237 $17.99 each

8. PRACTICE BOARD WITH PATTERNS.
Practice is a must for decorating that gets an A+. Slip practice pattern onto board under wipe-clean vinyl overlay and trace in icing. Includes stand and patterns for flowers, leaves, borders and lettering—31 designs included.
406-V-9464 $6.99 each

Flower Nails

Essential turntables for creating impressive icing flowers such as the rose.

9. FLOWER NAIL NO. 9 1¼ in. diameter.
402-V-3009 59¢ each

10. FLOWER NAIL NO. 7 1½ in. diameter.
402-V-3007 79¢ each

11. 2 IN. FLOWER NAIL
Use with curved and swirled petal tips, 116-123, to make large blooms.
402-V-3002 99¢ each

12. 3 IN. FLOWER NAIL
Has extra large surface, ideal with large petal tips.
402-V-3003 $1.09 each

13. 1-PC. LILY NAIL
1⅝ in. diameter.
402-V-3012 79¢ each

14. LILY NAIL SET
Essential for making cup flowers, such as poinsettias and lilies. To use 2-pc. nails: Place aluminum foil in bottom half of nail and press top half in to form cup. Pipe flower petals. Set includes ½, 1¼, 1⅝, and 2½ in. diam. cups. Sturdy white plastic.
403-V-9444 $1.99 8-pc. set

Bases and Boards

1. NEW! REVOLVING CAKE STAND
Plate rotates smoothly in either direction for easy decorating and serving; 3 in. high with 11 in. diameter plate in molded white plastic.
415-V-900 $9.99 each

2. LAZY DAISY SERVER
Stationary stand. Sturdy white plastic with scalloped edges, 5 in. high with 12 in. plate.
307-V-700 $8.99 each

3. PROFESSIONAL CAKE STAND
Heavy-duty aluminum stand is 4⅝ in. high with 12 in. rotating plate. Super strong; essential for decorating tiered wedding cakes.
307-V-2501 $36.99 each

4. TRIM 'N TURN CAKE STAND
Flute-edged. Plate turns smoothly on hidden ball bearings. Just turn as you decorate. White molded plastic; holds up to 100 lbs. 12 in.
2103-V-2518 $7.99 each

5. SHOW 'N SERVE CAKE BOARDS
Scalloped edge. Protected with grease-resistant coating.
8 IN. 2104-V-1125
$3.99 pack of 10
10 IN. 2104-V-1168
$4.49 pack of 10
12 IN. 2104-V-1176
$4.99 pack of 8
14 IN. 2104-V-1184
$5.49 pack of 6
14 X 20 IN. RECTANGLE
2104-V-1230 $5.99 pack of 6

6. CAKE CIRCLES & BOARD
Sturdy corrugated cardboard.
6 IN. 2104-V-64 $2.19 pack of 10
8 IN. 2104-V-80 $3.29 pack of 12
10 IN. 2104-V-102 $3.99 pack of 12
12 IN. 2104-V-129 $3.99 pack of 8
14 IN. 2104-V-145 $3.99 pack of 6
16 IN. 2104-V-160 $4.99 pack of 6
18 IN. 2104-V-180 $4.99 pack of 6
13 X 19 IN. 2104-V-552 $4.49 pack of 6

7. DOILIES
Grease-resistant, glassine-coated paper doilies are ideal for iced cakes. Round and rectangle shapes have lace borders sized to fit around your decorated cakes. Ideal for serving cookies and canapes, too!
10 IN. ROUND 2104-V-1310
$1.99 pack of 16
12 IN. ROUND 2104-V-1312.
$1.99 pack of 12
14 IN. ROUND 2104-V-1314.
$1.99 pack of 8
10 x 14 IN. RECTANGLE
2104-V-1324 $1.99 pack of 12

8. FANCI-FOIL WRAP
Serving side has a non-toxic grease-resistant surface. FDA approved for use with food. Continuous roll: 20 in X 15 ft. **$6.99 each**
ROSE 804-V-124
GOLD 804-V-183
SILVER 804-V-167
BLUE 804-V-140
WHITE 804-V-191

9. TUK-N-RUFFLE
Attach to serving tray or board with royal icing or tape. Order 60 ft. bolt or by the foot.

Color	Per Foot	
PINK	801-V-708	35¢
BLUE	801-V-200	35¢
WHITE	801-V-1003	35¢
Color	60-Ft. Bolt	
PINK	802-V-702	$13.99
BLUE	802-V-206	$13.99
WHITE	802-V-1008	$13.99

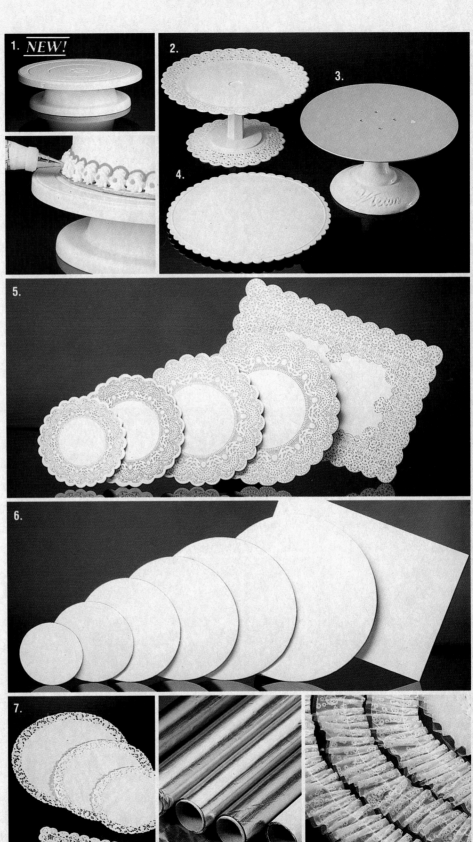

139

Press-on Patterns

Sturdy plastic tools leave easy-to-follow designs on cake tops and sides. Valuable timesavers for busy decorators.

1. 15-PC. DECORATOR PATTERN PRESS SET
Classic designs to use alone or combine together for unique effects. Many can be reversed for symmetrical designs.
2104-V-2172 $4.99 set

2. 9-PC. PATTERN PRESS SET
Fancy florals, classic curves–pretty for any occasion.
2104-V-3101 $4.29 set

3. SCRIPT PATTERN PRESS MESSAGE SET
Lets you put it into words so beautifully. Combine the words Happy, Birthday, Best, Wishes, Anniversary, Congratulations, and make a lasting impression.
2104-V-2061 $2.99 set

4. MESSAGE PATTERN PRESS SET
Makes it easy to imprint your cakes with exactly the right words! Includes the same six words as the Script Set. 2 x 6¾ x¾ in. high.
2104-V-2077 $3.49 set

More Tools

Essential tools for measuring and marking your cakes.

5. DIAL DIVIDER
Just turn dial to mark 6 to 16 in. cakes into exact intervals. Plastic.
409-V-8607 $2.79

6. CAKE DIVIDING SET
Wheel chart marks 2-in. intervals on 6 to 18-in. diameter cakes. Triangle marker for precise spacing for stringwork, garlands, more. Includes instructions.
409-V-800 $8.99

7. DECORATING COMB
Quick way to make ridges in icing. 12-in. long, plastic.
409-V-8259 $1.29 each

8. DECORATING TRIANGLE
Each side adds a different wavy effect to icing. 5 x 5-in. plastic.
409-V-990   99¢

9. DECORATOR'S BRUSHES
Great for smoothing icing, painting candy molds and colorful touches. Set of 3.
2104-V-846 $1.49 set

Stainless Steel & Rosewood Spatulas

Stainless Steel Spatulas with flexible, non-rust blades and durable rosewood handles.

10. 8 IN. TAPERED
409-V-517 $2.59 each

11. 8 IN. SPATULA
409-V-6043 $2.59 each

12. 11 IN. SPATULA
409-V-7694 $4.49 each

13. 8 IN. ANGLED SPATULA
409-V-738 $2.59 each

14. 12 IN. ANGLED SPATULA
409-V-134 $4.99 each

Decorating Bags & Tools

1. FEATHERWEIGHT DECORATING BAGS

Lightweight, strong, flexible polyester bags are easy to handle, soft, workable and never get stiff. Specially coated so grease won't go through. May be boiled. Dishwasher safe. Instructions included.

Size	Stock No.	Each
18 IN.	404-V-5184	$6.99
16 IN.	404-V-5168	$6.49
14 IN.	404-V-5140	$5.49
12 IN.	404-V-5125	$4.29
10 IN.	404-V-5109	$3.29
8 IN.	404-V-5087	$2.19

2. DISPOSABLE DECORATING BAGS

Use and toss—no fuss, no muss. Perfect for melting Candy Melts ™* in the microwave, too. Strong, flexible, and easy-to-handle plastic. 12 in. size fits standard tips and couplers.

2104-V-358 $3.89 pack of 12.
24-COUNT VALUE PACK
2104-V-1358 $6.29 pack of 24

3. PARCHMENT TRIANGLES

Make your own disposable decorating bags with our quality, grease-resistant vegetable parchment paper.

12 in. 2104-V-1206
$3.99 pack of 100
15 in. 2104-V-1508
$4.99 pack of 100

4. TIP SAVER

Reshape bent tips. Molded plastic.
414-V-909 $2.79 each

5. TIP SAVER BOXES

Keep decorating tips clean and organized.
A. 26-TIP CAPACITY
405-V-8773 $4.99 each
B. 52-TIP CAPACITY
405-V-7777 $6.99 each

PLASTIC COUPLERS

Use to change tips without changing bags when using the same color icing.

6. LARGE COUPLER

Fits 14 in. to 18 in. Featherweight Bags. Use with large decorating tips.
411-V-1006 $1.19 each

7. ANGLED COUPLER

Reaches around sharp angles. Fits all bags and standard decorating tips.
411-V-7365   79¢ each

8. STANDARD COUPLER

Fits all decorating bags, standard tips.
411-V-1987   59¢ each

9. TIP COVER

Slip over tip and save or take filled bags of icing along for touch-ups. Plastic.
414-V-915   99¢ pack of 4

10. MAXI TIP BRUSH

Gets out every bit of icing fast and easy.
414-V-1010 $1.59 each

11. TIP BRUSH

Plastic bristles clean tips thoroughly.
414-V-1123 $1.19 each

12. NEW! DESSERT DECORATOR

Easy-to-control lever lets you decorate cakes, pastries, cookies with one hand. Includes 5 easy-to-change decorating nozzles.
415-V-825 $10.99 each

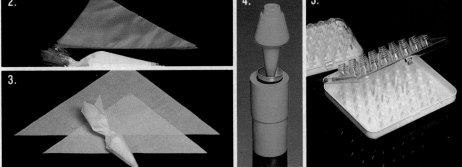
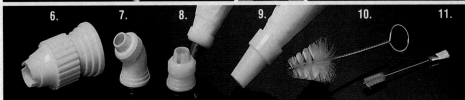

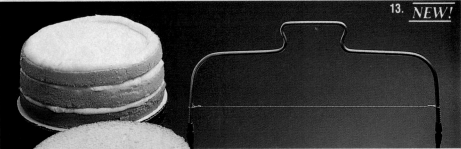

13. NEW! CAKE LEVELER
Levels and tortes cakes up to 10 in. wide and 2 in. high.
415-V-815 $2.99 each

Toppers and Candles

1. PETITE CLOWN CANDLES
6 mini mites clowning around. 1¼ to 2⅞ in.
2811-511 $1.99 set

2. JUGGLER CLOWN
A circus of fun. 4-in. high.
2113-V-2252 $2.09 each

3. COUNTDOWN CLOWN
Face turns from 1 to 6. 4½-in. high.
2113-V-2341 $1.39 each

4. COMICAL CLOWNS
A variety of fun faces. 2-in. to 2½-in.
2113-V-2635 $2.99 set of 4

5. DERBY CLOWNS
A barrel of laughs. On picks. 1¾-in. high.
2113-V-2333 $2.49 pack of 4

6. SMALL DERBY CLOWNS
Miniatures! Great for cupcakes.
2113-V-2759 $1.99 pack of 6

7. CAROUSEL CAKE TOP SET
A fast, easy circus decoration for 10 in. or
larger cakes.
1305-V-9302 $4.99 set

8. CIRCUS BALLOONS
12 in a bunch. 3 bunches per set.
2113-V-2366 $2.49 set

9. CLOWN SEPARATOR SET
Two funny guys balance a 6 in. round cake on top
plate. Perfect to set atop a large base cake (be
sure to dowel rod). They can stand on their hands
or feet. Set includes two 7 in. scalloped-edged
separator plates and two snap-on clown
supports. 4-in. high.
301-V-909 $6.99 each

10. CAROUSEL SEPARATOR SET
Contains: 2 brown and 2 white snap-on pony
pillars, two 10 in. round plates—one clear acrylic,
one plastic. Two 10 in. cardboard circles to
protect plates.
2103-V-1139 $9.99 set.

11. PETITE ANIMAL CANDLES
6 animal menagerie! 1¼-in. to 2⅞-in. high.
2811-V-513 $1.99 set.

12. HONEY BEAR
Hand-painted. 5 in. high.
2113-V-2031 $2.69 each

13. APPALOOSA ROCKING HORSES
Four painted ponies; 2½ in. high.
2113-V-2015 $3.49 set of 4

14. LI'L COWPOKE
Wee buckaroo; 5⅛ in. high.
2113-V-2406 $2.69 each

15. DOLLY DRESS-UP
High style; 4½ in. high.
2113-V-1485 $2.69 each

16. SPACESHIP TOPPER SET
Spacecraft is 3¾ in. high; 4⅛ in. wide
on 1¼ in. platform. 2¼ in. robot and 2⅛ in.
spaceman hold standard candles.
2111-V-2008 $3.69 set

Toppers and Candles

1. SESAME STREET SET.* BIG BIRD, OSCAR THE GROUCH, COOKIE MONSTER, BERT and ERNIE
2-in. to 3¼-in. high.
2113-V-1728 $2.99 set

2. COOKIE MONSTER PICK* 3⅜ in.
2113-V-3813 $1.99 pkg. of 6

3. BIG BIRD PICK* 3⅜ in. high.
2113-V-3815 $1.99 pkg. of 6

4. BIG BIRD WITH AGE*
Age indicator 1-6. 3⁹⁄₁₆ in. high.
2113-V-1430 $2.09

*1982, 1984 Children's Television Workshop BIG BIRD, COOKIE MONSTER, OSCAR THE GROUCH, BERT AND ERNIE © 1982, 1984 Muppets, Inc. All rights reserved.

5. JACK-O-LANTERNS 2-in.
2113-V-3135 $1.69 set of 4

6. HAPPY GHOST 4⅜ in. high.
2113-V-3356 $1.09 each

7. WACKY WITCH 5¼ in. high.
2113-V-6118 $2.09 each

8. WITCH CANDLE 3 in. high.
2811-V-1033 $1.49 each

9. PUMPKIN CANDLE 3 in. high
2811-V-1031 $1.49 each

10. HOLLY WREATH 3½ in.
2113-V-4784 $1.09 each

11. SANTA 'N TREE
Santa 2⅝ in. tall; tree 3⅜ in. high.
2113-V-1647 $1.69 2-pc. set

12. SNOWMAN CANDLE 3 in. high
2811-V-1229 $1.49 each

13. SANTA CANDLE 3 in. high
2811-V-1225 $1.49 each

14. JACK-O-LANTERN PICK
1⅝ in. on 1¾ in. pick.
2113-V-4328 $1.39 pack of 6

15. BLACK CAT PICK
1¼ in. on 1¾ in. pick.
2113-V-4301 $1.39 pack of 6

16. CHRISTMAS TREE PICK
Festive fir. 1⅝ in. on 1¾ in. pick.
2113-V-4344 $1.39 pack of 6

17. SNOWMAN PICK
Favorite roly poly. 1⅝ in. on 1¾ in. pick.
2113-V-4360 $1.39 pack of 6

18. HEART CHARM 3¾ in. wide
2113-V-3518 $1.09 each

19. VALENTINE PICK 1 in. heart on 1 in. pick.
1502-V-1011 $1.39 pack of 12

20. SHAMROCK PICK
1¼ in. shamrock on 1⅞ in. pick.
2113-V-4387 $1.39 pack of 6

21. EASTER BUNNY PICK 2 in. on 1¾ in. pick.
2113-V-4476 $1.39 pack of 6

22. GOOD LUCK KEY PICK
2113-V-3801 $1.39 pack of 6

23. MORTARBOARD & DIPLOMA PICK
2113-V-3803 $1.39 pack of 6

24. SUCCESSFUL GRAD 4½ in. tall.
2113-V-4549 $1.69 each

25. GLOWING GRAD 4½ in. tall.
2113-V-1833 $1.69 each

26. GLAD GRADUATE 4¾ in. tall.
2113-V-1817 $2.09 each

27. NEW! HAPPY GRADUATE 4¾ in. tall
2113-V-1818 $2.09 each

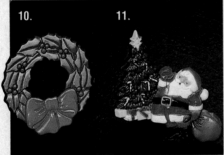

NEW!

Candles and Toppers

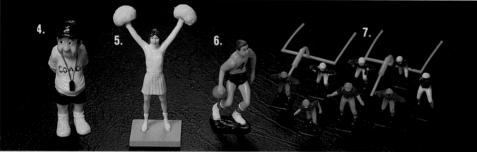

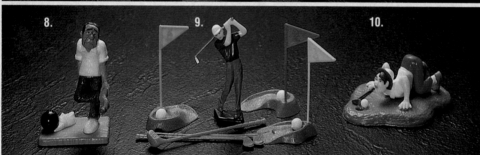

1. SOFTBALL PLAYER
2113-V-3705 $2.99 each

2. BASEBALL SET
Batter, catcher, pitcher and 3 basemen. Hand-painted. Each 2 in. tall.
2113-V-2155 $2.99 set

3. BASEBALL TOPPER SET
2113-V-2473 $2.99 3-pc. set

4. GOOD SPORT COACH
2113-V-4140. $2.69 each

5. CAMPUS CHEERLEADER
2113-V-2708. $1.69 each

6. BASKETBALL PLAYER
2113-V-9354 $1.99 each

7. SUPER BOWL FOOTBALL SET
Eight 2 in. high players and two 4½ in. high goal posts.
2113-V-2236 $2.99 10-pc.set

8. BUMBLING BOWLER
2113-V-2783 $2.69 each

9. GOLF SET*
Includes 4½ in. high golfer plus 3 each: 2½ in. wide greens, 4 in. high flags, 5 in. clubs and golf balls.
1306-V-7274 $2.09 set

10. COMICAL GOLFER
2 in. high, 4¼ in. wide, 5⅛ in. long.
2113-V-2554 $2.09 each

11. FISHY SITUATION
2113-V-2074 $2.69 each

12. END OF DOCK FISHERMAN
Just swirl icing with spatula to resemble water, set on top. 5 in. high.
2113-V-4832 $2.69 each

13. FRUSTRATED FISHERMAN
2113-V-2384 $2.99 each

14. GONE FISHIN' SIGN BOARD
Pipe on icing message. 4½ in. high.
1008-V-726 $1.39 pack of 2

15. SHARP SHOOTER
2113-V-2422 $2.99 each

16. JAUNTY JOGGER
2113-V-2066 $2.69 each

17. ARMCHAIR QUARTERBACK
Man 3⅜-in. high; TV 2¼-in. high.
2113-V-1302 $2.69 set

18. LAZY BONES
2113-V-2414 $2.69 each

19. PARTY GUY
2113-V-3739 $2.69 each

20. BACKYARD GARDENER
2113-V-1973 $2.09 each

21. ALL THUMBS
2113-V-2686 $2.09 each

22. OL' SMOKY
Man 5⅛ in. tall; grill 2⅜ in. high.
2113-V-2694 $2.09 set

23. BIG BOSS
2113-V-3798 $2.69 each

*CAUTION: Contains small parts. Not intended for use by children 3 years and under.

1. BIRTHDAY NUMBERS SET
Numbers 2 in. high. With picks, about 3¼ in. high, 11 numbers in set.
1106-V-7406 $1.39 set.

2. BIRTHDAY CANDLES
24 candles in assorted colors. 2½ in.
2811-V-1248   79¢ each

3. TAPERS
24 long, slender candles for all occasions. 6½ in. high.
2811-V-1188   79¢ each

4. TEEN DOLL PICK
7 in. tall
2815-V-101 $2.99 each

5. FRECKLE-FACED LITTLE GIRL
6½ in. tall.
2113-V-2317 $2.99 each

6. SMALL DOLL PICKS
4½ in. on pick.
1511-V-1019 $4.99 pack of 4

7. TELEPHONE TEENS
Get on the party line for fast cake decorating and lots of smiles. 3 girls, 3 boys. 2 x 2¾ in. high.
1301-V-706 $3.69 6-pc. set

8. COMMUNION ALTAR
Tulle veil on girl. Each, 3 x 2½ in.
BOY 1105-V-7886 $2.09 each
GIRL 1105-V-7878 $2.09 each

9. SHINING CROSS
Detachable pick. 3¾ in. high.
1105-V-7320 $1.09 each

10. SLEEPING ANGELS
2113-V-2325 $1.99 pack of 2

11. NEW! 3 A.M. FEEDING
2113-V-3333 $3.99 each

12. CRYSTAL-CLEAR BOOTIES
Add ribbon laces.
1103-V-9332 $1.69 pack of 2

13. BABY SHOES CAKE PICKS
2113-V-3811 $1.39 pack of 6

14. STORK CAKE PICKS
2113-V-3805 $1.39 pack of 6

15. DAINTY BASSINETTE
Fill with surprises.
2111-V-9381 $1.09 each

16. MAMA STORK
1305-V-6303 $1.69 each

17. MR. STORK
115-V-1502 $6.00 each

18. PETITE LULLABY
115-V-1987 $8.00 each

19. BABY BRACELETS
2111-V-72 $1.69 pack of 4

20. TINY TODDLER
5½-in. high.
BLUE 1103-V-7429 $1.99 each
PINK 1103-V-7437 $1.99 each

21. BABY RATTLES
Great as gift trimmers, too!
2113-V-3283 $1.09 pack of 2

*CAUTION: Contains small parts. Not intended for use by children 3 years and under.

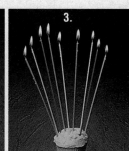

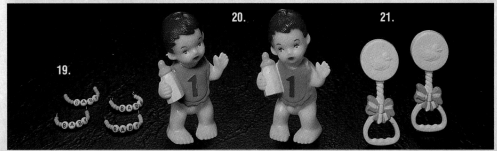
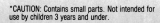

Instant Beauty

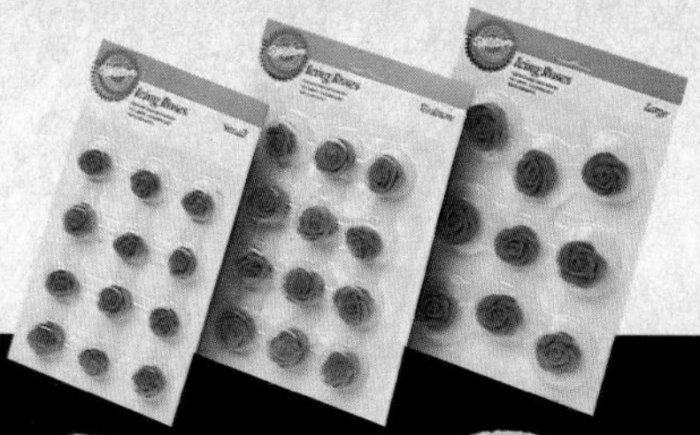

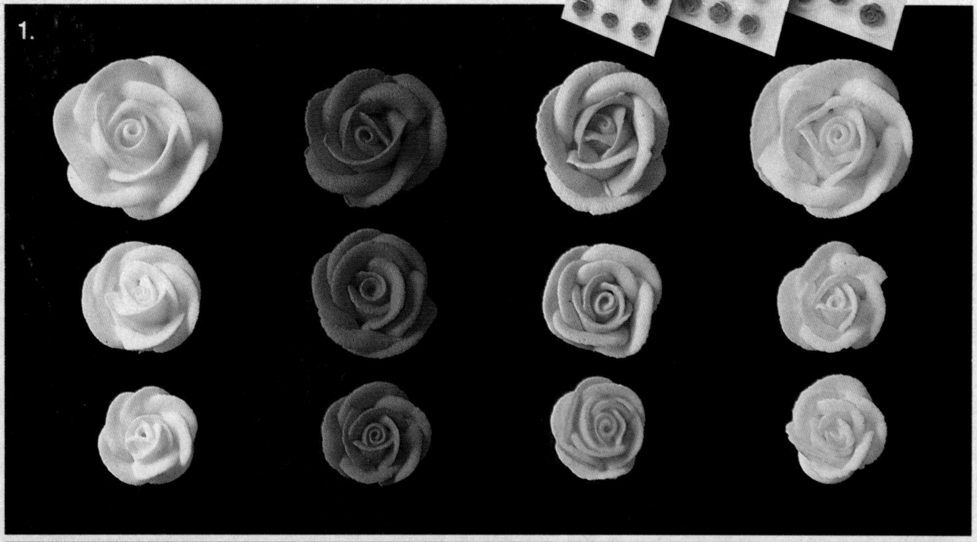

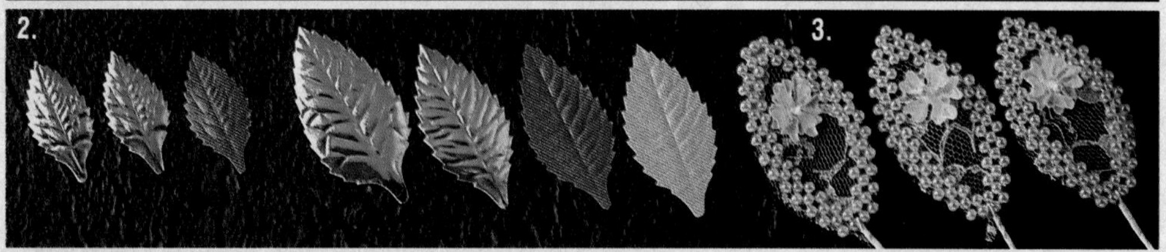

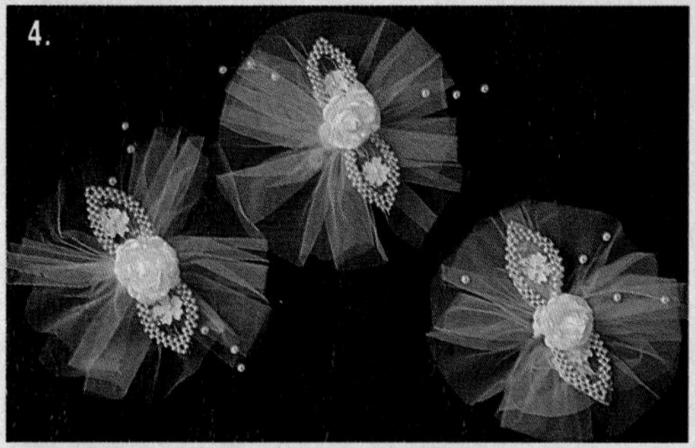

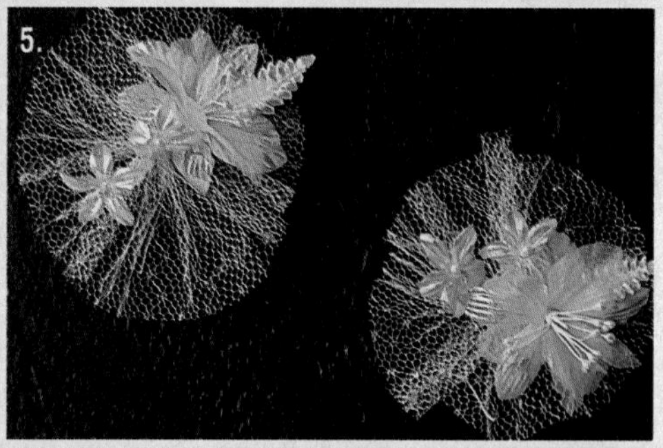

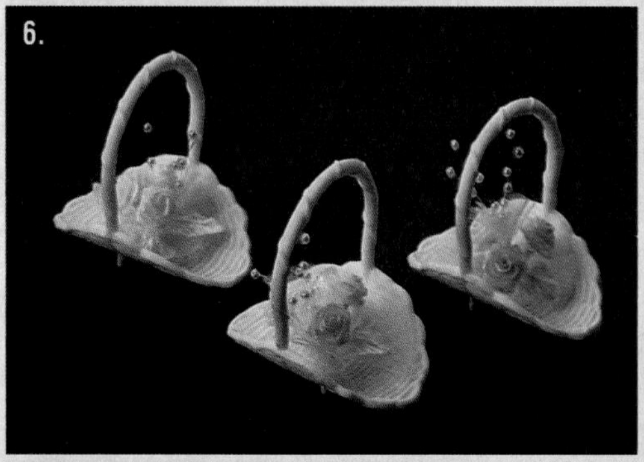

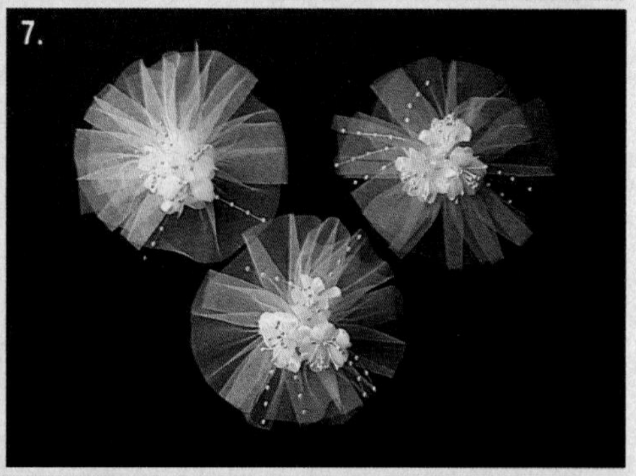

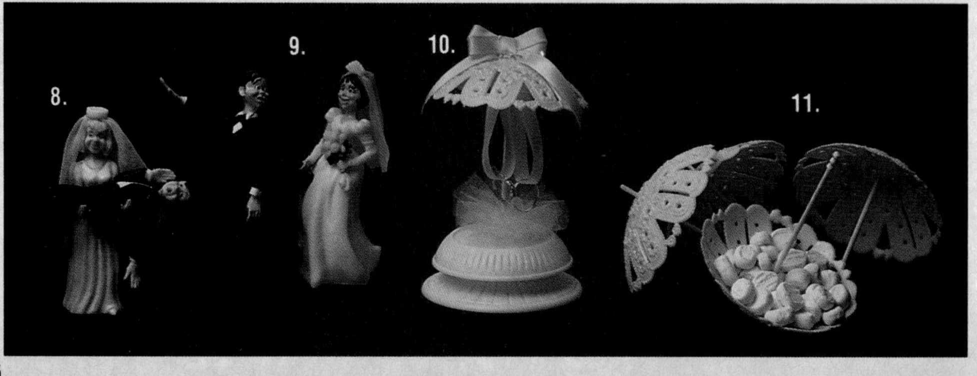

1. READY-TO-USE ICING ROSES
Save decorating time! Stock up on all colors and sizes for your next cake.

Color	Size		Stock No.	Price
WHITE	LARGE	1½ in.	710-V-411	$3.99 for 9
WHITE	MEDIUM	1¼ in.	710-V-311	$3.99 doz.
WHITE	SMALL	1 in.	710-V-211	$2.99 doz.
RED	LARGE	1½ in.	710-V-412	$3.99 for 9
RED	MEDIUM	1¼ in.	710-V-312	$3.99 doz.
RED	SMALL	1 in.	710-V-212	$2.99 doz.
PINK	LARGE	1½ in.	710-V-413	$3.99 for 9
PINK	MEDIUM	1¼ in.	710-V-313	$3.99 doz.
PINK	SMALL	1 in.	710-V-213	$2.99 doz.
YELLOW	LARGE	1½ in.	710-V-414	$3.99 for 9
YELLOW	MEDIUM	1¼ in.	710-V-314	$3.99 doz.
YELLOW	SMALL	1 in.	710-V-214	$2.99 doz.

2. ARTIFICIAL LEAVES
144 leaves per package. Green or white cloth; gold or silver foil. **Order 1005-V-number**

Color		1⅞ in.		1¼ in.
GOLD	6518	$2.59	6712	$2.29 pkg.
SILVER	6526	$2.59	6720	$2.29 pkg.
GREEN	4655	$2.59	4670	$2.29 pkg.
WHITE	6501	$2.59		

3. PEARL LEAVES
Dainty pearls edge appliqued tulle leaves. 2 per pkg.

WHITE	211-V-1201	$2.79 pkg
BLUE	211-V-1203	$2.79 pkg
PINK	211-V-1205	$2.79 pkg

4-6. FLORAL ACCENTS!
Use your imagination! Make your own ornaments, headpieces, party favors, gift accents, more!

4. PEARL LEAF PUFFS–5½″
WHITE 211-V-1125
PINK 211-V-1127
BLUE 211-V-1129
$4.49 each

5. PRETTY BOUTONNIERES–3½″
GOLD 2110-V-3950
SILVER 2110-V-3925
$1.99 each

6. BEAUTY IN A BASKET
Ever-so-dainty hand-crafted satin roses peek from tulle puffs in a lacy basket.
Plastic basket. 3 x 2 x 2-3/4 in.
$1.29 each
WHITE 2110-V-2309
PINK 2110-V-2305
BLUE 2110-V-2307

7. FLORAL PUFF ACCENT–5½″
BLUE 211-V-1015
PINK 211-V-1013
WHITE 211-V-1011
$2.89 each

8. LIBERATED BRIDE
Modern romance! 4½″ in. high.
2113-V-4188 $3.99 each

9. RELUCTANT GROOM COUPLE
1316-V-9520 $4.99 each

10. BRIDAL SHOWER DELIGHT
Umbrella of happiness. 6 in. high.
115-V-201 $8.00 each

11. PARTY PARASOLS
4 in. parasols; 5 in. snap-on handles.
2110-V-9296 $1.69 pack of 4

All items in this beautifully crafted collection of bridal accessories are attractively gift packed. They're perfect shower and engagement gifts.

1. NEW! WEDDING AND ANNIVERSARY CHAMPAGNE GLASSES.

Two elegant styles will highlight that all important wedding or anniversary toast. Sold in sets of 2 glasses. Leaded crystal, saucer style set. Embossed with our exclusive Loving Traditions design. Fancied with lace, satin, ribbon and pearly trim.

BRIDE AND GROOM 120-V-210
Leaded Crystal
$24.00 set

ANNIVERSARY WISHES 120-V-211
Leaded Crystal
$24.00 set

Traditional Sherbet style set enhanced with satin ribbons.

BRIDE AND GROOM 120-V-203
$14.00 set

ANNIVERSARY WISHES 120-V-205
$14.00 set

2. BRIDAL TOASTING AND ANNIVERSARY GLASSES

Leaded crystal glasses etched with our original couple. Pretty tiny flowers and satin ribbon accents. 8-3/8 in. high.

2 PC. BRIDAL SET 120-V-200
$24.00 set

2 PC. ANNIVERSARY SET 120-V-202
$24.00 set

3. CAKE KNIFE & SERVER

Gleaming stainless with elegantly detailed handles. Tenderly touched with sprays of satin ribbons, fabric flowers and pearls.

CAKE KNIFE 120-V-701
$13.50 each

CAKE SERVER 120-V-702
$13.50 each

KNIFE & SERVER SET 120-V-700
$24.00 set

4. WEDDING BELL

Delicate leaded crystal with our lovely etched bridal couple design. Adorned with lace and satin ribbon bow and crystal-look clapper. 6-in. high.

120-V-900 $17.50 each

5. WEDDING ALBUM

Romantic wedding memories will be sentimentally captured forever in this lace-covered satin album. Cover is handmade and beautifully adorned with a satin ribbon tie, fabric flowers and pearl accents. Contains 21 pages to keep a detailed account of everything from engagement, showers, wedding guests, gifts, family trees and much more.

120-V-301 $30.00 each

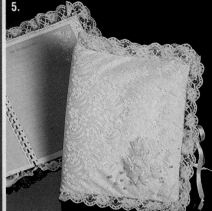

Loving TRADITIONS™

To have and to hold on that special day. Exquisite handmade bridal accessories of satin and lace that reveal or conceal, but the quality shines through. If invited to shower the bride-to-be, here are many thoughtful ways to make her wedding day perfect from beginning to end. Gift-packed.

BRIDE'S GARTER
Frilly and flirty. Satin band is lavished with lace. Prettied with ribbons, faux pearls and shimmery ''gem'' stone.
$5.00 each
WHITE   120-V-401
IVORY   120-V-403
PINK   120-V-400
BLUE   120-V-402
BLACK   120-V-404

BRIDE'S PURSE
An elegant hide-away of satin and lace. Adorned with fabric flowers and pearl accents. Closes with a drawstring cord. Nice and roomy. (11¼ x 13 in.).
120-V-601 $15.00 each

BRIDE'S HANDKERCHIEF
Pretty, tasteful and handmade. A wide band of white lace frames square of white, ivory or blue (for that traditional ''something blue'') cotton.
$5.00 each
WHITE   120-V-500
BLUE   120-V-502
IVORY   120-V-501

RING BEARER'S PILLOWS
Totally enchanting ways to present shining bands of love and unity. Shimmery satin lavishly or classically adorned with delicate lace, dainty tulle, pearls, fabric flowers and satiny ribbons. Pretty keepsakes forever after the wedding day!
PEARL HEART
WHITE   120-V-100   **$16.00 each**
FLORAL SQUARE
WHITE   120-V-104   **$16.00 each**
LACY SQUARE (not shown)
WHITE   120-V-106   **$20.00 each**
LACY SQUARE (not shown)
IVORY   120-V-107   **$20.00 each**

Wedding Couples

1-2. NEW! BISQUE PORCELAIN COUPLES
Beautifully detailed twosomes. Each
4½ in. high. **$12.99 each**

1. SIDE-BY-SIDE COUPLE
BLACK COAT   214-V-201
WHITE COAT   214-V-202

2. DANCING COUPLE
WHITE COAT   214-V-320
BLACK COAT   214-V-321

3. CLASSIC COUPLE
Plastic, 4½ in. **$4.49 each**; 3½ in. **$3.99 each.**

Couple	Coat	Height	Stock No.
WHITE	BLACK	4½ in.	202-V-8110
WHITE	WHITE	4½ in.	202-V-8121
WHITE	BLACK	3½ in.	2102-V-820
WHITE	WHITE	3½ in.	203-V-8221

SHOWN ON LOVER'S LACE, p. 156

BLACK	BLACK	4½ in.	214-V-301
BLACK	WHITE	4½ in.	214-V-302
BLACK	BLACK	3½ in.	203-V-302
BLACK	WHITE	3½ in.	203-V-301

4. ANNIVERSARY COUPLE
Gold or silver gown. Plastic, 4½ in. tall.
25TH SILVER   203-V-2828   **$3.99**
50TH GOLD   203-V-1821   **$3.99**

5. KISSING COUPLE
Endearing couple, 4 in. tall. Plastic.
202-V-172   **$4.49 each**

6-7. GLAZED PORCELAIN COUPLES
Choose with plate slot base (for displaying a plate) or without base.

6. 4⅝ IN. COUPLE
202-V-218   **$15.99 each**

7. 8¼ IN. COUPLE/BASE
202-V-234   **$22.99 each**

8. BRIDESMAIDS
Plastic, 3½ in. tall. **99¢ each**
WHITE   203-V-8324
PINK   203-V-8341
BLUE   203-V-8304
YELLOW   203-V-8325

9-10. PORCELAIN GROOMSMAN & BRIDESMAID Gown can be painted.
4½ in. tall. **$3.99 each**
9. BRIDESMAID   202-V-225
10. GROOMSMAN
WHITE COAT   202-V-221
BLACK COAT   202-V-223

11. GROOMSMAN
Plastic, 3½ in. tall. **99¢ each**
BLACK COAT   203-V-8402
WHITE COAT   203-V-8424
ALL WHITE   203-V-8829

12. CIRCLES OF LACE 10 in. high.
210-V-1986   **$8.99 each**

13. FLORAL ARCH 10-in. high.
210-V-1987   **$8.99 each**

14. FLORAL BASE
White, 1½ in. high, 4¾ in. diameter.
201-V-1815   **$1.99 each**

15. CRYSTAL-LOOK BASE
1¾ in. high, 4½ in. diameter.
201-V-1450   **$2.99 each**

16. PETITE PEDESTAL BASE
3½ in. top and 4 in. base. White.
201-V-1133   **$1.99 each**

17. HEART BASE
White openwork. 2 pcs. 1½ in. high.
4½-IN. 201-V-7332   **$2.99 each**
3¼-IN. 201-V-7847   **$2.49 each**

18. FLORAL SCROLL BASE
Victorian charm. 4½ x 2½ in. 2 pcs.
WHITE   201-V-1303   **$2.99 each**
NEW! IVORY   201-V-305   **$2.99 each**

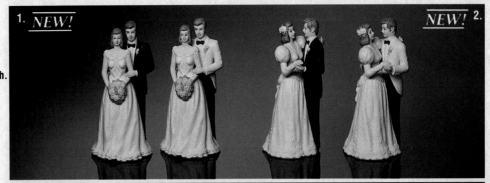

Wedding Ornaments

1. NEW! SOPHISTICATION
Bursting with excitement! Our lovely, new porcelain bride and groom are surrounded by breathtaking billows of tulle, dramatic lily of the valley sprays, dotted with shimmery pearls, and distinctive floral clusters. 8½ in. high. **$45.00 each**
BLACK COAT 117-V-201
WHITE COAT 117-V-202

2. LUSTROUS LOVE
A profusion of tulle peeks from behind lace leaves, dotted with forget-me-nots and rimmed with shimmery pearls. Satiny roses burst forth while pearls dance on transparent strings around porcelain lovers. 8 in. high. **$35.00 each**
WHITE 117-V-621
PINK 117-V-623
BLUE 117-V-625

3. SHIMMERING BELLS
Crystal-clear double arch and bells are delicately etched and trimmed with ribbon. Pretty puff of tulle, flowers, ribbon and pearls highlight embossed base. 9½ in. high. **$20.00 each**
BLUE 103-V-2501
PINK 103-V-2500

4. PROMISE
Sleek lucite-look heart frames white porcelain couple. Crystal-look base is covered with a profusion of tulle, ribbons and fabric flowers.
9⅝ in. high. **$25.00 each**
BLUE 117-V-309
WHITE 117-V-315
PINK 117-V-311

Wedding Ornaments

1. NEW! LOVE'S FANFARE
Lavish flourish and flair. Dramatic fan and ruffly froth of lace lavish our exquisitely detailed, new porcelain couple. A wreath of light-as-air flowers and shimmery pearl strands float on the lacy waves. 8 in. high.   **$50.00 each**
WHITE COAT 117-V-401
BLACK COAT 117-V-402

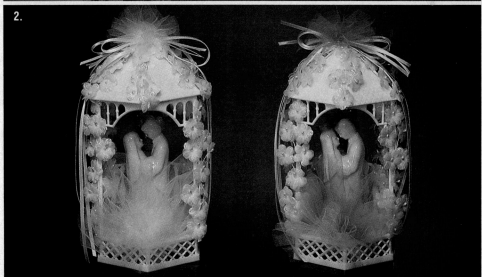

2. GARDEN ROMANCE
Our elegant porcelain couple stands in a dreamy gazebo entwined with flowery vines. Bold bursts of tulle and slender ribbons add impact to this romantic hideaway. 10½ in. high.   **$30.00 each**
IRIDESCENT 117-V-711
RAINBOW 117-V-713

3. REFLECTIONS
Sophisticated and trendsetting. Dramatic lucite-look backdrop reflects porcelain couple, tulle burst, pearl sprays and fantasy florals.
8¼ in. high.   **$25.00 each.**
BLUE 117-V-130
WHITE 117-V-268
PINK 117-V-297

4. NEW SHADE! SPLENDID
Dramatic sweep of lucite surrounds adoring porcelain pair. Cylindrical vase holds a matching spray of flowers that accents base. Add real flowers if you prefer. 10½ in. high.   **$28.00 each**
WHITE 117-V-506
PINK 117-V-507
BLUE 117-V-508
LILAC 117-V-509
NEW! PEACH 117-V-450

Wedding Ornaments

1. NEW! BRIDAL WALTZ

The meaningful commitment promised by two is beautifully reflected. Handsome arched windows share a view of our new porcelain couple gliding in graceful unison. Ruffles of lace and tulle flounce the bead embossed base and outline with windows. Delicate floral clusters adorn each side. 7½ in. high. **$40.00 each**

Coat	Color	Stock No.
WHITE	WHITE	117-V-321
WHITE	BLACK	117-V-322
WHITE	PINK	117-V-323
BLACK	PINK	117-V-324
WHITE	PEACH	117-V-325
BLACK	PEACH	117-V-326
WHITE	TEAL	117-V-327
BLACK	TEAL	117-V-328
WHITE	IVORY	117-V-329
BLACK	IVORY	117-V-330

2. ECSTASY

Columns of satiny flowers and lacy leaves, touched with pearls and bursts of tulle, surround adoring porcelain pair. Eye-catching strands of delicate blooms seem to float on air. 9½ in. high. **$40.00 each**
WHITE 117-V-831
PINK 117-V-833
BLUE 117-V-835

3. RHAPSODY

Contemporary belled arch is dotted with flowers and tulle. Stylized porcelain couple stands on crystal-look base, adorned with tulle puff and floral spray. 9½ in. high. **$25.00 each**
PINK 117-V-305
BLUE 117-V-313
WHITE 117-V-301

4. DEVOTION

Lucite arch is framed with ruffly tulle and lace. Glazed porcelain couple stands on sleek pedestal base in a burst of tulle, blooms and pearl strands. 9½ in. high. **$25.00 each**
BLUE 117-V-427
PINK 117-V-421
WHITE 117-V-425

Porcelain figures made in Korea; Taiwan.

Wedding Ornaments

1. NEW! ROMANCE & RUFFLES
Our vision of loveliness is bound to enamor with its glamour. Shimmery satin, edged with white or ivory lace, gets all gathered up in a captivating heart. A charming pompon ribbon bow repeats the two tones. Skirted in satin, base is adorned with pearly strands and flowers. 8½ in. high. **$25.00 each**

WHITE/WHITE	109-V-4001
IVORY/IVORY	109-V-4002
PINK/WHITE	109-V-4003
BLUE/WHITE	109-V-4004
PEACH/IVORY	109-V-4005
ROYAL BLUE/WHITE	109-V-4007
RED/WHITE	109-V-4008
TEAL/WHITE	109-V-4009

2. SPRING SONG
Perching lovebirds sing love songs in a profusion of posies and tulle. 9½ in. high.
111-V-2802 $16.00 each

3. VICTORIAN CHARM
Graceful ribbon loops and fantasy florals spill over resplendent satin five-bell cluster. 7½ in. high. **$20.00 each**
IVORY 103-V-1586
WHITE 103-V-1587
PINK 103-V-1588

4. NEW! UPDATED! CIRCLES OF LOVE
Symbolic double rings and fluttery doves are now nestled in a flowery hideaway. A double archway of lush, pearl-center flowers and pearl sprays curve around the lovely pairs. A single bloom dots the rings. 10 in. high. **$25.00 each**
PINK 103-V-300
PEACH 103-V-301
TEAL 103-V-302

5. EVERLASTING LOVE
Arches of lace, and filigree heart, dotted with tulle and wedding bands, surround floral filled bell. 10 in. high.
103-V-236 $16.00 each

6. HEARTS TAKE WING
Tulle-covered heart flatters the enchanting birds romancing beak-to-beak. 10½ in. high.
103-V-6218 $12.00 each

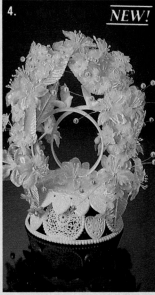

7. WEDDING BELLS
Filigree bell cluster is caught up in tulle, florals and arches of lace. 10½ in. high.
103-V-1356 $16.00 each

Plastic parts made in Hong Kong; Taiwan. Flowers made in Korea. All ornaments are hand-assembled in U.S.A.

Wedding Ornaments

1. NEW! HEARTS A FLUTTER

The stunning impact of glistening glass is here at last. Graceful swans put their heads together to form a heart so true. A pair of doves causes a flutter on the delicate open heart. Translucent bell-shaped base is wreathed with iridescent flowers.
8 in. high.   **$50.00 each**

WHITE	118-V-100
PINK	118-V-101
BLUE	118-V-102
PEACH	118-V-103
TEAL	118-V-104
ROYAL BLUE	118-V-105
RED	118-V-106
IVORY	118-V-107
PLUM	118-V-108

2. THE LOOK OF LOVE

Our exclusive porcelain cameo, framed in lace and tulle, beautifully expresses the joy of belonging to each other. Pedestal base is adorned with a graceful flower spray and a lavishness of tulle.
9 in. high.   **$35.00 each**
TEAL 117-V-955
PEACH* 117-V-956
WHITE 117-V-951
IVORY* 117-V-952
PINK 117-V-953
BLUE 117-V-954
*on ivory bases

3. SWEET CEREMONY

Seed pearl hearts frame glistening bell. Bride and heart frame are accented with tulle. 10 in. high.   **$14.00 each**
WHITE COAT 101-V-22028
BLACK COAT 101-V-22011

4. HEART-TO-HEART

Heart duo creates an eye-catching shadow-box effect around Kissing Couple. 9 in. high.
110-V-376 $17.00 each

5. BLESSED OCCASION

Surrounded by lush blooms, ribbon and tulle, the glowing cross stands out brilliantly. Lovely for religious occasions, too. 7¾ in. high.
103-V-1000 $14.00 each

Plastic parts made in Hong Kong; Taiwan. Flowers made in Korea. All ornaments are hand-assembled in U.S.A.

Wedding Ornaments

1-2. LAVISH SOFT SCULPTURED HEARTS are bound to delight. Two exquisite choices are available.

1. LACY ELEGANCE
A stunning spray of chiffon petal flowers accents lace-covered satin heart. A rose with pearl-edged leaves is planted in a bed of flowery lace and tulle. All set on sleek white or ivory pedestal base.
7 in. high. **$ 22.00 each**
PEACH* 109-V-2006
BLACK & WHITE 109-V-2007
PINK 109-V-2003
WHITE 109-V-2001
IVORY* 109-V-2002
BLUE 109-V-2004
TEAL 109-V-2005
*on ivory bases

2. SATIN ELEGANCE
Lace-edged satin heart bears a pair of wedding rings. Pearly stamens and dancing strands of pearls add luster to the enchanting satin and chiffon petal flowers. An exuberance of tulle veils pretty floral embossed base.
7 in. high. **$20.00 each**
TEAL 109-V-1005
IVORY* 109-V-1002
PINK 109-V-1003
PEACH* 109-V-1006
WHITE 109-V-1001
BLUE 109-V-1004
*on ivory bases

3. MORNING ROSEBUD
Doves flutter atop openwork gate. Pretty fabric flowers accent.
8 in. high **$10.00 each**
WHITE COAT 101-V-44020
BLACK COAT 101-V-44013

4. NEW! MOONLIT SNOW
Gazing into each others eyes, our striking couple resides in an archway of diaphanous flowers and shimmery pearl sprays. Base is veiled with a ruffle of lace. 9 in. high. **$25.00 each**

Coat	Couple	Color	Stock No.
WHITE	WHITE	WHITE	114-V-201
BLACK	WHITE	WHITE	114-V-202
WHITE	BLACK	WHITE	114-V-207
BLACK	BLACK	WHITE	114-V-208
BLACK	WHITE	PEACH	114-V-205
WHITE	WHITE	PEACH	114-V-206
BLACK	WHITE	PINK	114-V-204
WHITE	WHITE	PINK	114-V-203

1.

2.

3.

4. NEW!

Petite Wedding Ornaments

1. NEW! STYLE & COLORS!
LA BELLE PETITE
A pretty double ruffle of airy tulle now accents base. Iridescent petal flowers have shimmery pearl centers. 5½ in. high. **$9.00 each**
WHITE 106-V-248
PINK 106-V-249
PEACH 106-V-250

2. PETITE DOUBLE RING COUPLE
The perfect pairs of people, birds and bands. 5½ in. high. **$7.00 each**
BLACK COAT 104-V-42413
WHITE COAT 104-V-42420

3. PETITE BELLS & BUDS
Satin bells, adorned with dainty blooms, ring true. Filigree heart is glamorized with tulle. 6½ in. high. **$10.00 each**
PINK 106-V-1000
WHITE 106-V-1001
BLUE 106-V-1002

4. NEW COLORS!
PETITE SPRING SONG
Pretty paired with full-size Spring Song on p. 153. 7 in. high. **$11.00 each**
WHITE 106-V-159
PINK 106-V-160
PEACH 106-V-161

5. NEW VERSION! LOVERS IN LACE
Now also features a handsome black couple under lace-covered arches and a burst of tulle. 7 in. high. **$10.00 each**

COAT	COUPLE	
BLACK	BLACK	104-V-302
WHITE	BLACK	104-V-301
BLACK	WHITE	104-V-818
WHITE	WHITE	104-V-826

6. PETITE DOUBLE RING
Graceful doves land on bands of love. Adorned with tulle puff. 5½ in. high.
106-V-4316 $6.00 each

7. NATURAL BEAUTY
Filigree heart, floral spray and satin bow add charm to perched pair.
6 in. high. **$10.00 each**

LILAC	106-V-1147
PEACH	106-V-1104
PINK	106-V-1120
BLUE	106-V-1184
WHITE	106-V-1163

8. NEW COLOR!
PETITE BELLS OF JOY Now in pink!
Eye-catching cluster of white filigree bells are enhanced with fabric roses, lace-covered arches and puff of tulle.
7 in. high. **$12.00 each**

WHITE	106-V-2658
PINK	106-V-350

9. NEW! UPDATED! HAPPY HEARTS
Ruffles of lace now highlight the base of this lighthearted romantic. The ideal porcelain couple stands before sleek lucite-look heart. 6 in. high. **$22.00 each**

Coat	Color	Stock No.
BLACK	PINK	108-V-217
WHITE	PINK	108-V-219
BLACK	WHITE	108-V-525
WHITE	WHITE	108-V-526

Specialty Ornaments

1. CHRISTMAS JOY
Cathedral window views a pair of satin bells filled with showy poinsettias. A festive holiday centerpiece, too. 10 in. high.   **$16.00 each**
RED 103-V-3001
WHITE 103-V-3002

2. GOLDEN & SILVER JUBILEE
Threads of gold or silver glisten on impressive bursts of white tulle. Numeral wreath and couple boast handsome detailing. The shining fabric petals on orchids and ferns emit an elegant glow. 8½ in. high.   **$16.00 each**
GOLD 102-V-1250
SILVER 102-V-1225

3. PETITE ANNIVERSARY
Glistening numeral wreath is tastefully adorned with adoring doves. 5½ in. high   **$6.00 each**
25TH 105-V-4265
50TH 105-V-4273

4. NEW! UPDATED!
PETITE DOUBLE RING DEVOTION
Sprays of iridescent flowers with shimmery pearl stamens and fern leaves now add flair to the handsome couple and embossed wedding bands. 5 in. high.   **$9.00 each**
25TH SILVER 105-V-4613
50TH GOLD 105-V-4605

5. BRIDAL SHOWER DELIGHT
Pretty bowed umbrella is dainty and delightful for showering the bride-to-be with happy wishes. Pretty for wedding cakes, too.
115-V-201   **$8.00 each**

6. NEW! UPDATED!
25 OR 50 YEARS OF HAPPINESS
Impressive profusion of pearl accented blooms, shimmery leaves and pearly sprays give a totally new look to this classic choice. 10 in. high.   **$16.00 each**
25TH 102-V-207
50TH 102-V-223

7. NEW! UPDATED!
PETITE ANNIVERSARY YEARS
The addition of pretty blooms adds appeal to this versatile favorite. Embossed wreath holds snap-in numbers. 5¾ in. high.
105-V-4257   **$7.00 each**

Plastic parts made in Hong Kong; Taiwan. Flowers made in Korea. All ornaments are hand-assembled in U.S.A.

Beautiful Trims

1. SATIN BELLS
Radiant additions for holiday and special celebration cakes, too. Choose from a wonderful variety of colors in 2 and 3 in. sizes.

Color	Height	Stock No.	Price
WHITE	2 IN.	1001-V-9210	$4.99 pack of 3
WHITE	3 IN.	1001-V-9153	2.99 each
IVORY	2 IN.	1001-V-9206	4.99 pack of 3
IVORY	3 IN.	1001-V-9203	2.99 each
BLUE	2 IN.	1001-V-9212	4.99 pack of 3
BLUE	3 IN.	1001-V-9179	2.99 each
PINK	2 IN.	1001-V-9208	4.99 pack of 3
PINK	3 IN.	1001-V-9187	2.99 each
RED	3 IN.	1001-V-9200	2.99 each

2. FILIGREE BELLS

Height	Stock No.	Price/Pack
1 IN.	1001-V-9447	$1.79/12
2 IN.	1001-V-9422	$1.79/6
2¾ IN.	1001-V-9439	$2.29/6
3 IN.	1001-V-9404	$1.59/3
4½ IN.	1001-V-9411	$1.89/3

3. GLITTERED BELLS

Height	Stock No.	Price/Pack
1¼ IN.	1007-V-9061	$2.99/12
1¾ IN.	2110-V-9075	$1.09/6
2 IN.	1007-V-9088	$2.49/6
3 IN.	2110-V-9090	$2.49/6
5 IN.	1007-V-9110	$2.99/3

4. IRIDESCENT BELLS

Height	Stock No.	Price/Pack
1½ IN.	1001-V-8016	$3.59/12
1¾ IN.	1001-V-8025	$2.49/6
2 IN.	1001-V-8033	$2.99/6
3 IN.	1001-V-8041	$3.39/3

5. LARGE DOUBLE WEDDING RINGS
3⅜ in. diam.
WHITE 201-V-1008 $1.79 each.

6. SMALL WEDDING RINGS
⅝ in. diam
$1.59 pack of 24
SILVER 1002-V-1016
GOLD 1002-V-1008.

7. FLOWER SPIKES
Fill with water, push into cake and add flowers. 3 in. high.
1008-V-408 $2.49 pack of 12

8. LARGE FLUTTER DOVES
4 x 2¾ in.
1002-V-1806 $2.99 pack of 2

9. WHITE BIRD ON STAND.
4¾ in. high.
1316-V-1202 $3.99 each

10. PETITE WHITE BIRDS.   2⅛ in.
1316-V-1210 $2.99 each

11. KISSING LOVE BIRDS.
Beak-to-beak romantics. 5½ in. high.
1002-V-206 $4.99 each.

12. SMALL DOVES   2 x 1½ in.
1002-V-1710 $1.99 pack of 12

13. GLITTERED DOVES
Coated with non-edible glitter.
1006-V-166 $1.69 pack of 12

14. SERENE SWANS
A graceful and stately pair. 2½ in. high.
1002-V-11 $1.99 pack of 2

Beautiful Trims

It's fun to create your own bridal shower favors and wedding cake ornaments with these lovely trims. Start with one or more basics, add flowers, lace, birds, bells, ribbons of your choice for a personalized ornament.

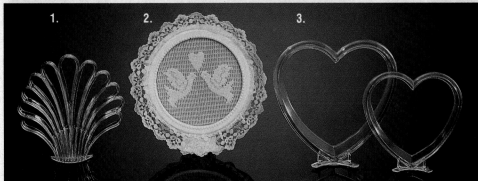

1. PETITE FANS
4⅞ in. high   **$1.99 each**
CLEAR 205-V-634
PINK 205-V-630
WHITE 205-V-632

2. LOVE BIRD DOILY PANELS
Embossed white plastic frame, edged with lace, stands on pedestal base. 5¼ in. diam.
$4.99 each
PINK 205-V-3010
LAVENDER 205-V-3011
BLUE 205-V-3012

3. CRYSTAL-LOOK HEARTS
4¼ IN. 205-V-1672   **$1.59 each**
5½ IN. 205-V-1674   **$1.79 each**

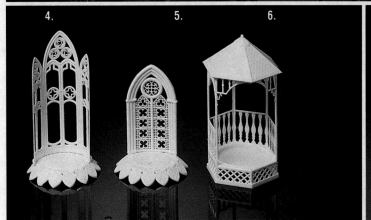

4. CURVED GOTHIC WINDOW
5 x 9 in. 2 pcs.
205-V-3059   **$3.99 each**

5. PETITE GOTHIC WINDOW ARCH
5 x 7¼ in. 2 pcs.
205-V-2672   **$2.99 each**

6. PETITE GARDEN HOUSE
5 x 9 in. Easy to assemble.
205-V-8298   **$4.49 each**

7. 6-PC. GOTHIC ARCH SET
Plastic pieces simply lock together for easy assembly. 10½ in. high.
205-V-3109   **$4.99 set**

8. ARCH CANOPY TRELLIS
Delicate latticework. 3½ x 6¾ in.
205-V-6015   **$2.99 each**

9. PICKET ARCHWAY
Gate swings. 5½ x 5¼ in.
205-V-344   **$2.99 each**

10. WISHING WELL
Handle turns. 3 x 4¾ in.
205-V-327   **$3.99 each**

11. OLD FASHIONED FENCE
2½ in. posts, 1 in. pegs, 144 snap-together links.
1107-V-8326   **$2.49 set**

12. HEART BOWL VASE
Pretty embossed floral design. 3 in. high.
1008-V-9685   **$2.29 each**

Lacy Filigree

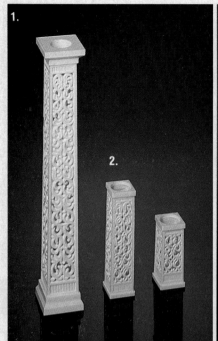

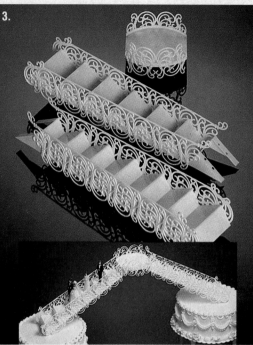

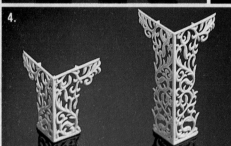

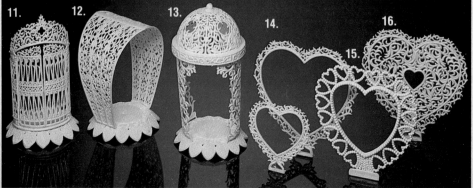

1. LACY-LOOK PILLAR
Add tulle or fabric to coordinate with bride's color scheme. 12-in. high.
303-V-8976 $2.99 each

2. SQUARE FILIGREE PILLARS
Delicate openwork design.
5 IN. 303-V-7717 $2.99 pack of 4
3 IN. 303-V-8071 $1.99 pack of 4

3. FILIGREE PLATFORM AND STAIRWAY SET
Bridge the gap between lavish tiers. Includes two stairways (16¾ in. long) and one platform (4¾ in. x 5 in.). White plastic.
205-V-2109 $11.99 set
ONE-STAIRWAY ONLY.
205-V-1218 $4.99 each

4. SNAP-ON FILIGREE
Gives Grecian pillars a romantic look.
FITS 3 IN. PILLARS.
305-V-390 $1.59 pack of 4
FITS 5 IN. PILLARS
305-V-398 $1.99 pack of 4

5. FILIGREE FOUNTAIN FRAME
Perfect around the Kolor-Flo Fountain. Eight white plastic scallops snap together. 9 in. diameter. 3½ in. high.
205-V-1285 $2.99 each

6. SWIRLS
Leaf-framed latticework. 1 x 2½ in.
1004-V-2100 $2.49 pack of 12

7. SCROLLS
Swirling and graceful. 2¾ x 1¼ in.
1004-V-2801 $2.29 pack of 24

8. LACY HEARTS Fancy! 3¾ x 3½ in.
1004-V-2306 $2.49 pack of 12

9. CURVED TRIANGLE Dramatic! 3 x 3½ in.
1004-V-3001 $2.49 pack of 12

10. CONTOUR
Lattice and leaves. 3¾ x 2⅔ in.
1004-V-2003 $2.49 pack of 12

11. GATETOP ARCH
Sentimental scene. 8 in. tall. 2 pcs.
205-V-3483 $2.99 each.

12. ITALIAN FILIGREE ARCHWAY
4½ x 7 in. 2 pcs.
205-V-8115 $4.49 each

13. GARDEN GAZEBO 4 pcs. 4¼ x 8½ in.
205-V-4100 $4.49 each

14. FILIGREE HEARTS
7 IN.
205-V-1501 $2.49 pack of 3
4 IN.
205-V-1527 $1.49 pack of 3

15. SEED PEARL HEART 7 x 6½ in.
205-V-1006 $3.49 pack of 3

16. LARGE FILIGREE HEART
1004-V-2208 $3.79 each

20th ANNIVERSARY ISSUE

Order Form

Most of the products in this book are available through your local Wilton dealer. In the event the items you want are not available locally, use this convenient, shop-at-home order form. You'll receive delivery within 10 working days after we receive your order.

Order Form

Caller Service No. 1604
2240 West 75th Street
Woodridge, IL 60517
(312) 963-7100

❶ SOLD TO: (PLEASE PRINT PLAINLY)

NAME _____
first · middle initial · last

ADDRESS _____

CITY _____ STATE _____ ZIP _____

AREA CODE _____ DAYTIME PHONE NO. _____

SHIP TO: (Fill in only if different from Sold To.)

NAME _____
first · middle initial · last

ADDRESS _____

CITY _____ STATE _____ ZIP _____

_____

❷ CREDIT CARD ORDERS   VISA   MasterCard

Use VISA or MasterCard!
Fill in the boxes:
Credit Card Number

Expiration
Month/Year _____   Signature _____

For Office Use Only
Please do not write in spaces

Date

Cash

Debit M.

Credit M.

Handling Charge

Air Mail

Foreign

Pal/Sam

Coupon

Gift Ct.

❸ PAGE	❹ STOCK NUMBER			❺ HOW MANY	❻ DESCRIPTION	PRICE OF ONE	TOTAL PRICE Dollars	Cents
121	1701	V	900		1990 Yearbook (No postage & handling)	$4.99		
	1607	V	728		Surprise Package I	$5.99		
	1607	V	805		Surprise Package II	$12.49		

Shipping and Handling Charges (See No. 8)
Orders up to $29.99 . . . . .add $3.50
Orders from $30-49.99 . . . . .add $4.00
Orders of $50 and more. . . . . .add $4.50

Enjoy Quick Delivery!
Your Wilton Order Arrives Within
10 Working Days, After We Receive It!

NO C.O.D. ORDERS

❼ TOTAL MERCHANDISE

❽ ADD SHIPPING, HANDLING & POSTAGE CHARGE
NOTE! Find the amount you pay on chart to the left.

❾ STATE & LOCAL TAXES—SEE TAX NOTE

❿ SPECIAL SHIPPING SERVICES

SUB TOTAL

⓫ COUPONS AND/OR
CREDIT MEMO DEDUCTIONS

TOTAL AMOUNT ENCLOSED

MONEY BACK GUARANTEE
If you are not completely satisfied with your Wilton purchase, return the item for an exchange or refund.

CF

← DETACH ENVELOPE HERE →

FOLD ALONG LINE AND SEAL FLAP
HAVE YOU ENCLOSED YOUR CHECK OR MONEY ORDER?

Please Send Cake Decorating/ Candy Making Information to:

Name

Address

City

State   Zip

CK

Introduce a Friend to the Joys of Cake Decorating and Candy Making!

You've already discovered the rewards of cake decorating and candy making. We're sure you'd like to share that satisfaction with a friend who'd like to receive our catalog and learn more about these wonderful self-satisfying arts.

Please include her/his name and address on the reverse side of this coupon and we'll add it to our mailing list.

Note: After you've filled in this information, just detach the coupon and place it in the envelope with your order.

↑ IMPORTANT: This coupon must be detached before mailing.

↑ IMPORTANT: This coupon must be detached before mailing.

Will Not Be Delivered Without Proper Postage

Enclose your signed check or money order with Order Form.

Wilton
ENTERPRISES, INC.
Caller Service No. 1604
2240 West 75th Street
Woodridge, IL 60517

How To Order

1 Print your name, address and phone no. clearly. If you wish your order sent to another address, be sure to include that information in the area designated: "SHIP TO."

2 You may pay by check, money order or credit card (Only VISA or MasterCard accepted.) SORRY, NO C.O.D. ORDERS. To charge an order to your VISA or MasterCard, enter your charge card number in the boxes. Supply card expiration date and your signature. Orders will not be processed without this information.

Make checks payable to Wilton Enterprises, Inc.

Wilton Enterprises is not responsible for cash sent by mail.

Orders from outside U.S.A. must be paid in U.S. Funds only.

3 Enter page number on which item is shown.

4 Fill in stock number of item.

5 Fill in the number of items desired. If an item includes more than one piece, DO NOT list number of pieces. Example: 14 piece set is listed as 1 item under quantity.

6 Fill in name of item.

7 Total your order.

8 Add appropriate amount to your order for shipping, handling and postage for inside U.S.A. (See chart inside Order Form to determine charges.) Wilton ships via United Parcel Service. Allow 10 working days for delivery. (HI and AK allow 17 working days.)

Outside the U.S.A. shipping, handling and postage totals $7.00. Allow 3 months for delivery (except Canada).

9 Add state and local taxes *where you live** to your total amount, including shipping and delivery charges. See Tax Chart below. Wilton Enterprises, Inc. is required by law to collect state taxes on orders shipped to:

AZ 5%; CA 6%; CO 3%; FL 6%; GA 4%; IA 4%; IL 6.75%; IN 5%; KS 4%; KY 5%; LA 4%; MD 5%; MA 5%; MI 4%; MN 6%; MO 4.225%; NC 3%; NJ 6%; NY 7%; OH 6%; PA 6%; TN 5.5%; TX 7%; UT 6.25%; VA 4.5%; WA 7.5%.

***Tax rates are subject to change according to individual state legislation.**

10 Air Service add 50% of your total order cost. Air Service outside U.S.A. add 100% of your total order cost.

11 When Your Order Arrives...Should you be missing an item from your order (1) check to be sure you have not overlooked the merchandise (2) check over your receipted order form. If any item is temporarily out of stock we forward the balance of your order with out of stock notification and the reorder date. If payment is check or money order you will receive a credit memo for the amount of the missing item. The memo may be applied to your next order or returned to Customer Service for a cash refund. Charge Accounts will be charged only for merchandise shipped.

Wilton Return Policy: Inspect all merchandise upon arrival. If you're dissatisfied in any way with any item, notify Wilton Customer Service in writing with a copy of your invoice and all available information regarding your order *before* returning merchandise. A Customer Service Representative will contact you. You have 60 days to return merchandise. Handle returns promptly, as they take approximately 30 days to process.

SAVE MAILING TIME! Phone in your charge order. 1-312-963-7100. Ask for mail order. Remember! Only charge orders (VISA or MasterCard) will be accepted by phone.

Prices in this book supersede all previous Wilton publications. Wilton reserves the right to change prices without notice.

For inquiries on your previous order send all available information and a copy of your invoice to:

Wilton. 2240 West 75th Street Woodridge, IL 60517

FROM

Name

Address

Apt. No.

City

State   Zip

If your name and/or address has changed since you last ordered from Wilton, please fill in previous address here.

Name

Address

Apt. No.

City

State   Zip

50% OFF!

Surprise Packages!

Twice the Fun at Half the Price! Here's an opportunity to get lots of great baking, decorating and candy making products to help you make wonderful, fun, pretty treats for family and friends.

Treat yourself to one or both of these super surprise packages... Save 50% on each! It's a bargain you can't pass up. Order yours now.

Package 1
Contains $12.95 worth of quality products for just
$5.99*

Package 2
Contains $25.00 worth of quality products for just
$12.49*

Order both or just one. Indicate quantity and total price on the Order Form.

*Products in package change periodically. Sorry, no returns or substitutions accepted.

Order Form

Caller Service No. 1604
2240 West 75th Street
Woodridge, IL 60517
(312) 963-7100

❶ SOLD TO: (PLEASE PRINT PLAINLY)

NAME _____
 first   middle initial   last

ADDRESS _____

CITY _____ STATE _____ ZIP _____

AREA CODE _____ DAYTIME PHONE NO. _____

SHIP TO: (Fill in only if different from Sold To.)

NAME _____
 first   middle initial   last

ADDRESS _____

CITY _____ STATE _____ ZIP _____

❷ CREDIT CARD ORDERS VISA' MasterCard.

Use VISA or MasterCard!
Fill in the boxes:
Credit Card Number

Expiration
Month/Year _____ Signature _____

For Office Use Only
Please do not write in spaces

❸ PAGE	❹ STOCK NUMBER			❺ HOW MANY	❻ DESCRIPTION	PRICE OF ONE	TOTAL PRICE	
							Dollars	Cents
121	1701	V	900		1990 Yearbook (No postage & handling)	$4.99		
	1607	V	728		Surprise Package I	$5.99		
	1607	V	805		Surprise Package II	$12.49		

For Office Use Only column entries:
Date
Cash
Debit M.
Credit M.
Handling Charge
Air Mail
Foreign
Pal/Sam
Coupon
Gift Ct.

Shipping and Handling Charges (See No. 8)
Orders up to $29.99 . . . . .add $3.50
Orders from $30-49.99 . . . . .add $4.00
Orders of $50 and more . . . . .add $4.50

Enjoy Quick Delivery!
Your Wilton Order Arrives Within
10 Working Days, After We Receive It!

NO C.O.D. ORDERS

❼ TOTAL MERCHANDISE

❽ ADD SHIPPING, HANDLING & POSTAGE CHARGE
NOTE! Find the amount you pay on chart to the left.

❾ STATE & LOCAL TAXES–SEE TAX NOTE

❿ SPECIAL SHIPPING SERVICES

SUB TOTAL

⓫ COUPONS AND/OR
CREDIT MEMO DEDUCTIONS

TOTAL AMOUNT ENCLOSED

MONEY BACK GUARANTEE
If you are not completely satisfied with your Wilton purchase, return the item for an exchange or refund.

CF

DETACH ENVELOPE HERE ⟶

FOLD ALONG LINE AND SEAL FLAP

HAVE YOU ENCLOSED YOUR CHECK OR MONEY ORDER?

Introduce a Friend to the Joys of Cake Decorating and Candy Making!

You've already discovered the rewards of cake decorating and candy making. We're sure you'd like to share that satisfaction with a friend who'd like to receive our catalog and learn more about these wonderful self-satisfying arts.

Please include her/his name and address on the reverse side of this coupon and we'll add it to our mailing list.

Note: After you've filled in this information, just detach the coupon and place it in the envelope with your order.

Please Send Cake Decorating/ Candy Making Information to:

Name

Address

City

State   Zip

CK

↑ IMPORTANT: This coupon must be detached before mailing.

↑ IMPORTANT: This coupon must be detached before mailing.

How To Order

1 Print your name, address and phone no. clearly. If you wish your order sent to another address, be sure to include that information in the area designated: "SHIP TO."

2 You may pay by check, money order or credit card (Only VISA or MasterCard accepted.) SORRY, NO C.O.D. ORDERS. To charge an order to your VISA or MasterCard, enter your charge card number in the boxes. Supply card expiration date and your signature. Orders will not be processed without this information.

Make checks payable to Wilton Enterprises, Inc.

Wilton Enterprises is not responsible for cash sent by mail.

Orders from outside U.S.A. must be paid in U.S. Funds only.

3 Enter page number on which item is shown.

4 Fill in stock number of item.

5 Fill in the number of items desired. If an item includes more than one piece, DO NOT list number of pieces. Example: 14 piece set is listed as 1 item under quantity.

6 Fill in name of item.

7 Total your order.

8 Add appropriate amount to your order for shipping, handling and postage for inside U.S.A. (See chart inside Order Form to determine charges.) Wilton ships via United Parcel Service. Allow 10 working days for delivery. (HI and AK allow 17 working days.)

Outside the U.S.A. shipping, handling and postage totals $7.00. Allow 3 months for delivery (except Canada).

9 Add state and local taxes *where you live*• to your total amount, including shipping and delivery charges. See Tax Chart below. Wilton Enterprises, Inc. is required by law to collect state taxes on orders shipped to:

AZ 5%; CA 6%; CO 3%; FL 6%; GA 4%; IA 4%; IL 6.75%; IN 5%; KS 4%; KY 5%; LA 4%; MD 5%; MA 5%; MI 4%; MN 6%; MO 4.225%; NC 3%; NJ 6%; NY 7%; OH 6%; PA 6%; TN 5.5%; TX 7%; UT 6.25%; VA 4.5%; WA 7.5%.

*Tax rates are subject to change according to individual state legislation.

10 Air Service add 50% of your total order cost. Air Service outside U.S.A. add 100% of your total order cost.

11 When Your Order Arrives...Should you be missing an item from your order (1) check to be sure you have not overlooked the merchandise (2) check over your receipted order form. If any item is temporarily out of stock we forward the balance of your order with out of stock notification and the reorder date. If payment is check or money order you will receive a credit memo for the amount of the missing item. The memo may be applied to your next order or returned to Customer Service for a cash refund. Charge Accounts will be charged only for merchandise shipped.

Wilton Return Policy: Inspect all merchandise upon arrival. If you're dissatisfied in any way with any item, notify Wilton Customer Service in writing with a copy of your invoice and all available information regarding your order *before* returning merchandise. A Customer Service Representative will contact you. You have 60 days to return merchandise. Handle returns promptly, as they take approximately 30 days to process.

SAVE MAILING TIME! Phone in your charge order. 1-312-963-7100. Ask for mail order. Remember! Only charge orders (VISA or MasterCard) will be accepted by phone.

Prices in this book supersede all previous Wilton publications. Wilton reserves the right to change prices without notice.

For inquiries on your previous order send all available information and a copy of your invoice to:

Wilton® ENTERPRISES, INC. 2240 West 75th Street Woodridge, IL 60517 (312) 963-7100

FROM

Name

Address   Apt. No.

City

State   Zip

If your name and/or address has changed since you last ordered from Wilton, please fill in previous address here.

Name

Address   Apt. No.

City

State   Zip

Wilton® ENTERPRISES, INC.
Caller Service No. 1604
2240 West 75th Street
Woodridge, IL 60517

Enclose your signed check or money order with Order Form.

Will Not Be Delivered Without Proper Postage

Angelic Bliss

1. ARCHED TIER SET*

Impressive with Kolor-Flo Fountain. Includes: Six 13 in. arched columns, two 18 in. round separator plates, six angelic cherubs to attach to columns with royal icing or glue.
301-V-9752 $44.99 set
18 IN. PLATE
302-V-504 $12.99 each
13 IN. PILLARS
303-V-9719 $3.99 each
13 IN. PILLARS
Save $4.95 on pack of six.
301-V-9809 $18.99 pack

*Use Arched Tier Plates and Pillars together only.

2. HARVEST CHERUB SEPARATOR SET
Includes four 7 in. Harvest Cherub pillars, two 9 in. separator plates (lower plate has 12 in. overall diameter).
301-V-3517 $11.99 set

3. DANCING CUPID PILLARS 5½ in.high.
303-V-1210 $7.99 pack of 4

4. SNAP-ON CHERUBS
Accent Corinthian and Grecian pillars. (Pillars not included.) 3½ in. high.
305-V-4104 $1.29 pack of 4

5. FROLICKING CHERUB
A graceful eye-catcher. 5 in high.
1001-V-244 $2.79 each

6. TINY KNEELING CHERUB
Fits in with his melody of love.
206-V-150 $1.49 each

7. WINGED ANGELS
Angelic adornments. A pair per package. 2½ x 2in.
1001-V-457 $1.80 per package.

8. MUSICAL TRIO
Adds the right note. Each 3 in. high.
1001-V-368 $2.29 pack of 3

9. KNEELING CHERUB FOUNTAIN
Accent with tinted piping gel and flowers. 4 in. high.
1001-V-9380 $1.99 each

10. ANGELINOS
Captivating cutie for birthday and holiday cakes, too. 2 x 3in.
1001-V-504 $3.29 pack of 6

11. CHERUB CARD HOLDER
Charming place markers too! (Cards not included.) 1⅝ x 3⅜ in.
1001-V-9374 $3.49 pack of 4

12. ANGEL WITH HARP
Elegant and composed. 3½ in. high.
1001-V-7029 $4.49 pack of 4

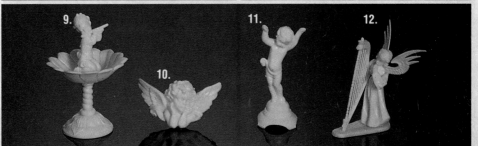

Majestic Enhancers

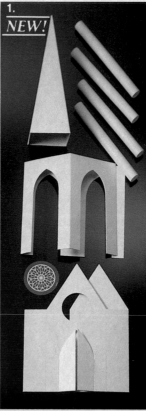

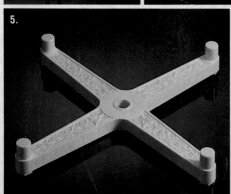

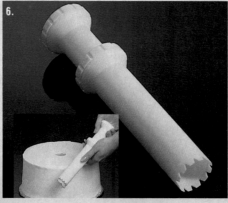

1. NEW! CATHEDRAL CAKE KIT

Transform basic wedding cakes into magnificent masterpieces. Kit includes: 5 easy-to-assemble white church pieces, 4 white plastic cake supports and a church window that can be illuminated from within.

2104-V-2940 $12.99 Kit

2. CRYSTAL-CLEAR CAKE DIVIDER SET

White plastic separator plates; ½ in. diameter 7½ in. high clear plastic twist legs penetrate cake and rest on plate (dowel rods not needed). Includes 6 in., 8 in., 10 in., 12 in., 14 in., 16 in. plates plus 24 legs. Save 25% on set.

301-V-9450 $45.99 set

Plates	Number	Price
6 IN.	302-V-9730	$ 2.99 each
8 IN.	302-V-9749	$ 3.99 each
10 IN.	302-V-9757	$ 4.99 each
12 IN.	302-V-9765	$ 6.99 each
14 IN.	302-V-9773	$ 8.99 each
16 IN.	302-V-9780	$10.99 each

7½ IN. TWIST LEGS
303-V-9794 $3.99 pack of 4

9 IN. TWIST LEGS
Add more height.

303-V-977 $3.99 pack of 4

3. TALL TIER STAND SET

Five twist-apart columns 6½ in. high with 1 bottom and 1 top bolt; 18 in. footed base plate; 16 in., 14 in., 12 in., 10 in., 8 in. separator plates (interchangeable, except footed base plate). White plastic. Save 25% on set.

304-V-7915 $45.99 set

Plates	Number	Price
8 IN.	302-V-7894	$ 3.99 each
10 IN.	302-V-7908	$ 4.99 each
12 IN.	302-V-7924	$ 5.99 each
14 IN.	302-V-7940	$ 8.99 each
16 IN.	302-V-7967	$11.99 each
18 IN.	302-V-7983	$14.99 each

COLUMNS

6½ IN.	303-V-7910	$ 1.59 each
7¾ IN.	304-V-5009	$ 2.59 each
13½ IN.	303-V-703	$ 4.29 each

TOP COLUMN CAP NUT
304-V-7923   79¢ each

GLUE-ON PLATE LEGS
304-V-7930   59¢ each

BOTTOM COLUMN BOLT
304-V-7941   99¢ each

4. FLOATING TIERS CAKE STAND SET

Display three tiers on this lovely metal cake stand. Fast and easy to use! Set includes stand and 8 in., 12 in., 16 in. smooth-edged separator plates.

307-V-825 $59.99 set

Additional plates available (same plates as Crystal-Clear Cake Divider Set).

Plates	Number	Price
8 IN.	302-V-9749	$ 3.99 each
12 IN.	302-V-9765	$ 6.99 each
16 IN.	302-V-9780	$10.99 each

5. TALL TIER 4-ARM BASE STAND

Replace Tall Tier Base Plate (See No. 3) with this heavy-duty white plastic support; add separator plates up to 12 in. For proper balance, add up to 3 graduated tiers to center column. Includes base bolt.

304-V-8245 $11.99 each

BASE BOLT ONLY
304-V-8253   59¢ each

6. CAKE CORER TUBE

Prepare tiers quickly and neatly for the Tall Tier Stand column. Serrated edge removes cake centers with one push. Ice cake before using. 7 in. long solid center fits into 6½ in. long hollow corer to eject cake bits. Cleans easily.

304-V-8172 $1.99 each

Crystal Beauty

1. CRYSTAL BRIDGE AND STAIRWAY SET
Set up a masterpiece. Includes two stairways (16¾ in. long) and one platform (4¾ in. x 5 in.). Plastic.
205-V-2311 $14.99 set
ONE STAIRWAY ONLY
205-V-2315 $7.99 each

2. THE KOLOR-FLO FOUNTAIN
Cascading waterfall with sparkling lights is the perfect way to enhance elegant formal tiers. Water pours from three levels. Top levels can be removed for smaller fountain arrangement. Intricate lighting system with two bulbs for extra brilliance. Plastic fountain bowl is 9¾ in. diameter. 110-124v. A.C. motor with 65 in. cord. Pumps water electrically. Directions and replacement part information included.
306-V-2599 $89.99 each
PUMP   306-V-1002 $34.99
PISTON   306-V-1029 $2.99
PUMP/BULB BRACKET   306-V-1037 $2.79
LAMP SOCKET   306-V-1045 $4.49
LIGHT BULB   306-V-1053 $2.49
CASCADE/PUMP CONNECTOR
306-V-1088 $2.29
FLOATER SWITCH   306-V-1096 $11.99
UPPER CASCADE   306-V-1118 $6.99
MIDDLE CASCADE   306-V-1126 $7.99
LOWER CASCADE   306-V-1134 $8.99
BOWL   306-V-1142 $12.99
BOTTOM BASE   306-V-1169 $6.99

3. FOUNTAIN CASCADE SET
Dome shapes redirect water over their surface in undulating rivulets. Set includes 4 pieces: 2½, 4½, 8 and 11½ in. diameter. (Kolor-Flo Fountain sold separately.)
306-V-1172 $14.99 set

4. FLOWER HOLDER RING.
White plastic. 12½ in. dia. x 2 in. high. Put at base of Kolor-Flo Fountain.
305-V-435 $4.99 each

5. CRYSTAL-LOOK TIER SET
Teams with the Kolor-Flo Fountain. Plastic. Two 17" plates; four 13¾" pillars.
301-V-1387 $39.99 set
17 IN. CRYSTAL-LOOK PLATE
(Use only with 13¾ in. crystal pillars.)
302-V-1810 $13.99 each
13¾ IN. CRYSTAL-LOOK PILLAR
(Use only with 17 in. crystal plate.)
303-V-2242 $3.99 each

6. CRYSTAL-LOOK PLATES
Use with crystal-look pillars.
7 IN. 302-V-2013 $2.99 each
9 IN. 302-V-2035 $3.99 each
11 IN. 302-V-2051 $4.99 each
13 IN. 302-V-2078 $6.99 each

7. CRYSTAL-LOOK BOWL
Perfect for blooms. 4½ x 1½ in deep.
205-V-1404 $2.49 each

8. CRYSTAL-LOOK SPIKED PILLARS
Double cake circles for support.
7 IN. 303-V-2322 $3.99 pack of 4
9 IN. 303-V-2324 $4.99 pack of 4

9. CRYSTAL-LOOK PILLARS
Combine with crystal-look plates and Crystal Bridge and Stairway Set.
3 IN. 303-V-2171 $2.99 pack of 4
5 IN. 303-V-2196 $3.99 pack of 4
7 IN. 303-V-2197 $3.99 pack of 4

Note: The cut crystal design and slender railings of this set are fragile. Please take special care when using and storing them to prevent damage.

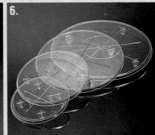

10. IRIDESCENT GRAPES
1099-V-200 $3.79 pack of 4

11. IRIDESCENT DOVES
1002-V-509 $3.49 pack of 6

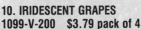

All plastic products made in Hong Kong. Kolor-Flo Fountain made in Germany.

Stately Pillars

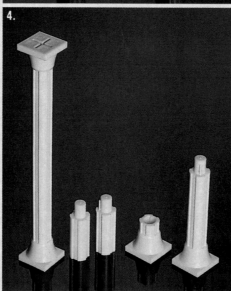

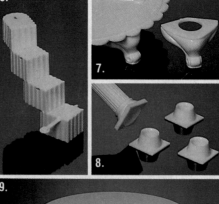

1. ARCHED PILLARS
Grecian-inspired with arched support structure. Embossed leaf motif adds impact. Pack of 4.
4½ IN. 303-V-452   **$2.99 pack**
6½ IN. 303-V-657   **$4.99 pack**

2. CORINTHIAN PILLARS
Another popular choice. Resembling authentic Greek columns, they're an impressive addition. Pack of 4.
5 IN. 303-V-819   **$3.59 pack**
7 IN. 303-V-800   **$4.59 pack**

3. ROMAN COLUMNS
Handsome pillars may be used with Kolor-Flo Fountain (remove one fountain tier if using 10¼ in.). Sleek lines, classic simplicity!
13¾ IN. 303-V-2129   **$2.99 each**
10¼ IN. 303-V-8135   **$2.59 each**

4. EXPANDABLE PILLARS
Striking, simple column is made up of six individual sections. It can adjust from 3 ins. to an impressive 10 ins. high! Ideal for busy decorators!
303-V-1777   **$8.99 pack of 4**

5. FIVE-COLUMN TIER SET.
Includes five 13¾-in. Roman columns and two 18-in. round scalloped-edged separator plates. A lovely set to use with the Kolor-Flo Fountain. White plastic.
301-V-1980   **$29.99 set**
13¾ IN. ROMAN PILLARS
303-V-2129   **$2.99 each**
18 IN. ROUND SEPARATOR PLATE
302-V-1225   **$10.99 each**

6. STAIRSTEPS
24 1 in. high stairs with 3 in. candleholders.
1107-V-8180   **$5.49 set**

7. SEPARATOR PLATE FEET
Elegant Queen Anne-inspired feet with scrollwork details are a perfect finishing touch. They'll fit all separator plates. Set of 4.
301-V-1247   **$1.59 set**

8. PLASTIC STUD PLATES
Just glue these studs on to sturdy cardboard cake circles to create an elegant separator plate for cake top or base. Real money-savers, especially when cake is to be given away. Studs fit all white (not crystal) pillars, except 13 in. Arched Pillars.
301-V-119   **$1.79 pack of 8**

9. SUPER STRONG CAKE STAND
Molded embossed base holds up to 185 pounds of cake! High impact polystyrene material and underweb of ribbing make this stand super strong. 2¾ in. high with arched sides. Full 18 in. diameter accomodates larger cake bases.
307-V-1200   **$12.99 each**

1. 54-PC. GRECIAN PILLAR AND PLATE SET

Deluxe collection provides you with round scalloped-edged separator plates and 5 inch pillars. Includes: 2 each 6, 8, 10, 12 and 14 inch plates; 20 Grecian pillars; and 24 pegs.
301-V-8380 $45.99 set

2. CLASSIC SEPARATOR PLATE SETS

Grecian pillars and scalloped-edged plates in 5 plate diameters and 2 pillar heights. Set includes 2 plates, 4 pillars and 4 pegs.

6 IN. PLATE SET WITH 3 IN. PILLARS
2103-V-639 $5.99 set
8 IN. PLATE SET WITH 5-IN. PILLARS
2103-V-256 $6.99 set
10 IN. PLATE SET WITH 5-IN. PILLARS
2103-V-108 $8.99 set
12 IN. PLATE SET WITH 5 IN. PILLARS
2103-V-124 $10.99 set

3. SWAN PILLARS

Grecian pillars with romantic swan base add flowing grace to your masterpiece. 4 in. high. Pack of 4.
303-V-7725 $2.99 pack

4. GRECIAN PILLARS.

Our most popular pillars will add grace and beauty to small and grand tiers. Elegantly scrolled and ribbed. Pack of 4.
5 IN. 303-V-3703 $2.99 pack
3 IN. 303-V-3606 $1.99 pack

5. PLASTIC PEGS

Add to insure that cake layers and separator plates atop cakes will stay in place. These pegs do not add any support, so dowel rod your cake properly before using. See page 106 for more details. 4 in. long. Set of 12.
399-V-762 $1.44 set

6. GRECIAN SPIKED PILLARS

Classic, sleek and impressive. Spiked pillars eliminate the need for separator plates on tier tops. Pillars push into cake to rest on separator plate or cake circle beneath. To prevent pillars from going through, be sure to double cake boards, or use separator plate when cakes are stacked.
5 IN. 303-V-3708 $1.99 pack
7 IN. 303-V-3710 $2.99 pack
9 IN. 303-V-3712 $3.99 pack

7. PLASTIC DOWEL RODS

Heavy-duty hollow plastic; strong sanitary support for all tiered cakes. Can be cut with serrated knife to desired length. 12¾ in. long x ¾ in. diameter.
399-V-801 $1.99 pack of 4

8. WOODEN DOWEL RODS

Essential for supporting stacked cakes and tiers. Complete assembling instructions, on page 106. Cut and sharpen with strong sheers and knife. 12 in. long. ¼ in. wide. Set of 12.
399-V-1009 $1.99 set

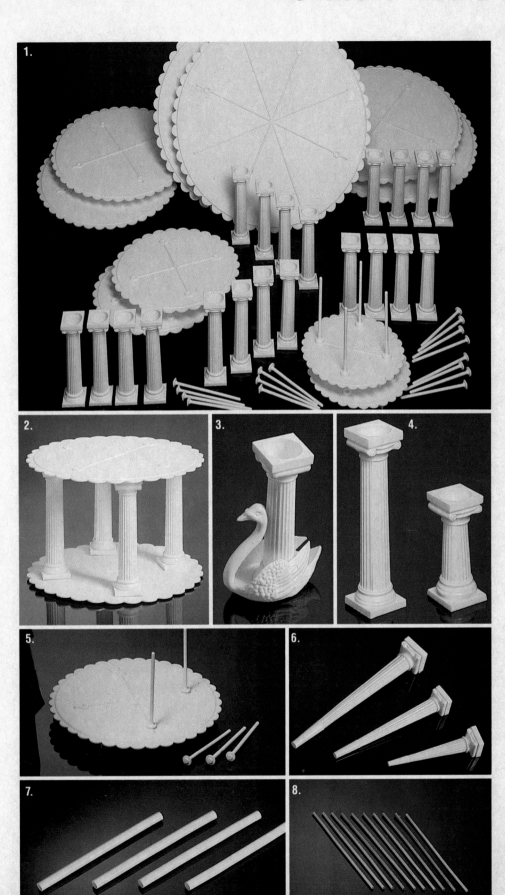

Separator Plates

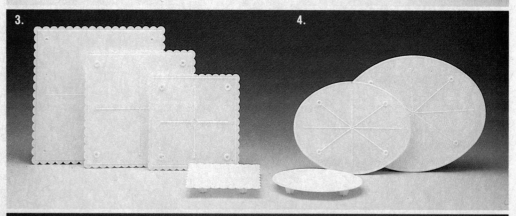

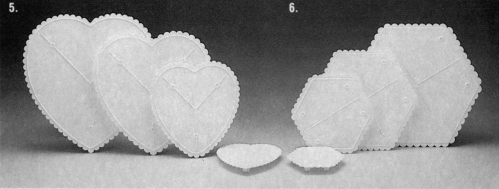

1. NEW! DECORATOR PREFERRED ROUND SEPARATOR PLATES
Super strong. Scalloped edge is interchangeable and compatible with other Wilton separator plates and pillars. See full description on inside back cover.

6 IN.	302-V-6	$1.79 each
7 IN.	302-V-7	$1.99 each
8 IN.	302-V-8	$2.29 each
9 IN.	302-V-9	$2.79 each
10 IN.	302-V-10	$3.29 each
11 IN.	302-V-11	$3.79 each
12 IN.	302-V-12	$4.29 each
13 IN.	302-V-13	$4.99 each
14 IN.	302-V-14	$5.29 each
15 IN.	302-V-15	$6.49 each
16 IN.	302-V-16	$7.29 each

2. ROUND SEPARATOR PLATES
Scalloped-edged plates in standard and odd sizes. Keep your plates in place, be sure to order Plastic Pegs (p. 165).

6 IN.	302-V-67	$1.79 each
7 IN.	302-V-1306	$1.99 each
8 IN.	302-V-83	$2.29 each
9 IN.	302-V-1322	$2.79 each
10 IN.	302-V-105	$3.29 each
11 IN.	302-V-1349	$3.79 each
12 IN.	302-V-120	$4.29 each
13 IN.	302-V-1365	$4.99 each
14 IN.	302-V-148	$5.29 each
15 IN.	302-V-1403	$6.49 each
16 IN.	302-V-946	$7.29 each

3. SQUARE SEPARATOR PLATES
Edges are gracefully scalloped.

7 IN.	302-V-1004	$2.99 each
9 IN.	302-V-1020	$3.99 each
11 IN.	302-V-1047	$4.99 each
13 IN.	302-V-1063	$5.99 each

4. OVAL SEPARATOR PLATES
Perfect support for oval tiers.

8½ IN.		
302-V-2130	$3.99 each	
11½ IN.		
302-V-2131	$4.99 each	
14½ IN.		
302-V-2132	$5.99 each	

5. HEART SEPARATOR PLATES
Scalloped-edged; perfect with our Heart Pans.

8 IN.	302-V-2112	$2.99 each
11 IN.	302-V-2114	$3.99 each
14½ IN.		
302-V-2116	$7.99 each	
16½ IN.		
302-V-2118	$8.99 each	

6. HEXAGON SEPARATOR PLATES
Scalloped-edged; combine with hexagon, square or round pans.

7 IN.	302-V-1705	$2.99 each
10 IN.	302-V-1748	$3.99 each
13 IN.	302-V-1764	$5.99 each
16 IN.	302-V-1799	$7.99 each

PLEASE NOTE: All prices, certain products and services, reflect the U.S.A. domestic market and do not apply in Australia and Canada.

1. ROUND TIER SET
The ideal choice for engagement parties, anniversaries, religious occasions and more. Set includes 5 x 2½-in, 7⅛ x 2½-in. and 9⁵⁄₁₆ x 2⅝-in. aluminum rounds; eight 5-in. Grecian Spiked Pillars; 6 and 8-in. scallop-edged round white plastic separator plates; instructions. Takes 2 cake mixes.
2105-V-2531 $21.99 set

2. ROUND MINI-TIER SET
Takes one cake mix. Set includes 5, 6 and 8-in. pans, 1-in. deep; 5, 7 in. separator plates; 8 clear plastic twist legs; decorating instructions.
2105-V-98042 $10.99 set
ROUND MINI-TIER PLATE SET ONLY
301-V-9817 $2.99 set

3. CLASSIC ROUND PAN SET
Set includes 6, 8, 10 and 12-in. aluminum pans. 2 in. deep.
2105-V-2101 $22.99 set

4. 2-PC. OVAL PAN SET
Set includes two 9 x 6¾ x 1¾ in. pans.
2105-V-1553 $8.99 set

5. 4-PC. OVAL PAN SET
Set includes four 2 in. deep aluminum pans. Sizes are 7¾ x 5⅝ in.; 10¾ x 7⅞ in.; 13 x 9⅞ in.; 16 x 12⅜ in.
2105-V-2130 $22.99 set

6. BEVEL PAN SET
Bakes beveled cake edges that can be positioned with layers. Set includes 8, 10, 12-in. tops and 14 and 16-in. bases.
517-V-1200 $25.99 set

7. 5-PC. SQUARE PAN SET
Classic tiers. Set includes 8, 10, 12, 14, 16-in. pans, 2-in. deep. If purchased separately, $54.99.
505-V-104 $49.99 set

8. 5-PC. ROUND TIER SET
Set includes 6, 8, 10, 12, 14-in. 2-in. deep aluminum pans.
504-V-118 $31.99

9. 3-IN. DEEP ROUND PAN SET
Set includes 8, 10, 12, 14-in. aluminum pans.
2105-V-2932 $31.99 set

10. 4-PC. HEXAGON PAN SET
Set includes 6, 9, 12, 15 in. pans, 2 in. deep.
2105-V-3572 $26.99 set
Also available (not shown)
9 IN. x 2 IN.
2105-V-5125 $6.99 each
12 IN. x 2 IN.
2105-V-5133 $8.99 each

11. PETAL PANS
Also available
9 IN. x 2 IN.
2105-V-5109 $6.99
12 IN. x 2 IN.
2105-V-5117 $8.99

12. 4-PC. PETAL PAN SET
Set includes 6, 9, 12 and 15 in., 2-in. aluminum deep.
2105-V-2134 $26.99 set

Plastic products made in Hong Kong.

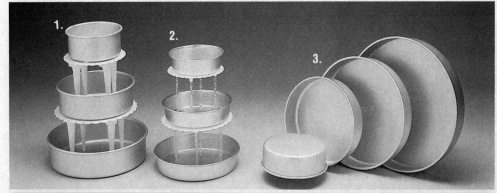

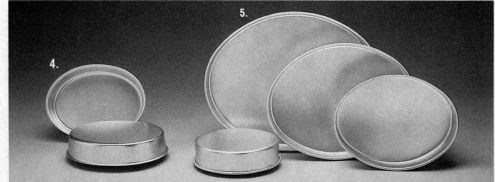

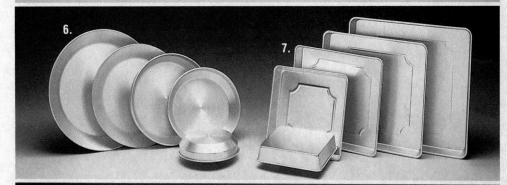

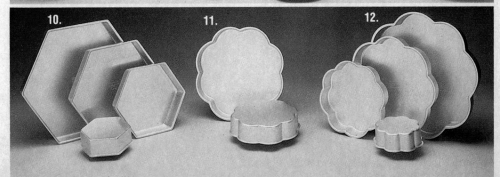

Performance Pans

2 IN. DEEP

NEW!

1. ROUND PANS...THE BAKING CLASSICS

Your options for baking lovely cakes are limitless.

2 IN. DEEP

16 IN. ROUND
2105-V-3963 $14.99
14 IN. ROUND
2105-V-3947 $11.99
12 IN. ROUND
2105-V-2215 $8.99
10 IN. ROUND
2105-V-2207 $6.49
8 IN. ROUND
2105-V-2193 $5.49
NEW! 7 IN. ROUND
2105-V-2190 $5.29
6 IN. ROUND
2105-V-2185 $4.99

2. 9 IN. ROUND PAN SET

Bake two 9 in. layer cakes at one time. Great Value! Easy to store.
2105-V-7908 $8.99 set of 2

3. 3 IN. DEEP

Bake impressive high cakes. Perfect for tortes, fruit and pound cakes, and cakes to be covered with fondant icing.
8 IN ROUND
2105-V-9104 $6.99
10 IN. ROUND
2105-V-9945 $8.99

4. CAKE SAVER

Designed to carry most elaborately decorated cakes. Generous size accommodates borders and top decorations easily. Use to carry or store all types of cakes, including bundt, angel food, cheese cakes, even pies, as well as layer cakes. Maintains freshness. Wide enough for a 10 in. cake with borders or a 12 in. cake without borders. Includes one 14 in. round base and one 6 in. high cover.
415-V-905 $9.99

5. BAKE-EVEN CAKE STRIPS.

At last, an ingenious way to bake perfectly level, moist cakes. Avoid high-rise centers, cracked tops or crusty edges. Just dampen strips and wrap around the pan before baking. Each band is 1½ in. wide x 30 in. long, with 1 in. overlap.

SMALL SET
Contains 2 bands, enough for two 8 or 9 in. round pans.
415-V-260 $5.49

LARGE SET
Contains 4 bands, enough for one of each of the following: 10, 12, 14 and 16 in. round pans.
415-V-262 $13.99

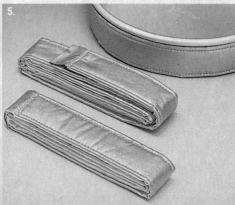

2 IN. DEEP

3 IN. DEEP

Rely on Wilton Performance Pans Premium Bakeware for baking your very best. You'll achieve repeated success with these professional-quality anodized aluminum pans. Not only are they durable, they're dishwasher safe. An unequaled variety of sizes and shapes gives you countless possibilities. Whether you're creating tall-tiered cakes or roasting prime rib, you can depend on Performance Pans for the finest results.

6. SQUARE PANS...THE BAKING VERSATILES

The most basic shape to bake plain or fancy cakes. A variety of sizes to create a first-class feast from bread to dessert. 2 in. deep.

16 IN. SQUARE
2105-V-8231 $15.99
14 IN. SQUARE
2105-V-8220 $13.99
12 IN. SQUARE
2105-V-8213 $10.99
10 IN. SQUARE
2105-V-8205 $8.49
8 IN. SQUARE
2105-V-8191 $6.49
6 IN. SQUARE
507-V-2180 $4.99

7. 9 x 13 CAKE PAN COVER

Cover, protect and transport decorated cakes in the pan with this cover. Designed for use with the Wilton 9 x 13 in. Performance Pan*, this cover has a raised dome lid which allows you to cover decorated cakes with ease. Keeps cakes and other foods fresh in the pan, even after slicing.

415-V-903 $3.99 each

*Cake pan not included.

8. SHEET PANS . . . THE BAKE ALLS

Essential for the all-around cook and baker. The versatility coupled with dependability makes these pans the ones to always have on hand. 2 in. deep.

12 x 18 IN. SHEET
2105-V-182 $12.99
11 x 15 IN. SHEET
2105-V-158 $10.99
9 x 13 IN. SHEET**
2105-V-1308 $6.99
7 x 11 IN. SHEET
2105-V-2304 $5.99

**Cover cakes-to-go and left overs with the Wilton Cake Pan Cover sold above. Made of natural polypropylene, this is a ''must-have'' for anyone who takes cakes to picnics and get-togethers.

Ovencraft Pans

3 IN. DEEP

2 IN. DEEP

Cake Pans for the Professional. Every hardworking kitchen should be equipped with this line of exceptional bakeware! The most discriminating bakers and decorators can get superb results again and again with these expertly crafted pans. Their special design produces perfect straight-sided cakes. The smooth anodized finish releases cakes with ease. The durable, extra-heavy gauge aluminum produces even heating for the best baking results. The labels feature a cake cutting guide, baking hints and icing recipes.

3 IN. DEEP ROUND PANS
Bake higher, more impressive cakes.

18 IN. HALF-ROUND
Use to bake an 18 in. round cake in a conventional oven.
2105-V-5622 $12.99 each
14 x 3 IN.
2105-V-5610 $12.99 each
12 x 3 IN.
2105-V-5609 $10.99 each
10 x 3 IN.
2105-V-5608 $8.99 each
8 x 3 IN.
2105-V-5607 $6.99 each
6 x 3 IN.
2105-V-5620 $4.99 each

2-IN. DEEP ROUND PANS
Ideal for two-layer cakes and tier cakes.
16 x 2 IN.
2105-V-5606 $14.99 each
14 x 2 IN.
2105-V-5605 $11.99 each
12 x 2 IN.
2105-V-5604 $8.99 each
10 x 2 IN.
2105-V-5603 $6.49 each
9 x 2 IN.
2105-V-5619 $5.99 each
8 x 2 IN.
2105-V-5602 $5.49 each
6 x 2 IN.
2105-V-5601 $4.99 each

SHEET PANS
Create luscious cakes with this versatile shape and 2-3/16 in. depth.
12 x 18 IN.
2105-V-5618 $16.99 each
11 x 15 IN.
2105-V-5617 $14.99 each
9 x 13 IN.
2105-V-5616 $11.99 each

SQUARE PANS
Perfectly square corners and 2-3/16 in. depth produce professional quality cakes.
14 IN.
2105-V-5614 $16.99 each
12 IN.
2105-V-5613 $13.99 each
10 IN.
2105-V-5612 $10.99 each
8 IN.
2105-V-5611 $7.99 each

With today's lifestyle, you want products that can fit into your busy schedule. Microwave cake and dessert baking is fast, easy and convenient . . . and very suitable to modern living. Now you can add fun to your microwave baking with Wilton MicroBakes. The pans are made in the U.S.A., and are designed especially for use with microwave cake and dessert mixes. MicroBakes are available in a wide variety of basic, novelty and holiday shapes. All are reusable. And with MicroBakes, you can bake in the summer without the heat of conventional ovens.

The exclusive MicroGrid™ baking system at the bottom of the flat pans distributes heat, providing more consistent baking results.

MicroBakes are top rack, dishwasher-safe.

For the ease of microwave baking with the fun of a Wilton pan, choose MicroBakes. They're sized to fit *any* Microwave cake mix.

$4.49 each

Row 1
DOUBLE MIX
RECTANGLE	2106-V-104
SQUARE	2106-V-102
HEART	2106-V-106

Row 2
FLAN	2106-V-112
RING	2106-V-118
FANCY RING *	2106-V-124

Row 3
ROUND	2106-V-100
CLOWN	2106-V-114
BIG BIRD	2106-V-116

Row 4
MINI HEART	2106-V-120
JUMBO MUFFIN *	2106-V-130
SHORTCAKES 'N TREATS	2106-V-126

Row 5
STAR	2106-V-110
CHRISTMAS TREE	2106-V-122
TEDDY BEAR	2106-V-108

*available 10/1/89

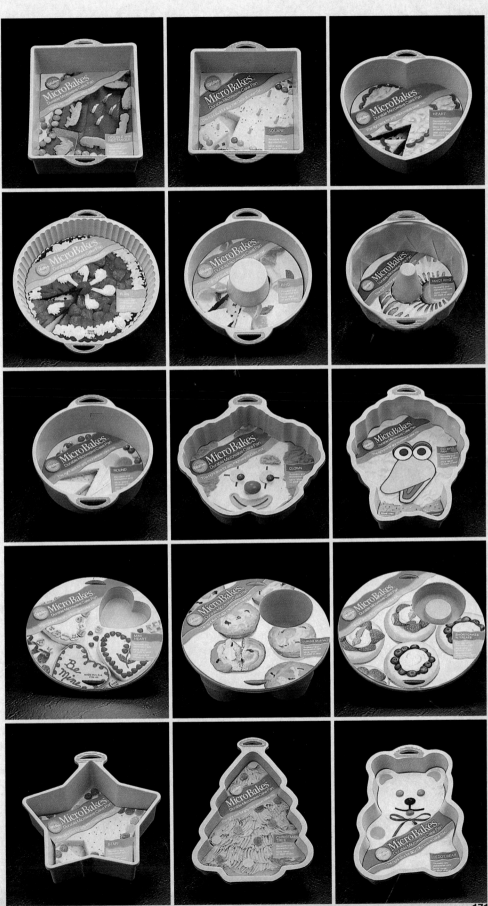

Specialty Bakeware & Tools

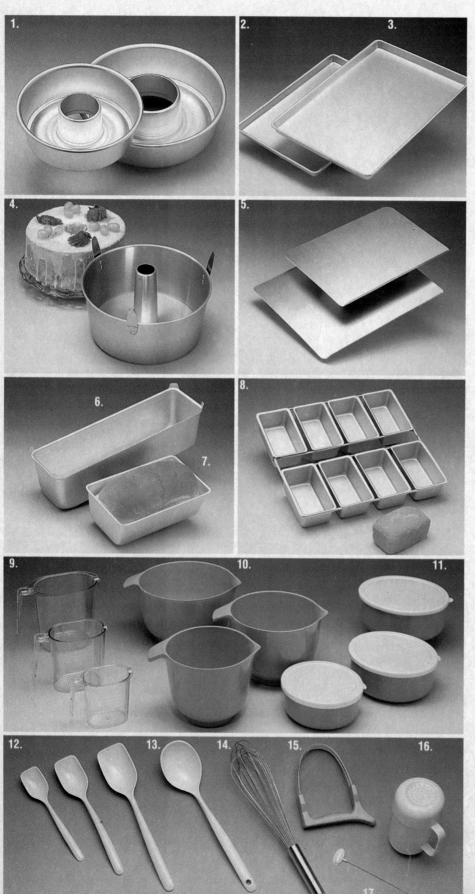

1. RING MOLDS/PANS
Two great sizes. Each 3 in. deep.
8 IN. RING MOLD/PAN
2105-V-190 $6.49
10 IN. RING MOLD/PAN
2105-V-4013 $7.99

2. JELLY ROLL PAN/COOKIE PAN
10½ x 15½ x 1 in.
2105-V-1269 $8.99

3. COOKIE/JELLY ROLL PAN, 12 x 18 x 1 in.
2105-V-4854 $9.99

4. ANGEL FOOD PAN
For angel food and chiffon cakes; it even bakes pound or fruit cake. 2-piece, 10-in. diameter, 4½-in. deep. Takes 1 standard angel or chiffon cake mix.
2105-V-2525 $12.99

5. COOKIE SHEETS
10 x 15 IN. 2105-V-1265 $5.99
12½ x 16½ IN. 2105-V-2975 $7.49

6. LONG LOAF PAN
Bake classic cakes or angel food. Takes 9 cups of batter or standard angel food mix.
16 in. x 4 in. x 4½ in.
2105-V-1588 $9.99

7. LOAF PAN
Perfect for sandwich loaf, cakes, bread, more.
8¾ in. x 4½ in. x 2¾ in.
2105-V-3688 $5.99

8. MINI LOAF PAN SET
2105-V-3844 $14.99

9. MEASURING CUP SET
Clear plastic with standard and metric measurements. 1, 2 and 4-cup. (Hong Kong.)
415-V-555 $5.99 set

10. 3-PC. MIXING BOWL SET
Easy to grip with non-skid base ring to prevent slipping. Spill-proof pouring. Includes 1, 2 and 3 quart sizes. See color code below.
2520-V-01 $24.99

11. 6-PC. STORAGE BOWL SET
Snap on lid for secure storage. 3, 4 and 6-cup bowls won't discolor or absorb stains. Dishwasher and freezer safe. See color code below.
2520-V-28 $12.99
COLOR CODE NO. Use when ordering 10 & 11:
BISCUIT 01   RED 20
BLUE 03   DUSTY ROSE 21
SLATE BLUE 10   WHITE 24

12. SCOOP SET
White melamine scoops in 1, 2 and 4 Tbls.
2530-V-2824 $2.99

13. COOKING SPOON, 12 in. white plastic spoon.
2530-V-3224 $1.59

14. WIRE BALLOON WHISK
Stainless steel wires are sealed in handle; 12 in. long. (Taiwan)
415-V-816 $5.99

15. PASTRY BLENDER
Stainless steel wires, plastic handle. (Taiwan)
415-V-820 $2.99

16. ALL-PURPOSE SHAKER
White plastic, dishwasher safe. (Hong Kong.)
415-V-679 $1.99

17. CAKE TESTER
6-in. length makes it safe to use. Stainless steel with easy grip handle. (Taiwan.)
415-V-625   69¢

Specialty Bakeware

NEW! 1.

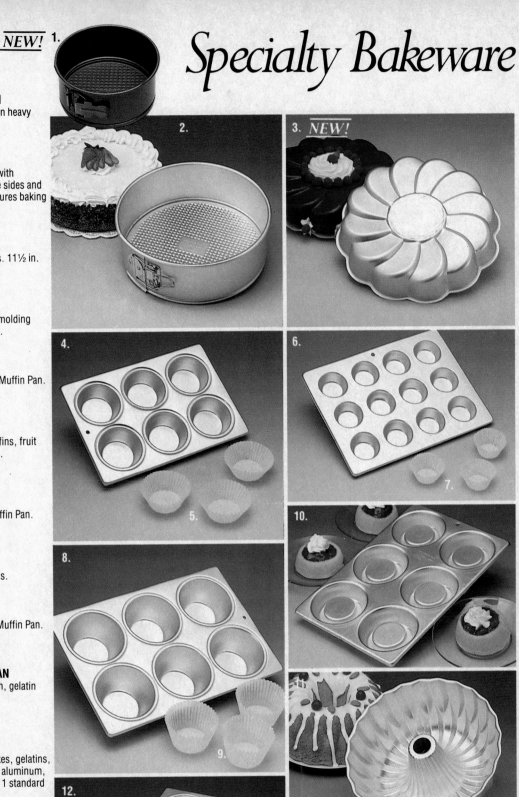

1. NEW! 6 IN. SPRINGFORM PAN
Unique size. Quality non-stick finish on heavy gauge steel. 3 in. deep.
2105-V-218 $6.99 each

2. 9 IN. SPRINGFORM PAN
Party-perfect cheesecakes come out with ease. Just release springlock, remove sides and serve. The waffle textured surface insures baking success. 3 in. deep.
2105-V-5354 $9.99

3. NEW! VIENNESE SWIRL PAN
Make lovely continental style desserts. 11½ in. diameter.
2105-V-8252 $8.99 each

4. SIX-CUP MUFFIN PAN
From muffins to cupcakes! Great for molding desserts, too. 7⅜ x 10¾ x 1 in. deep.
2105-V-5338 $6.99

5. MUFFIN BAKE CUPS
Paper liners for use with the Six-Cup Muffin Pan. 75 per carton.
415-V-1115 $1.49 carton

6. MINI-MUFFIN PAN
Make multiple bite-size delights. Muffins, fruit cakes, cupcakes, cheesecakes, more.
7¾ x 10 x ¾ in.
2105-V-2125 $6.99

7. MINI-MUFFIN CUPS
Paper liners for use with the Mini-Muffin Pan. 100 per carton.
415-V-1117 $1.49 carton

8. JUMBO MUFFIN PAN
Bake super-size cupcakes and muffins.
2105-V-1820 $11.99

9. JUMBO BAKE CUPS
Paper liners for use with the Jumbo Muffin Pan. 50 per carton.
415-V-1113 $1.59 carton

10. SHORTCAKES 'N' TREATS PAN
It's easy to make brownies, ice cream, gelatin and lots of other original treats.
8 x 12½ x 1 in. deep.
2105-V-5966 $6.99

11. FANCY RING MOLD/PAN
This unique pan offers a menu of cakes, gelatins, ice cream, mousse, more! Anodized aluminum, 10 in. diameter, 3 in. deep and takes 1 standard bundt-type cake mix.
2105-V-5008 $9.99

12. PETITE FANCY RING MOLDS/PANS
Diminutive desserts in elegant form.
2105-V-2097 $15.99

13. CONTINENTAL FLAN
So many international recipes are possible with this elegant pan. 11-in. diameter.
2105-V-2046 $7.99

All Occasion Pans

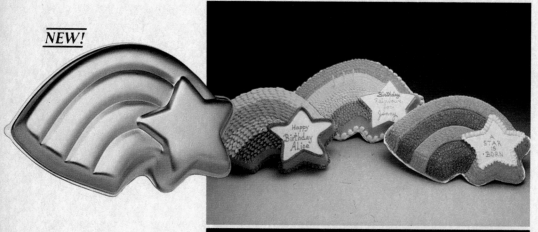

NEW!

NEW! SHOOTING STAR PAN
Blaze a radiant trail of party colors. This natural wonder is always a good omen signaling fun and happy times. Perfect for any star-rating event. One mix aluminum pan is 15½ x 10 in.
2105-V-804 $8.99 each

STAR PAN
What an illustrious way to give someone the star treatment. Brighten birthdays and a galaxy of other stellar occasions. New possibilities shine through again and again with so many ways to decorate. One-mix aluminum pan is 12¾-in. across.
2105-V-2512 $8.99 each

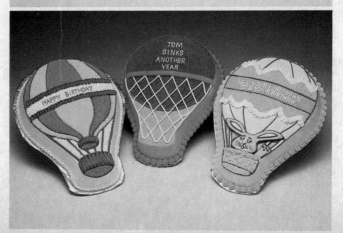

HORSESHOE PAN
Here's a good luck charm to convey the very best. It's a perfect sign of good fortune for graduations, baby showers, promotions and so much more. The classic shape also takes on many other exciting decorating ideas. One-mix aluminum pan is 12 x 1¾-in.
2105-V-3254 $8.99 each

UP 'N AWAY BALLOON PAN
Reach new heights in celebrating birthdays and other high-flying events. This cake also successfully carries off greetings of "congratulations" and "bon voyage". Four ways to decorate included. One-mix pan is 14½ x 10½ x 1⅞-in.
2105-V-1898 $8.99 each

174

All pans made in Korea.

WONDER MOLD KIT

In every season, you'll find our fair lady at the loveliest affairs —birthdays, graduations and bridal showers. Use the mold alone or as a part of another cake design. Aluminum pan (8-in. diam., 5-in. deep) takes 5-6 cups of firm-textured batter. Heat-conducting rod assures even baking. Kit contains pan, rod, stand, 7-in. doll pick and instructions.

2105-V-565 $11.99 kit

WONDER MOLD PAN ONLY

(without doll pick)

502-V-682 $8.99

TEEN DOLL PICK

7-in tall, same as in kit.

2815-V-101 $2.99 each

PETITE DOLL PAN

Couple this pan with the Small Doll Picks for a petite feminine quartet. Alone, it lends itself to all sorts of inventive cake ideas. Great assembled wtih the Wonder Mold Kit as a color-coordinated bridal party centerpiece.

508-V-302 $8.99 each

SMALL DOLL PICKS

4½-in. on pick.

1511-V-1019 $4.99 pack of 4

GUITAR PAN SET

From Country & Western to Heavy Metal, music fans will rave about this cake. Just ice, place plastic trims and pipe simple borders. Strings (not included) can be added for even more musical effect. Includes plastic neck, bridge and pick guard. One-mix aluminum pan is 17¾ x 8½ x 2-in.

501-V-904 $8.99 set

GUITAR ACCESSORY KIT ONLY

503-V-938 $1.59 set.

DOUBLE-TIER ROUND PAN

Bake up a special effect! Just use one 2-layer cake mix in one pan. Create two classic tiers – 6 and 10-in. Decorate this unique shape with either sophistication or whimsy. A year round party pleaser. Aluminum pan is 9¾ x 3-in.

2105-V-1400 $8.99 each

PIANO KIT

A concerto in cake and icing – such sweet music to enliven a birthday or usher in the New Year! In fact, our baby grand is a well-tuned addition to most any celebration. Pans take one mix. Kit includes two 1-in. deep aluminum pans (6¾ x 7¾-in. and 9½ x 7-in.), plastic top, base, 4 snap-on legs, props, stick, 2 candelabras, pedals, music board and keyboard.

501-V-8093 $12.99 kit.

PIANO ACCESSORY KIT ONLY

503-V-8084 $7.49 each

All Occasion Pans

NEW!

NEW! MINI-BELL PAN
Six cakes baked at once that ring true with the festive spirit! A classic shape for birthdays, Christmas and wedding showers. The single-serving size can also be set on larger cakes with remarkable results. Aluminum pan is 9½ x 13 in.
2105-V-8254   **$8.99 each**

GUMBALL MACHINE PAN
Children of all ages can't resist the lure of the gumball machine. In cake and colorful icing, it will be even more irresistible. The alternate decorating ideas are equally exciting. Takes one cake mix. 8 x 13½-in.
2105-V-2858   **$8.99**

DOUBLE BELL PAN
For whom the bells toll? Future brides, anniversary couples, and Christmas merry-makers—just to name a few. Throughout the calendar, there's always an occasion to ring out a special sentiment. One-mix aluminum pan is 13½ x 10½ x 2-in.
2105-V-1537   **$8.99 each**

CONGRATULATIONS PAN
For those jolly good fellows that nobody can deny, here's a cake that fits perfectly. Wish them the best of everything! Our one-mix aluminum pan is 15 x 9½ x 1⅞-in. and includes alternate decorating ideas.
2105-V-3523   **$8.99 each**

QUESTION MARK PAN
Pose any question. This quick and easy cake answers the who, what, when and why of every occasion. After all, inquiring party-goers want to know. One-mix aluminum pan is 14⅞ x 11 x 12-in.
2105-V-1840   **$8.99 each**

All pans made in Korea.

All Occasion Pans

NEW!

NEW! USA PAN
Put yourself on the map by creating the All-American cake. Besides the Fourth of July, there's a long list of occasions to celebrate with this pan—a new move, a bon voyage or a political victory. Aluminum pan is 14½ x 9¼ in.
2105-V-8251 $8.99 each

BOOK PAN
Publish special messages on cakes that always receive rave reviews. This open book details every one of life's important chapters – birthdays, baby showers, graduations and much more. Create a colorful greeting card cake, too. Five ways to decorate included. One-mix aluminum pan is 13 x 9½ x 2-in.
2105-V-972 $8.99 each

TWO-MIX BOOK PAN
Bake a cake of epic proportions. For larger parties, this great volume serves up to 30 guests. The story unfolds as the crowd gathers to celebrate most any major occasion. 11½ x 15 x 2 ¾-in. aluminum pan.
2105-V-2521 $12.99 each

HAMBURGER PAN
Top off an all-American fast food party with this colorful cake with everything on it. Hundreds will be served at birthdays, school parties, promotions and a whole lot more. One-mix aluminum pan is 11 3/8 x 11 x 2-in.
2105-V-3306 $8.99 each

T-SHIRT PAN
Fit any occasion to a ''T'' with a cake that's always dressed to thrill. This pan adapts easily to birthdays, baby showers and any other celebration you can imagine. One-mix aluminum pan is 13¼ x 12½ x 2-in.
2105-V-2347 $8.99 each

PLEASE NOTE: All prices, certain products and services reflect the U.S. domestic market and do not apply in Australia and Canada.

All Occasion Pans

NEW! HAPPY CLOWN PAN
Color a happy face of classic comedy. This circus funny man brings on smiles at kids' parties. Modify his looks to entertain at all sorts of occasions. Aluminum pan is 12 x 12 in.
2105-V-802 $8.99 each

BUTTERFLY PAN
This delightful pan is all aflutter with design possibilities. Decorate simply or with intricate detail. This lovely creature will spread its fanciful wings at all sorts of social events. 10½ x 13-in. aluminum pan takes one cake mix.
2105-V-5409 $8.99 each

CHOO CHOO TRAIN PAN
Here's the little 3-D engine that could – pulling through again with a trainload of fun. All aboard! Two-part aluminum pan snaps together. Pan is 10 x 6 x 4-in. Takes 6 cups of firm-textured batter. Instructions included.
2105-V-2861 $10.99 each

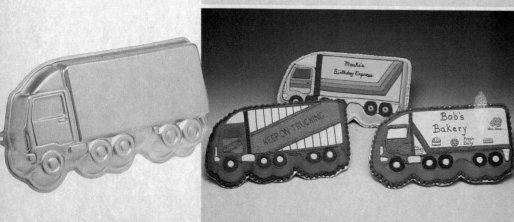

18-WHEELER TRUCK PAN
Here's the perfect vehicle for transporting tons of warm wishes. Deliver special greeting on Dad's Day, moving day and at life's major milestones. One-mix aluminum pan is 8¾ x 17 x 2-in.
2105-V-0018 $8.99 each

All pans made in Korea.

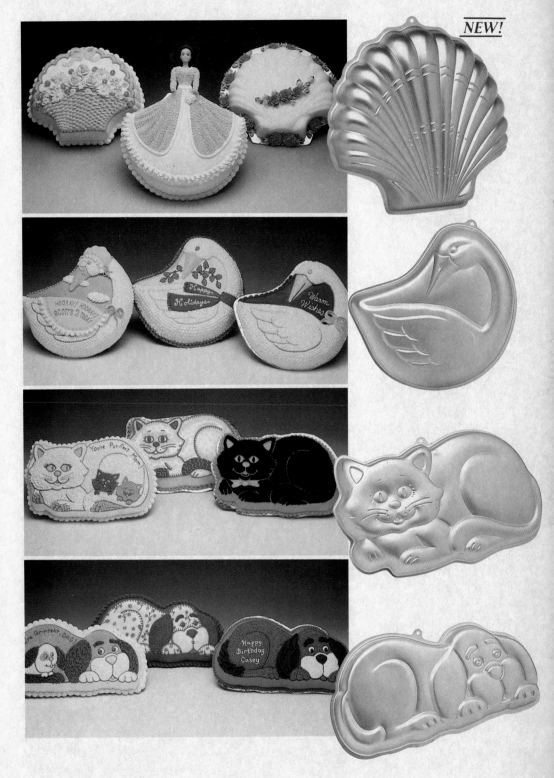

NEW!

NEW! SHELL PAN
Include simple elegance in your collection of bakeware. With the recipe for delicate lemon cake printed on the label, create a delectable dessert topped with gorgeous yellow fondant. Here's a shaped pan that you'll turn to time and time again. Aluminum pan is 11 x 12 in.
2105-V-8250 $8.99 each

GOOSE PAN
Take a gander at our graceful goose. What perfect casting as Mother Goose for kids' parties and baby showers. It also adds sweet country charm to the Christmas season. Aluminum pan is 11½ x 12 inches and takes one cake mix.
2105-V-2499 $8.99 each

KITTY CAT PAN
There's more than one way to decorate a cat – especially with this pan. Create sleek or long-haired breeds for fans of felines everywhere. 9 x 15 x 2-in. aluminum pan takes one cake mix.
2105-V-1009 $8.99 each

PUPPY DOG PAN
So many folks are smitten with puppy love. Here's the cake bred especially to make them feel all warm inside. He's a loyal mascot to have at a variety of celebrations. 17½ x 8⅞ x 1⅞-in. aluminum pan takes one cake mix.
2105-V-2430 $8.99 each

All Occasion Pans

CUDDLES THE COW PAN
Our very own queen of the barnyard is certainly not the bossy type. This bovine beauty "mooves" in the very best circles of kids' parties. She'll even charm grown-ups with her fun, light-hearted attitude. Takes one mix. Aluminum pan is 12¾ x 12½ in.
2105-V-2875 $8.99 each

PARTYSAURUS PAN
Back from extinction and ready to rock 'n' roll! The continued celebrity of dinosaurs makes our pre-historic party animal a must-have at all sorts of fun fests. It's fun casting him in countless new roles. One mix pan is 16 x 10 x 1⅞-in.
2105-V-1280 $8.99 each

LITTLE MOUSE PAN
He seems to be saying "CHEESE". This cute little guy has a friendly smile for every birthday boy or girl. His happy face makes any day a special event. One-mix pan is 15¾ x 9½ x 2-in.
2105-V-2380 $8.99 each

HUGGABLE TEDDY BEAR PAN
Now here's an old friend who's enjoying more popularity than ever. Maybe it's because he makes folks feel so good. He'll bring his happy mood to any occasion. Ideas for birthdays and baby showers included. One mix aluminum pan is 13½ x 12¼ x 2-in.
2105-V-4943 $8.99 each

All pans made in Korea.

All Occasion Pans

TEDDY BEAR STAND-UP PAN
This beloved buddy in 3-D adds a dimension of delight to special days year 'round. He gladdens hearts, both young and old, with his classic charm and sweetness. Includes many ingenious decorating ideas. Two-piece aluminum pan is 9½ x 8½ x 5-in. Core, stand and clips.
2105-V-2325 $15.99 set

BAKING CORE ONLY*
503-V-504 $3.59

*Although slightly smaller than the core included with the pan, this works as well.

ROCKING HORSE PAN
Indulge your hobby for decorating with this perennial favorite. The Wild West, carnival or Christmas-time are just a few of the themes to give this lovable toy. It's a winner for birthdays and baby showers. One-mix aluminum pan is 13½ x 13½ x 2-in.
2105-V-2388 $8.99 each

PRECIOUS PONY PAN
A little horseplay is always expected at a kid's party. Create a colt or a filly to prance about with warm birthday wishes. Captivating alternate ways to decorate are included. One-mix aluminum pan is 16 x 11 x 2-in.
2105-V-2914 $8.99 each

PANDA PAN
Here's one of the cutest cakes in captivity! With so many great ways to decorate it, this 3-D delight is a hit at all sorts of happy events. Two-piece aluminum pan takes 6½ cups of firm-textured batter. Includes 6 clips, heat conducting core and instructions. Pan is 9½ x 8⅝-in. tall.
2105-V-603 $15.99 each

BAKING CORE ONLY
503-V-504 $3.59

PANDA MOLD
Aluminum 2-pc. mold/pan is perfect for baking cakes and molding candy, ice cream, sugar. About 5 in. high.
518-V-489 $4.99 each

181

Favorite Characters

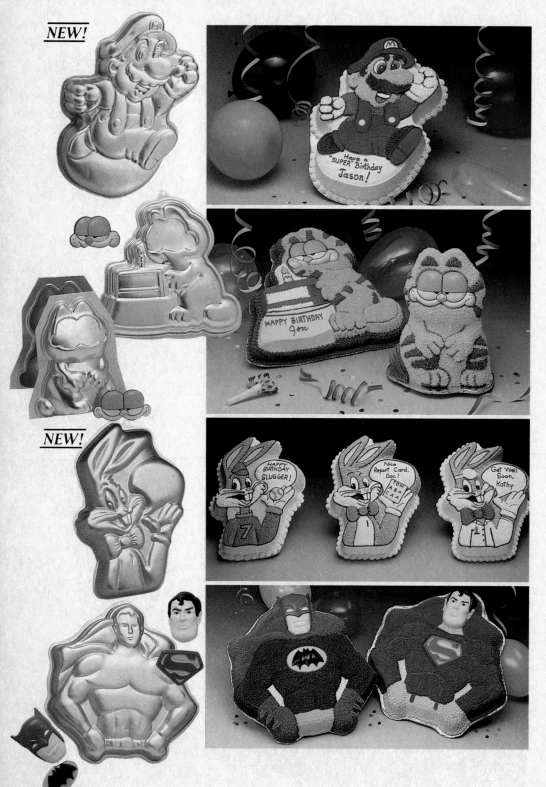

NEW! SUPER MARIO BROTHERS®
Now it's your turn to have some fun. You can be sure your man will win every time! Aluminum pan takes one cake mix. 14¼ x 9½ in. Available 10/15/89.
2105-V-2989 $9.99 each
© 1989 Nintendo of America, Inc.

GARFIELD® ONE-MIX PAN
Count on this fussy feline to be on his best behavior on birthdays, holidays, graduation, more. Five ways to decorate are included. The plastic facemaker is a super decorating timesaver. Pan is 11½ x 12½ x 2-in.
2105-V-2447 $9.99 set

GARFIELD® STAND-UP CAKE PAN SET
This cool cat will have everyone under his paw at the party scene. Plastic facemaker included. Set also contains a 2-pc. aluminum pan, clips, baking stand and instructions. Finished cake will be 6 x 6 x 9-in. high.
2105-V-3147 $14.99 set
© 1984 GARFIELD. United Feature Syndicate, Inc.

NEW! BUGS BUNNY PAN
This kwazy wabbit gets top billing at parties for folks of all ages. On the cartoon balloon, pipe in a special message to suit the situation. Aluminum pan takes one cake mix. 14 x 9 in.
2105-V-8253 $8.99 each

All pans made in Korea. Plastic facemakers made in Hong Kong.
NOTE: LICENSED CHARACTER PANS CANNOT BE SOLD FOR COMMERCIAL USE.

SUPER HEROES PAN
There are a couple of great guys in this one pan. Whomever you choose, he's perfect for birthdays, Dad's Day, promotions, graduation and lots more. Set includes 13 x 13 x 2-in. pan, SUPERMAN* and BATMAN plastic face masks and chest emblems.
2105-V-8507 $9.99 set
BATMAN MASK & EMBLEM
503-V-814 $1.99 set
SUPERMAN MASK & EMBLEM
503-V-857 $1.99 set
*TRADEMARKS LICENSED BY DC COMICS, INC.
© 1978

Favorite Characters

NEW!

SESAME STREET CELEBRITIES

NEW! BIG BIRD PAN
Here's a brainy bird with the smarts to teach our children well. From Sesame Street, this ever-popular star in his new setting still maintains a faithful following among pre-schoolers. One-mix aluminum pan. 13 x 11 in.
2105-V-0805 $8.99 each

ERNIE CAKE PAN
He's bound to give his all to see that the party is a real ball! One-mix aluminum pan is 14½ x 10 x 1⅞-in.
2105-V-3173 $8.99 each

COOKIE MONSTER CAKE PAN
Indescribably delightful! This wide-eyed monster whips up a happy birthday surprise. Alternate designs turn his cake into a card or a gift. One-mix aluminum pan is 14½ x 11½ x 1⅞-in.
2105-V-4927 $8.99 each

© 1985 Children's Television Workshop. BIG BIRD AND COOKIE MONSTER are trademarks of Muppets, Inc. SESAME STREET and SESAME STREET SIGN are trademarks and service marks of the Children's Television Workshop. All rights reserved.

NEW! TEENAGE MUTANT NINJA TURTLES
Here's one guy who'll be a winner at every event. Your decorating prowess will make him the center of attention at birthdays, graduations, and other fun party times. One mix aluminum pan. 15 x 9½ in. Available 10/15/89.
2105-V-3075 $9.99 each

© 1989 Teenage Mutant Ninja Turtles® is a registered trademark of Mirage Studios, U.S.A.

ALF™ PAN
Audacious and disarming, this alien life form has worked his way into the hearts of millions. He'll put fun into any occasion—especially birthdays! The plastic facemaker does justice to the old ALFer! One-mix aluminum pan is 11½ x 12 x 1⅝-in.
2105-V-2705 $9.99 each

ALF is a Registered Trademark of Alien Productions®
© 1987 Alien productions. All Rights Reserved.

Sports Pans

BASEBALL GLOVE PAN

Root for the home team by baking this all-star cake! Sandlot sluggers and big league players alike will get caught up in the sweet taste of victory. One-mix aluminum pan is 12 x 12¼ x 1¾ in.
2105-V-1234 $8.99 each

BALL PAN SET

The fans will go wild as they all keep their eyes on the ball. Bake up this treat to celebrate a winning score. This imaginative cake can also be adapted to any occasion. Set includes two 6-in. diameter half ball aluminum pans and two metal baking stands. Each pan half takes 2½ cups batter.
502-V-3002 $7.99 each
BALL PAN BAKE STAND ONLY.
503-V-881. $.99 each

BOWLING PAN SET

Strike up a rousing response with a cake entirely in its own league. Or use this pan lots of other clever ways for birthdays and holidays. Set includes two 14-in. aluminum pans and two baking racks. Takes one cake mix for 2 halves.
502-V-4424 $9.99 each

MINI-BALL PAN

Score really big on the party circuit with cakes-for-one. These little treats are perfect in any championship season. Ice balls and push together for a 3-D effect. One cake mix will yield 12 to 15 balls. 11½ x 7½ x 1½ in. aluminum pan.
2105-V-1760 $8.99 each

FOOTBALL HERO PAN

Tackle all sorts of sporting occasions. Give this cake the colors and insignias of any team. Put any number on the jersey. It's an unbeatable way to touch down on any particular sports favorite. One-mix aluminum pan is 12 x 12½ x 2 in.
2105-V-4610 $8.99 each

GOLF BAG PAN

Tee off for all sorts of celebrations! Here's a cake bound to be popular at the clubhouse. It links perfectly to birthdays, retirement parties and much more. One-mix aluminum pan is 15 x 8½ x 2½ in.
2105-V-1836 $8.99 each

Halloween Pans

NEW! SCARECROW PAN
Let this charming little man of straw brighten your harvest table with colorful character. Suit every season with all kinds of alternative decorating schemes. One-mix aluminum pan is 15 x 11½ in.
2105-V-801 $8.99 each

NEW!

BOO GHOST PAN
Conjure up this spooky spirit for fright night. It's a fun and easy way to create a bit of a light-hearted scare. Goblins and ghoulies of all ages will love it! One-mix aluminum pan is 14¼ x 11¾ x 1⅞ in.
2105-V-1031 $8.99 each

JACK-O-LANTERN PAN
Carve out a Halloween classic in cake and icing. It's a quick, easy way to brighten the October holiday. One-mix aluminum pan is 12¼ x 11⅝ x 2 in.
2105-V-3068 $8.99 each

MINI-PUMPKIN PAN
Bake little treats for Halloween tricksters. Or create kid-pleasing party cakes year 'round. Easy alternate ideas include a bunny, clown and monster. Each well of this 12¼ x 8 x 1⅜ in. aluminum pan takes a ½ cup of cake batter.
2105-V-1499 $8.99 each

NEW! HAUNTED HOUSE KIT
Construct a gingerbread mansion to conjure up some Halloween fun. For Christmas and other occasions, remodel this gingerbread house with the appropriate candies and cookies. Kit includes patterns, sturdy plastic cookie cutters, 4 disposable bags, 1 round tip, and easy-to-follow instructions.
2104-V-1031 $6.99 each

NEW!

Gingerbread Centerpiece Kit
Haunted House

Valentine Pans

NEW!

NEW! HEART QUARTET PAN
A hearty foursome arranged in an unusual shape provides unlimited decorating ideas. To start with, the label includes 3 designs for Valentine's Day, St. Patrick's Day and birthdays. With your imagination, the possibilities are endless. One-mix aluminum. 11 x 11 in.
2105-V-1414 $8.99 each

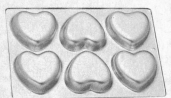

HEART MINI-CAKE PAN
Set of dainty hearts with sweet words of love and friendship. A true delight for Valentine's Day, bridal showers and kids' parties. Each heart of this 8 x 11⅛ in. aluminum pan is 3½ x 1¼ in. deep. One cake mix makes 12 hearts.
2105-V-11044 $8.99 each

HAPPINESS HEART PAN SET
Two hearts that eat as one! Create a lovely layer cake to convey sweet sentiments on any occasion. It takes just one mix to fill both pans; each 9 x 1½ in. deep, aluminum.
2105-V-956 $8.99 each

DOUBLE TIER HEART PAN
Put romance on the menu with a cake of two pretty heart tiers. It's a lovely show of affection for birthdays, Mother's or Father's Day, wedding showers and so much more. Instructions show 4 delightful ways to decorate. One-mix aluminum pan is 11½ x 11 x 2¼ in.
2105-V-1699 $8.99 each

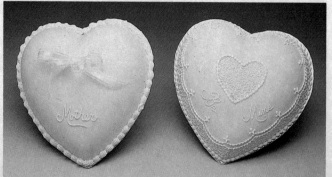

PUFFED HEART PAN
Stir the senses with a sculpted heart. This luscious cake can be decorated with either elegance or whimsey. The one-mix pan includes instructions for exquisite fondant-covered cakes, a butterfly and a bundle of joy. 11 x 11 x 2½ in., aluminum.
2105-V-214 $8.99 each

Valentine Pans

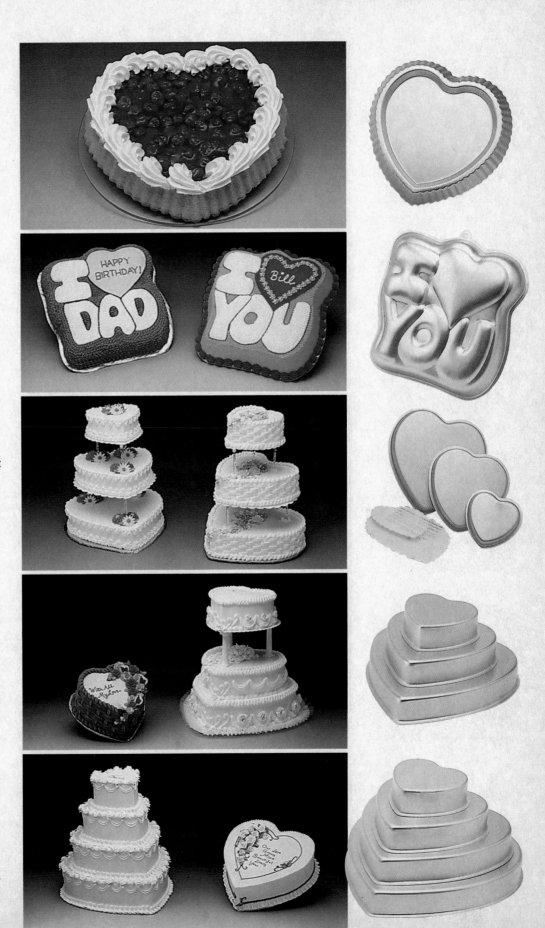

HEART FLAN PAN
How unique – Fill a flute-edged heart cake with richness – Choose pudding, ice cream, fruit, more! Of course, it can be trimmed with icing or whipped cream also. Aluminum, 11 x 10½ in.
2105-V-3218 $7.99 each

I LOVE YOU PAN
What a lovely valentine. It delivers a light-hearted expression of love 365 days a year. Decorating is so quick and easy with this one-mix aluminum, 10¼ x 10¾ in. pan.
2105-V-215 $8.99 each

HEART MINI-TIER SET
Creates a delightful effect! Make a petite masterpiece using only one cake mix in three sweetheart tiers. Set includes 5, 7½ and 9 in. pans, two scallop-edged white separator plates and six crystal-look plastic twist legs.
2105-V-409 $10.99 each
SEPARATOR PLATE SETS
301-V-9728 $2.99 set of 2

HEART DELIGHTS
Discover romance in full bloom with three lovely tiers. Just wonderful for dates lovingly remembered with a heart – anniversaries, bridal showers, birthdays and of course, weddings. Our 2-in. deep aluminum pans are sold separately in three essential sizes, 6, 9, 12½ in.
6 IN HEART
2105-V-4781 $3.99 each
9 IN HEART
2105-V-5176 $5.99 each
12½ IN HEART
2105-V-5168 $8.99 each

HEART PAN SET
Love is at its grandest in four lovely tiers. Lavishly celebrate showers, weddings and more with the ultimate heart-shaped cake. Set includes 6, 9, 12 and 15½ in. diam. aluminum pans.
504-V-207 $24.99 set

Easter Pans

NEW!

NEW! LITTLE DUCKY PAN
In the dictionary, his picture should be featured to illustrate "cute". He's an adorable addition to baby showers, kids' birthdays and Eastertime celebrations. One-mix aluminum, 13 x 10 in.
2105-V-2029 $8.99 each

SUNNY BUNNY PAN
Smiles and grins will burst out everywhere when our own little hare hops on an Easter table. With his floppy ears, he's an enchanting centerpiece for baby showers, birthdays, more! See label for ideas. One-mix aluminum pan is 12⅝ x 10¼ in.
2105-V-2435 $8.99 each

COTTONTAIL BUNNY PAN
Here comes a hoppy-go-lucky hare to signal that spring has sprung! He's an adorable addition to birthdays and baby showers, too. The label includes a bunny-quick way to decorate. One-mix aluminum pan is 14 x 12 in. x 2 in.
2105-V-2015 $8.99 each

LOVABLE LAMB PAN
Wherever there's a springtime celebration, this lamb is sure to go. This easy-to-do cake is also a hit for birthdays and baby showers. Several designs included. One-mix aluminum pan is 13⅝ x 10¾ x 1⅞ in.
2105-V-2514 $8.99 each

LITTLE LAMB PAN
Create a classic little lamb. This 3-D delight is perfect for birthdays and baby showers, too. Two-piece aluminum pan is 10 x 7-in. tall and takes 6 cups of pound cake batter. Baking and decorating instructions included.
2105-V-2010 $10.99 each

All pans made in Korea.

Easter Pans

CROSS PAN
Celebrate a blessed day with a symbol of faith. Bake and decorate this meaningful cake for holidays, christenings and other religious occasions. Instructions include a birthday and family reunion cake. One-mix aluminum pan is 14½ x 11⅛ x 2 in.
2105-V-2509 $8.99 each

GREAT EGGS!™ KIT
Create a springtime fantasy! Make Easter basket sugar and candy confections. Kit includes 2 egg molds, tips, coupler, brush, 2 candy mold sheets, recipes and instructions.
2104-V-3616 $8.99 each

EGG PAN SET
Decorate the ultimate Easter egg. This sumptuous cake makes a great holiday centerpiece. Two-piece aluminum pan takes just one cake mix. Each half is 8¾ x 5⅜ in. and includes a ring base for level baking.
2105-V-700 $10.99 each

EGG PAN RING ONLY.
503-V-954 $.99 each

EGG MINI-CAKE PAN
You can put all these "eggs" in one beautiful Easter basket. Or use them as colorful place markers at the holiday table. The label includes a variety of versatile decorating ideas. One cake mix yields about 24 cakes. Each oval well is 3½ x 2⅜ in.
2105-V-2118 $8.99 each

Create a panorama of Easter cake, cookie and candy treats for baskets, centerpieces and Easter Sunday dinner. For more adorable Easter ideas, see pp. 56-59.

Christmas Pans

NEW!

NEW! SNOWMAN PAN
Bake up a roly-poly figure of winter fun. Sprinkled with coconut and decorated with candies, this cake makes a tasty Christmas treat. Inventive ideas to adapt for all seasons included on the label. One-mix aluminum. 15¼ x 10¼ in.
2105-V-803 $8.99 each

RUDY REINDEER PAN
It's Rudy, our irresistible reindeer. He'll soon be leading the fun at all holiday festivities. One-mix aluminum pan is 10¾ x 16¾ x 1¾ in.
2105-V-1224 $8.99 each

TREELITEFUL PAN
Here's holiday decorating made quick and easy. Just cover with one-squeeze stars, add simple garlands and candy or cookie ornaments. Instructions include several ideas for throughout the year. One-mix aluminum pan is 15 x 11 x 1½ in.
2105-V-425 $8.99 each

JOLLY SANTA PAN
Send sweet season's greetings with the smiling face of old St. Nick. He's great fun to decorate! One-mix aluminum pan is 13¼ x 11½ x 2 in.
2105-V-1225 $8.99 each

STAND-UP SNOWMAN PAN KIT
Here's a cheerful chap with a grin for Old Man Winter. Create a flat or 3-D cake. One-mix aluminum pan is 11½ x 6½ x 2¾ in.
2105-V-1394 $9.99 each

HOLIDAY TREE PAN KIT
Bake a tree-trimming party treat. You have two wonderful options: A cake that lies flat or a crowd-pleasing 3 dimensional centerpiece. One mix aluminum pan is 10½ x 8 x 3 in.
2105-V-1510 $9.99 each

MINI-CHRISTMAS TREE PAN
O Christmas trees! Lots of little ones to serve individually. Pan includes alternate ideas for year 'round versatility. 13 x 10½ x 1¼ in., aluminum.
2105-V-1779 $8.99 each

GINGERBREAD BOY PAN
Simple decorating creates great effects with this versatile pan. Cast him in all sorts of delightful roles in every season. One-mix aluminum pan is 14 x 10½ x 2 in.
2105-V-2072 $8.99 each

HOLIDAY HOUSE KIT
Build an enchanted cottage of cake candy and icing. One-mix pan is 8⅝ x 9 x 3 in.
2105-V-2282 $9.99 each

HOLIDAY KITS
Make fabulous holiday centerpieces with these fun kits.

NEW! 12 DAYS OF CHRISTMAS KIT
Holiday magic! The words and music of a favorite Christmas ballad come to life in an elaborate gingerbread centerpiece decorated with sweets. Kit includes patterns, 4 sheets of candy molds and easy-to-follow instructions.
2104-V-2950 $7.99 each

NEW! SANTA'S STABLE KIT
A Christmas fantasy for the whole family to enjoy. Recreate the reindeer's North Pole headquarters on a holiday tabletop. Kit includes patterns, sturdy plastic cookie cutters and easy-to-follow instructions.
2104-V-2949 $5.99 each

GINGERBREAD HOUSE KIT
Construct a dream house in a winter wonderland. The kit includes a Tudor castle design and 3 plastic gingerbread people cutters, sturdy pattern pieces and instruction book.
2104-V-2946 $5.99 each

CHRISTMAS COOKIE TREE
Begin a new holiday tradition. Ice, stack and trim cookie stars. Kit includes 10 plastic star cutters in graduated sizes, plus instruction book.
2105-V-3424 $5.99 each

NEW!

NEW!

Decorator's Index

Pan Index